FLORENCE MADDEN & ELENI S

EVERYDAY NLP

for life, work and relationships

"The field of NLP has needed this book on *Everyday NLP* for a long time. I am grateful to Eleni and Florence for finally giving it birth. Bravo!"
Robert Dilts Co-Founder, NLP University

Everyday NLP

Cover (illustration) by AST Signs Ltd.

Designed and Set by Philippa French, Little Frog Design
Printed in the United Kingdom
First Printing, 2019
ISBN: 978-1-9999643-2-0 (Paperback)
ISBN: 978-1-9999643-3-7 (eBook)
Everyday NLP
Carlisle
Cumbria
United Kingdom
CA5 7BA.

www.everydaynlpbook.com

Foreword

When Eleni and Florence invited me to write the foreword to their book, I was both honoured and excited. I knew that Florence, as an ANLP accredited trainer and Eleni, one of our International Ambassadors would combine their skills, warmth and friendship to create an accessible everyday book about NLP.

Throughout the book, Eleni and Florence delve into so many NLP topics and bring them to life by weaving their passion for NLP with references and citations…and then they throw in a good mix of personal anecdotes to illustrate and clarify these points.

My personal favourite always has been the NLP Communication Model – if you were able to apply this model to all your communications in future, I am confident it would give you greater insight into your own life, work and relationships…and that is before you start to explore such gems as values and beliefs, the NLP Presuppositions (what a great philosophy for life)…and many other well known NLP tools and techniques.

Florence and Eleni inject their passion and enthusiasm into every page as they lead you on the NLP journey which they know will empower you to be the best you can be.

Karen Falconer

CEO of the Association of NLP

Feedback From the World of NLP and Beyond...

Congratulations to Florence and Eleni for this thoughtful, rich and comprehensive overview of NLP and its applications to everyday life situations. As Eleni and Florence show us, the greatest value of learning NLP is in how it can be applied to improve almost any situation that you encounter in your daily life. By presenting stories and examples from their own personal experience, Florence and Eleni bring NLP to life in a way that illustrates both its simplicity and power without needing to be sensational. The field of NLP has needed this book on Everyday NLP for a long time. I am grateful to Eleni and Florence for finally giving it birth. Bravo!

Robert Dilts, Developer, Author, Trainer and Consultant in the field of NLP and Co-Founder NLP University

This rich book reconnects us with what NLP is really about and how it relates to so many other concepts that have emerged in recent years such as Neuroplasticity. And this at a time when the essence of NLP is at risk of being diluted because of its popularity. And Florence and Eleni do so with such wisdom and depth. And more than this they model what NLP is all about with their friendship and teamwork. Writing a book in partnership is no mean feat. I congratulate you both. And I wish you success whatever that means to you. We need a tipping point in the world today towards the 'good'. And you are key contributors to this.

Sue Knight, International Master NLP Trainer and Coach and Author of NLP at Work

This new book by Florence and Eleni has been written very much from a pragmatic perspective and they have both shared in a very personal way, many stories and experiences that have shaped their understanding of NLP. They give a good explanation of the early background to NLP and how it came about and you will also learn about a number of NLP models. In each chapter, Florence and Eleni give examples of where they have used their experiences of NLP to great effect in achieving good outcomes and at the end of each chapter, there are some great questions for reflection, practice and learning. Reading this book reminded me of my early experiences with NLP and was a great refresher of the models and techniques. As a 'reflector' I loved reflecting at the end of each chapter too.

Louise Fisher, MA, Chartered FCIPD, Portfolio Non-Executive Director

Feedback From the World of NLP and Beyond...

Reading this book is a real pleasure; it successfully combines carefully explained theory with great examples of how to turn that theory into practice; it also invites us, their readers, to experience NLP and its processes in our own lives, and then feel the positive difference that choosing to do that can make to the ways in which we perceive the world around us, and, perhaps sometimes more importantly, to the impact we have on the people with whom we interact on a daily basis.

This is a wide-ranging manual, described, and expressed, personally and powerfully by Florence and Eleni. We readers quickly feel the passion they have for what they do and how they do it; the extensive knowledge they have individually and together gained from working for so many years in the NLP arena; the integrity in the way in which they pass on the gift of their knowledge and personal experience in the field; and the clear dialogue between the two different writing styles which enlivens, enriches our reading. What I particularly love and am impressed by is that they are using their own examples, their own choices of stories, poems and quotations to illustrate the points they are making so persuasively. This is a very different text book , one that that oozes soul and joyfulness. Thank you for asking me to read it. It's extraordinary.

Sarah Frossell, Speaker, Consultant and NLP Trainer Frossell Associates Ltd

It's my belief that everyone can benefit from a clear understanding of 'how we work as human beings' and NLP helps us become aware of patterns and programs that can both hinder and help us. More importantly, it provides the tools and techniques to create rapid shifts.

Over the years, NLP has become part of who I am rather than simply tools, techniques and a set of powerful beliefs. Through Everyday NLP, Eleni and Florence are offering you the gift of shifting 'how you think and do what you do' so you open your eyes to new possibilities and a new way of being that may at first seem impossible and yet, with their clear examples and engaging way of sharing, is actually so simple. This colorful book is filled with examples, clear explanations, lovely illustrations and humor. This is more than just a book to read... it is a definitive guide that really does allow you to incorporate NLP into YOU and enjoy the magic that unfolds every day!

Carol Talbot, NLP Master Trainer, Author, Professional Speaker, Master Fire-walk Instructor

Feedback From the World of NLP and Beyond...

As someone who has known of NLP for years, and has done a bit of research into the models and psychology behind it, I came away from Eleni and Florence's new book with such a better understanding around the history of, background behind, and benefits of NLP. I love their practical advice, the masterful way they have weaved stories in, and the accessible way they have shared what some may have had only a passing understanding of. If you want to know the benefits or NLP, understand it in a way you haven't before, if you want to access the power of NLP, and enjoy an enlightening read; grab yourself a copy of Everyday NLP today.

Corey Poirier, Multiple-Time TEDx Speaker and Bestselling Author of The Book of WHY (and HOW)

This lively book is woven together through personal journeying; a series of revelations with resonance for all, whether a time-served NLPer, or an NLP novice. Eleni and Florence pepper the book with apt quotes to illuminate or inspire and I enjoyed that they provide many personal examples to ground the work firmly in application.

The authors' writing style is eclectic and curious, (very much in the spirit of the original attitude of NLP). I particularly enjoyed the short section at the coda of each chapter: 'Everyday thinking and doing'; an invitation to activity, in order to assist the reader to transfer knowledge learning into understanding.

'Everyday NLP' was a joy to read and is eminently 'thumb-through-able'! I feel sure I will enjoy coming back to it time and again and I know that future students and readers will value it as a treasure trove of models, examples and activities to inform and accompany their own NLP journey.

Reb Veale, INLPTA Master Trainer of NLP, mBIT Trainer & Master Coach

Feedback From the World of NLP and Beyond...

A wonderful and empowering treasure trove of practical advice and tools to build your best self.

Orly Wahba, Motivational Speaker, Author of Kindness Boomerang & Founder of the Nonprofit Life Vest Inside

As a communications coach, I've always wanted to understand NLP to add it to my "toolbox", but felt intimidated by the concept and how to go about learning it. But thanks to Eleni Sarantinou and Florence Madden's "conversation between friends", I do. I think they've written a masterful book, with a simple clear roadmap of the principles of NLP and how to apply them in everyday life. A must read for anyone who wants to understand themselves, how they "speak to themselves", and use that knowledge to communicate powerfully and meaningfully. Aka: Giving Great Voice!

Tasia Valenza, Emmy Nominated Actress, Voiceover Artist and CEO of Giving Great Voice! Communication Coaching.

Being a fan of the pioneering work of Bandler and Grinder, there are big shoes to fill when writing an NLP book. The reader will enjoy the writing style, interactive exercises, and personal outcomes from reading this text. The authors have truly made learning about NLP enjoyable and will motivate the reader to begin the journey today. It is refreshing to pick up a book crafted with a foundational level of knowledge and structure for the reader to build upon.

Kyle S. Ferroly, PhDc. Psychophysiology The Center for Mind Brain Balance

Contents

Contents

Part 1

Setting The Scene

John Grinder the Co-Creator of NLP pointed out that the conscious mind records all the little details that the conscious mind ignores.

So in this first part we learn what opportunities NLP can open up for us and about NLP's key foundations and pillars of success, how our unconscious mind works, and how we process information.

Chapter 1

Approaching NLP …

… Introducing NLP and our approach to this book

By Florence

Approaching NLP…My Starting Point!

The following poem has stayed in my mind ever since I first heard it. I didn't fully understand it to begin with, but I was drawn to it, and it kept popping up in my mind until I did understand it. (Have you noticed how your 'unconscious mind' can do that – re-presenting things until you work them out?)

Out beyond ideas of wrongdoing and rightdoing,
there is a field. I'll meet you there.
When the soul lies down in that grass,
the world is too full to talk about.
Ideas, language, even the phrase "each other"
doesn't make any sense.
The breeze at dawn has secrets to tell you.
Don't go back to sleep.
You must ask for what you really want.
Don't go back to sleep.
People are going back and forth across the doorsill
where the two worlds touch.
The door is round and open.
Don't go back to sleep.

Extract from 'A Great Wagon' by Rumi,
a 13th-century Persian Sunni Muslim poet.

My English teacher at school, Mr Seymour, said that poetry can *move* us before we understand it. How right he was. My interpretation of this poem beautifully describes my learning journey with NLP.

My first NLP training was back in 1998–99 with an NLP Master Trainer called Sarah Frossell. I went to a 'taster' day and came away with a strong feeling that this thing called NLP was going to be important for me, both as a trainer and as a person. I struggled to put into words just why I felt so strongly about it, which was a problem because I had to 'sell' it to my employer at the time to get time off work, (I needed four weeks to complete my NLP Practitioner and Master Practitioner). Achieving this was my new goal or, as I learnt to call it, my outcome.

In the pack of notes I came away with after that taster session was a sheet of paper describing a process called the Well-Formed Outcome. We hadn't had a chance to do it during the session. Nevertheless, I took my 'outcome' (to do the NLP Practitioner and Master Practitioner courses) through this process. Afterwards, my feelings shifted even more – I felt as if I could walk through steel! Although I would never have said it out loud to anyone, I was prepared to walk away from my job, if that's what it took to make this training happen for me. The right words still hadn't come to me for explaining it to my boss, but the *way* I spoke to her about it was different; she saw the change in me and was determined to help me get the time off and financial support to do it – and I got both! Because of her reaction, I was even more convinced that I was 'on to something' – even though I still didn't quite have the words to describe what it was!

So, my journey with NLP began. My initial approach was naively to look for the 'right answer' – about what NLP was all about, partly for myself, and partly as the trainer I wanted to be – so that I could relate that 'right answer' to others. But my thinking was binary – right or wrong, good or bad – and in a rainbow world this black-and-white approach was limiting me and my development. Although I didn't realise it at the time, new thinking was dawning!

So What Is NLP?

NLP is an acronym that stands for 'Neuro Linguistic Programming'. There are a number of definitions of NLP, but the one that most resonates with me (and my learning now) is that of Richard Bandler, one of the original creators of NLP, who described it as "an attitude and a methodology" which has given rise to a number of techniques. This is an attitude of curiosity about ourselves and how things work, and wanting to use this to influence for the better.

When I began thinking of NLP as an *attitude*, rather than a collection of facts and ideas, Rumi's words in the poem – which speak to me about the value of curiosity and openness – really began to make sense to me.

My learning in NLP has been an awakening in my thinking – about myself, about others, and about the world around me. NLP is about how you can be the best version of yourself. How you think about yourself and others influences how you interact with them and therefore how effective you are in your life and work. And the learning process, to my delight, continues. Crucially, it became apparent to me quite early on that the starting point had to be *me*, and then my approach shifted. As one wise person pointed out:

If it is peaceful and calm life you are seeking
it will be better to change yourself
rather than seeking to change others.
Which will you find easier to protect
your feet with slippers or
to carpet the whole earth?

The words of Ghandi from 'The Salmon of Knowledge' by Nick Owen.

NLP…Where It All Began

NLP was born back in 1972 to the strains of *Changes* by David Bowie, *Smoke on the Water* by Deep Purple and *Tumbling Dice* by the Rolling Stones. Meanwhile, Eleni and I were children growing up on opposite ends of Europe, Greece and Northern Ireland, with no notion of the ideas forming that would shape so much of our work and life later on.

I have no idea, of course, if the creators of NLP were actually listening to Bowie et al., but in my mind's eye they were! This was also the era of flower power in response to the Vietnam War, flared trousers, the first handheld calculators, and the first digital watches; there were advances in the use of satellites and space travel, and the Watergate scandal began, leading to the ignominious fall of President Nixon. Against this backdrop of invention and change, the curiosity that gave birth to NLP began with the search for new answers and new approaches to the issues and challenges of life.

Bandler, Roberti and Fitzpatrick in their book *How to take Charge of Your Life. A User's Guide to NLP*, draw the comparison between traditional psychology and the NLP approach: instead of focussing on the 'why' problems have occurred, NLP focusses on 'how' people can make the changes they want.

The development of what became known as NLP, which was originally called Meta, started in California. It was based on studying the thinking and behaviour of people who demonstrated excellence in their field, and it arose from great thinkers working in the areas of cybernetics*, therapy and philosophy in the 1960s and 1970s.

Richard Bandler and Frank Pucelik were both students at the University of California. They had a shared interest in Gestalt therapy**, co-founded by Fritz Perls, and were curious about how he and other high-performing people got the results they did. Their aim was to identify exactly what these people were doing, so that they could reproduce the same results. This is the process described in NLP as 'modelling'.

Bandler needed some help in identifying the linguistic patterns that their models (successful people) used, so he approached John Grinder for help, who was Associate Professor of Linguistics at the university at the time.

---

*The word cybernetics comes from the Greek for Helmsman: 'one who steers a ship'. It is an umbrella term for the body of work on how actions are taken to achieve a goal and the flow of feedback that keeps a living organism or machine on track to achieving it. This is now more often referred to as 'systems thinking'.

**Gestalt Therapy, created in 1940s is a form of psychotherapy where the patient is encouraged to become aware of their feelings/emotions in the present moment. It is interested in a patient's past only from the viewpoint of how these are affecting them in the present.

Together, Bandler and Grinder went on to 'model' a highly regarded family therapist called Virginia Satir. From their observations of Perls and Satir, the NLP Meta Model emerged, (a model of language patterns explored in Ch.18). They had connections with an anthropologist and social scientist called Gregory Bateson, who introduced them to Milton Erickson, widely considered to be the father of modern hypnotherapy. Indeed, John Grinder in his book *The Origins of Neuro Linguistic Programming* acknowledges the contribution of Bateson, who according to L. Michael Hall was a teacher of almost everyone involved in NLP in the early days. Moreover, he believes that without Bateson's endorsement at the early stages of its development, that NLP would never have achieved the prominence it has.

They modelled Erickson too, which resulted in the development of the Milton Model for hypnotic language. Together, the Meta Model and the Milton Model formed the core language models of NLP.

So the first three people Bandler and Grinder modelled were:

- Fritz Perls – co-founder of Gestalt therapy.
- Virginia Satir – an expert in family therapy.
- Milton H. Erickson – the 'father' of modern hypnotherapy.

The Theories Underpinning NLP

The initial work of Bandler and Grinder has continued to be developed over the years, both by themselves and by others, creating a growing and diverse body of work. So as you start this book it is perhaps useful to recognise the key theoretical basis that underpins NLP. Fran Burgess addresses this point in her book *The Bumper Book of Modelling* and I hope you will find her explanation, shown diagrammatically in **Fig. 2**, useful for giving you some context as you read through this book.

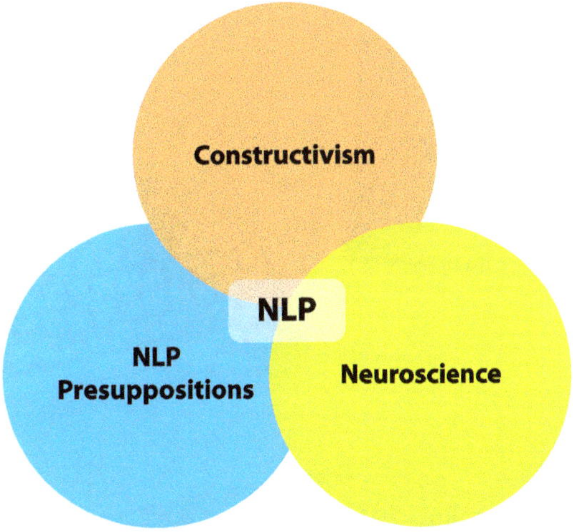

Fig. 2: The Theory Underpinning NLP – Burgess 2012, from *'The Bumper Book of Modelling'*

Fig. 1: Dateline 1972!

Philosophical base: Constructivism

NLP comes under the school of thought known as constructivism, which itself comes from the field of epistemology (the study of knowledge). The central tenet of constructivism is that we each see the world in our own unique way – we in fact construct our own reality. When we identify what makes up our own or other people's reality i.e. how people view the world, it can be *re*structured to generate personal change – if we so wish.

Scientific base: Neuroscience

NLP is about exploring how the mind works and how we process information internally. It helps us discover patterns that work for us and those we may want to change. Neuroscience is also about how the brain works, but from a functional point of view. Our knowledge of the brain and nervous system helps explain some of the reasons behind the effectiveness of NLP processes.

Burgess pointed out that linking these fields of study only came about in the mid-2000s – long after the initial work of Bandler and Grinder. One example of this linkage is in our understanding of 'intuitive' modelling, whereby we can 'stand in someone else's shoes' and unconsciously absorb how they do what they do. NLP modellers knew about 'intuitive modelling', but it was much later that the discovery of a specific type of neurons in the brain which were called 'mirror neurons', explained how it worked. (Eleni expands on this discovery and the role of 'mirror neurons' in Ch.5, and I explain more about intuitive modelling in Ch.27.)

Older scientific methods viewed the brain as a machine – one that 'is as it is' and therefore cannot be changed. But thanks to developments in neuroscience we are now aware of neuroplasticity – this is the brain's ability to change and adapt over the course of a person's lifetime. Knowing that the wiring of the brain can be altered, opens up huge possibilities for all of us. We can literally 'change our minds' and are therefore able to stop negative and repeated patterns, and introduce positive patterns of empowerment.

Thinking base: NLP presuppositions

What we believe about anything shapes our thinking about it. The 'presuppositions' of NLP are, in essence, beliefs or attitudes that we can adopt which shape our thinking in a more resourceful way. For this reason they are also known as 'resourceful beliefs', or 'beliefs of excellence'. They come from a variety of thinkers, in addition to the original NLP modelling subjects. These ways of thinking are transformative in themselves: they shape how we view ourselves and others. Espousing these ways of thinking can really challenge us and so totally change how we see the world around us. Examples of these are:

- *Milton H. Erickson:* There is no such thing as a resistant person – only information about their behaviour, or in other words, there is no such thing as resistant clients, only inflexible communicators.
- *Virginia Satir:* All behaviour is positively intended, or otherwise expressed as behind every action is an (unconscious) positive intention.

How My Approach To NLP Changed

From the dawning that I described earlier, my approach to NLP shifted away from 'finding the right answer' to opening up huge possibilities for achieving personal change for myself and helping others to do so too. Behind this shift in attitude, there were five key learnings for me, which will echo through this book. Here is a brief summary:

It is about 'being it' – not just 'knowing it'

As referred to earlier in the chapter, what matters is being open and curious in our thinking, and maintaining our awareness to the world outside us and within us – not simply being able to remember the theory behind it all. That means being open to possibilities for ourselves and in our attitudes to others. It starts with us thinking differently, rather than expecting others to change. With this respectful approach we are likely to be much more influential.

For those of you who want to embark on formal training in NLP, this is something you will hear more about. Achieving the required standards in training is assessed in both of these ways – being it and knowing it.

Don't go on discussing what a good person should be.
Just be one.

Marcus Aurelius, Emperor of Ancient Rome.

It is about being 'at Cause' rather than 'at Effect'

Closely related to 'being it' is this idea of putting ourselves 'at cause' in a situation, i.e. rather than blame others or complain, think instead '*What can **I** do about this?*' When we blame others and think in terms of what they have done to us we are 'at effect', and in this position we have to rely on others to change. When we put ourselves *at cause,* we are taking personal responsibility rather than blame, and this is a much more powerful position in which to place ourselves. You will see this theme reflected again and again as you read on.

We can model excellence in ourselves and others

The genesis of NLP was in modelling excellence. The basic idea is that if you see someone doing something really well, and can break it down into logical steps, then you have a recipe (a model) to follow in order to achieve similar results. That model is also then available, as Bandler points out, to change unhelpful patterns of mental and emotional behaviour.

The exciting thing for me, both then and now, is that we can use other people's models to make the changes we want, and so share in their success; AND in addition to that we can model any successful strategies we have in ourselves that may have gone unnoticed. Very often a behaviour we might want to have 'more of' in one circumstance may be the very same thing we demonstrate at other times. Frequently we do not realise this or make the link. Marilyn Monroe once quipped it was a waste of your own qualities wanting to be someone else, and yet the thrill of modelling for me is that we can have both. (More in Ch.27.)

Excellence does not remain alone. It is sure to attract neighbours.

Confucius, Chinese politician and philosopher.

We can shift our thinking and change our reality

NLP can help us change our perspective and to 'change our story'. The way things have been for us in the past do not have to dictate how things pan out for us in the future. If we do not like the results we are getting in our lives, it doesn't have to be like that – we can change it!

The powerful message from NLP is that we experience the world, and what happens around us, from within ourselves (more on this in Ch.3). So when we *change* what is happening inside our heads – what we think of as our reality – then we can also alter our view of another person, or situation or indeed ourselves.

I have a favourite scene in *Harry Potter and the Deathly Hallows* by J.K. Rowling, where Harry asks Professor Dumbledore if what is happening is real or just in his head. Dumbledore asks a little incredulously why because something is in our head it would not be real ! Philosophy is everywhere, don't you think?

What we think, we become.

Buddha, philosopher and spiritual teacher.

Here is a simple example of what I mean. This is a brief exercise I did while sitting on a plane. Note that no other passengers were involved or startled by what you are about to read.

Travelling alone during a flight, I started to mull over a conversation I was unhappy with. Trapped there, in my seat, I felt surrounded by the frustration of how I felt and this 'image' in my mind just wouldn't go away. So I started to play about with this unhelpful picture.

First, I quickly turned the coloured picture in my head to black and white, and to my amazed delight, already I felt its potency seeping away. So then I reduced the size of the image, from a dominant picture in front of my face, down to the size of a postage stamp. In my mind's eye (with no danger to myself or other passengers!) I pushed it out of the window and watched as it floated away onto a distant cloud – taking the negative feelings with it! What was left was a feeling of calmness and clarity about the conversation, as well as a sense of wonder of course, over what could be achieved without even getting out of my seat!

When we make changes about how we experience or remember people or situations, it can give us more control over our 'state', which provides us with many more options for the way that we subsequently handle things.

Consider the ecology of our actions

From my story above, you may start to infer another important principle about NLP that I learnt early on in my journey. It relates to 'ecology'. What is meant by ecology, (in the context of NLP), is that we do not just consider what is good for ourselves in a particular situation, but also the wider impact of our actions on other people, or even on ourselves in the longer term. This is a much more sustainable way of thinking, both for ourselves and others around us. The thinking and processes of NLP can be very powerful and – like anything that is powerful – they need to be used with care and consideration. You will come across many references to ecology as you read through this book. (Indeed, the organisations which have grown up to promote professional standards and best practice in NLP each has a code of ethics that enshrine the key principle of ecology.)

Forests precede civilizations and deserts follow them.

François-René de Chateaubriand, French writer and politician.

Our Approach To Everyday NLP

For both Eleni and I, our learning, the shifts in our thinking, and the changes in our stories continue to this day, as you might expect. This also happened when Eleni and I decided to write this book. The conversation went like this:

Florence: "I think we should write our own NLP book!" (Jokingly.)
Eleni: "Yes let's!" (Not joking!)
Florence: "Oh!" (In an 'I wish I hadn't said that' tone.)
Eleni: "Cool. You write half and I'll write half. Split the work." (Warming to the idea.)
Florence: "Okay. Let me finish the current book I am writing first, though!"

And so, on the first of January 2018, we began writing this book. Our friend Mike Rawlins movingly describes it as: "A conversation between friends". Like all friends (I hope!), we have had times of love and gratitude, as well as times of frustration, while bringing our own views and experiences to the book. In expressing our opinions, we have criss-crossed the fields of what is right and what is wrong … and I am pleased to say we have met on the other side.

Fig. 3: 'A conversation between friends in Kuala Lumpur.'

In our book we present the concepts and thinking behind NLP in relation to our 'everyday' experiences. And through these we also explain many of the techniques of NLP, that have been developed over the years. We have aimed not just to present the key models and concepts, but to illustrate their relevance to everyday life and to leave you at the end of each chapter with some thoughts and exercises to relate these to your own experience. We have included along the way quotes from a wide range of people who we believe have something valuable to say, and whose insights we think you will enjoy. The chapters are written in our own contrasting styles and we hope you will enjoy the variety. After all, it is a conversation between friends!

We have grouped the chapters to sit logically together into eight parts, with 'signposts' along the way, to help your understanding and to help you make connections. This first part of the book, for example, is about setting the scene with some of the key foundations of NLP.

Remember, as you read through this book, that NLP is not something you *do* to someone else; it is first and foremost about how *you* show up in the world. What we present are ways of thinking and approaching life (and work) that can influence ourselves, in the first place, and then others too, in ways that we think are worthwhile!

Everyday Thinking And Doing: Consider This …

So you may be wondering what difference learning about NLP can make to your life or how quickly you can make real change for yourself and others? To start this process, consider the following questions and perhaps write down your answers. (In fact, a journal to capture your thoughts and ideas would be a useful accompaniment to this book!):

- What are your reasons for reading this book and what are the top three outcomes you want to achieve as you do so?
- What have you read so far that has piqued your interest most?
- Who else could you discuss your learnings with as you read on through the book?

The Unconscious Mind …

… the role and functions of the hidden part of our mind

by Eleni

Don't get caught by the words 'conscious' and 'unconscious.' They are not real.

They are just a way of describing events that is useful in the context called therapeutic change.

'Conscious' is defined as whatever you are aware of at a moment in time. 'Unconscious' is everything else.

Richard Bandler and John Grinder from 'Frogs Into Princes', edited by Steve Andreas.

Dubai 2006. The first day of my NLP Practitioner course, and the buzz word was 'the unconscious'. For me, up until that point, the term had represented something secretive, mysterious, unpredictable, that was, frankly, best left alone. I thought it was an interesting area for people with serious psychological issues. Little did I know, back then, that the answer to so many of the questions I had about life came down to the connection between the conscious and the unconscious minds. With my strong academic upbringing, having been programmed to focus on my 'conscious logic', I felt a little lost on that first day.

And for the first time in my life, I also felt ... found!

I was in awe, and impatient to learn more about the unconscious. Was it in my stomach, my heart, my cells? What did it want? What did it do? Where did it come from? And did it, just perhaps, hold the ultimate truth?

As the NLP founders beautifully put it, the conscious and unconscious minds are in fact our own constructs – meaning they do not necessarily exist. They are our creations; words destined to make a distinction between what we focus on (conscious) and things that involve involuntarily processes (unconscious). What is conscious becomes unconscious after a while, and vice versa. One minute, we turn our focus to the door and it is in our conscious, and the next minute we stop thinking about the door and the door has moved to our unconscious.

NLP is about continuous growth and lasting change, because it involves our unconscious mind. What makes NLP effective is that it offers tools and techniques that by-pass the conscious mind and directly access the unconscious mind, where true change takes place.

Back then, on my first day, I also had three other major revelations:

Negative emotions are my friends, not my enemies. They are not negative because they carry important information for me that can propel me to a higher level of awareness, and eventually personal freedom. They are 'messengers', indicating where to look next for clues to lead to more learning and progress.

I could see my unconscious more clearly – childlike, playful, sweet, pure and with a cheeky side! Just like a child, exquisitely embracing innocence and fun.

Sharing my new-found knowledge of this conscious–unconscious connection with everyone on earth became important to me. You could say, the first seeds of inspiration for this book were planted that day.

The conscious–unconscious connection plays a key role when it comes to the results we achieve, our happiness, and how harmonious our relationships are. Working together, our conscious and unconscious minds make us stronger. The difference between a moment of bliss and one of darkness could be defined by the degree and quality of communication and synergy between the two.

Just maybe, all the hardship and obstacles I had encountered up until that point in my life were not just 'bad luck' after all. Maybe they also somehow represented how 'I', my conscious and unconscious, operated together. And perhaps that meant I could now learn more about how they could talk to each other more efficiently, feel internally freer and happier as a result.

The conscious mind may be compared to a fountain playing in the sun and falling back into the great subterranean pool of subconscious from which it rises.

Sigmund Freud, neurologist and founder of psychoanalysis.

What Is In The Unconscious?

Well, plenty of things! It is a collection of what we believe about ourselves and the world around us, and pretty much everything and everyone else that has been processed through our senses and been inside our head.

In our unconscious, there is what is important to us (our values), our experiences, our memories, our body's blueprint of how it works in vibrant health and what needs to happen to get there, our emotions, our decision-making mechanisms and internal strategies (how we do things), our likes and dislikes, our connections to every other human being (living or not living), our place in the universe – and pretty much everything that we are not consciously aware of every day!

The unconscious mind is made up of all those mental processes in our brain that continue without our knowledge – the millions of 'efficiently working dedicated helpers' who make sure that our heart keeps on beating every second, that all our organs keep running day and night, and keeps us breathing without us even noticing.

The Relevance Of Our Developmental Periods

As we grow up, there are some distinct periods in our life during which our main values are formed. Understanding these periods helps us understand the roles of our unconscious and conscious during our life and how to integrate them more effectively.

Morris Massey, a sociologist, described three major periods where our values are developed:

- The imprinting period (ages 0–7). During the first seven or so years of our life, due to lack of previous experience, we act like sponges, copying our main caregivers, parents and siblings. We are just beginning to develop mental filters, and most of our memories from this period will remain out of our conscious awareness in the future.
- The modelling period (ages 7–14). As young as the age of seven or eight, we start developing our 'conscious logic', and have some experiences and 'critical thinking' of our own. We start to question and doubt what we previously simply accepted as being true. Teenagers challenging the status quo is an essential step in them becoming adults. For the first time, their own captain now has a say about what enters their unconscious.
- The socialisation period (ages 14–21), This is when we form a lot of our ways of relating to others. Our focus switches from our family to friends, peers and social circles. We see the bigger picture and we develop a notion of belonging and being part of groups.

The Conscious Unconscious Ship Metaphor

Imagine we are a gigantic and powerful ship, with billions of crew members, assigned different tasks. The ship is us as a whole, our conscious is our captain, and our crew is our unconscious. Every day, the entire crew provides feedback on how each team is doing, and reports on the needs and wants of each group. Imagine the cooks, the engineers, the sailors on deck, the safety officers, the radio officers, the plumbers, the entertainers – every single role on the ship – coming together and exchanging views. They all do their part. They are all parts of our whole self – our ship.

In my mind, when I was aged somewhere between seven and twelve, my own ship's captain, (who was gradually taking over from my parents' captains), started to slowly disconnect from the crew (my unconscious). Then some time during my adolescence years, my captain (my conscious logic) began to believe that she alone was in charge of what happened to her. My captain stopped thinking about who prepared her food and who oiled the engines.

On reaching adulthood, around the age of eighteen, my ship's captain set out to find the island she wanted (her purpose in life). Every island was a great adventure, and yet not quite the island she was looking for.

As a young person, she started exploring the Mediterranean Sea and communicating on the radio with other ships. She became experienced in navigating. Later, she explored new seas and open oceans and felt safer and more confident at the helm.

Then, one day, she caught a glimpse of a shadow behind her. She did not pay much attention at first. The same thing happened the next day ... and the next. She finally left the helm to go and find out more. Was there anybody else on her ship? A feeling of anticipation, fear and great confusion overtook her. Then she saw them! Billions of crew members (her unconscious). Some were pale. Some had an empty look about them. Some were hanging from the sides of the deck. For the most part, though, everyone was there, in good condition, smiley and happy the captain had finally come out to greet them, once again.

That same evening, my captain joined the crew members for dinner and that was the first day of my NLP Practitioner course in Dubai. It was a bit overwhelming for her to reunite with all the crew – consciously. What a profound moment that was! My captain acknowledged her crew's contributions over the past decades and showed immense gratitude for the way they had held their posts no matter what. They had waited for this moment to come – without any guarantee that it ever would!

Of course, I had been listening to and discussing things with my unconscious all throughout my life – I just did not realise I was doing it. I did not consciously understand the mechanisms behind it, appreciate its power and how it cared for me. When I did, my purpose instantly changed. As a ship, the idea was never to find one specific island and remain there – the voyages of ships carry on for a lifetime.

At the dawn of this new understanding, a ray of light filled my captain's head, signalling how much she had yet to learn about and from the members of her crew. From now on, they would play a greater role in deciding their destinations, and she would listen to what they had to say. Right away, they asked for more fun and more rest. She saw a chance for more sleep and holidays! After all, she had her crew to count on!

Let us now sail forth to understand more about our crews and how they operate.

Prime Directives of The Unconscious Mind

'So what are they, these crew members?' I hear you ask. Well, they are the unconscious mind's guiding principles, their duties and job descriptions. In NLP, we call them **'prime directives'** as listed by Tad James in the book *Lost Secrets of Ancient Hawaiian Huna* in 1997, which he collated during his studies of the ancient philosophies. When you reflect on the prime directives and seek to understand the hidden treasures they hold, things start to fall into place and make sense!

The striking thing is that most, if not all of them, have been supported by neuroscience in the last 10 or 15 years.

Let's have a look at them. Take a deep breath! I will try to keep my descriptions succinct as there's quite a lot to take in. In fact, there are twenty-one directives in all. The first ones relate to our memories.

1 **It stores memories.** We cannot possibly be conscious of all our memories all of the time. So memories live in our unconscious and only come to the surface when we specifically recall them. We do not wake up every day thinking about everything. That would be insane ... or drive us insane! Or both!

2 **It makes associations.** It links similar things and ideas (and it learns quickly), for example, like the way we memorise a telephone number by making associations with a significant sequence or someone's date of birth. It is how we learn everything. We connect data to make sure we remember it!

3 **It organises all our memories.** It puts them together, in different 'cabins', into different categories. There are our childhood memories, our work memories, our summer-of-1972 memories, and so on. Once one memory is retrieved, more come to mind.

Memory is the diary that we all carry about with us.

Oscar Wilde, Irish poet and playwright.

4 **It represses memories that are associated with unresolved negative emotions.** Imagine if you were to wake up with all your 'negative' experiences, right there, in your conscious. You would not be able to operate! So, for our own protection, our memories of negative experiences are 'saved' in our unconscious minds, in a cabin of their own. They are still with us, but we are not fully aware of their influence every minute of the day. They do affect us unconsciously, though!

I used to believe that if I did not think about the bad things, I would not suffer, and they would not hurt me. I felt empowered because I could 'get on' with my life. Strangely enough, at the same time, I could feel that the negativity was still there, and certain triggers would remind me of it. In fact, the more I denied those negative feelings, the more they persisted as self-defeating voices in my head, or as bad dreams.

And this is because our unconscious does the following:

5 **It presents repressed memories for resolution.** Those negative experiences, the ones we repress because they are too painful to explore, eventually need to come out. Our unconscious tries to relieve our body and mind from the negativity they create, and this is the reason that they get presented to us by way of triggers – a movie, a phone call, someone's response to a situation. This is how our unconscious keeps us healthy, by helping us face what is unresolved somewhere within, so we can move forward.

To be able to move on, we have got to face and acknowledge our negative experiences; to change their meaning and try to see what we can learn from them. What can we do differently next time? What could possibly have created the event that caused us pain or trauma in the first place? The more insight we gain, the easier it is to look back, and let trapped negative emotions find their way out, so that we learn – even if the learning is just forgiveness and letting go. Keeping these memories locked inside accumulates negative emotions and causes pain. Whereas the more insight we get from them, the 'lighter' we feel.

6 **It keeps memories repressed for our protection.** If consciously we decide that we still do not want to 'go there', despite the triggers, these memories go back into the same cabin in our unconscious, where we keep unresolved events. And they wait there for another opportunity to resurface.

The next four directives are specific to our body's well-being:

7 **It runs the body.** It seems so obvious now, and I admit that I missed this one, big time! It was only because of this list of directives, and NLP, that I finally understood what should be crystal clear. Who runs my digestive system, and my muscles, and makes my heart beat? I do not sit here all day consciously saying, 'Beat, beat, beat…'. This realisation made me more mindful of how much is done 'for me' – for my survival and enjoyment through my own organs – and that made me express far more gratitude!

8 **It preserves the body.** Our body is our home and our temple, and this is where our self-healing mechanisms come into play. Our unconscious keeps our body safe. Our immune system never sleeps, it is always awake and ready to protect us every minute of every day. Our crew takes care of our ship's various functions to ensure smooth sailing at all times. Even if our unconscious is overwhelmed and filled with limitations, we still have a strong 'fight or flight' mechanism. When it comes to matters of life and death, we start moving – unconsciously and without hesitation! Our habits are forced to change instantly when the ship is about to sink.

The natural healing force in each one of us is the greatest force in getting well.

Hippocrates, Greek physician.

9 **It generates, stores, distributes and transmits 'energy'.** We wake up in the morning and expect to have high energy levels – then realise that the energy level we wanted simply is not there. We cannot consciously create energy on the spot. We can make ourselves *believe* that we have plenty of energy and convince ourselves we will be fine after a cup of coffee. But if we have not slept enough, and have not eaten well, and if our thoughts have tortured us through the night, then our energy levels will suffer, and we will feel it. The unconscious knows this, and it communicates it to the conscious. It is up to the conscious to learn to listen better to what the unconscious knows and is vocal about, rather than trying to fool itself. There are lessons to be learnt and changes to be made.

10 **It functions best as a whole integrated unit.** The unconscious dislikes fragmentation. This is one of my favourite directives, because I thought I did not really have any 'bad' parts. This was because I had supressed them so much, and I thought I had deleted them!

It turns out, we all have *everything*, and *every* part needs to be acknowledged. When we systematically promote more of our 'good' side and hide our 'darker' or 'naughty' thoughts, the suppressed parts make a lot of 'noise' – because they are there for a reason! There is a place, a time, and a way to give these parts their space, and NLP techniques can really help to reconcile them (Ch.16).

Okay, we are almost half way through the directives, and you are doing well. Grab a coffee or a cup of tea if you need to, then we will crack on with the remainder.

Ready to go again? Good. Just as with memories, the unconscious is the domain of perceptions, emotions, instincts, habits and values. The unconscious mind has an important role with these too.

11 **It controls and maintains all perceptions.** The unconscious mind receives and transmits perceptions to the conscious mind – via our senses. We feed our brain with all these perceptions and they in turn become images, sounds, feelings, beliefs, and – eventually – our reality.

12 **It is the domain of emotions.** Our emotional world is what drives us, and our memories get coloured by the feelings we experienced with each of those memories. We talk about happy memories and sad memories. When we feel happy, we tend to want to do more of what keeps us happy; but when we face negativity and gloom, we would rather run away from or avoid the feelings. Our decision-making mechanisms operate as a result of a mixture of memories and emotions.

We cannot create anger consciously in the same way that we cannot blush consciously. Sensations and feelings reside in the unconscious; they are the way our unconscious mind communicates with our conscious. When we experience a certain emotion, it carries messages for us to learn from and act upon.

So what else does our unconscious mind do?

13 **It maintains instincts and generates habits.** Again, we can gain great insight from knowing that all of our learning is done in our unconscious mind. You could argue that we only really know how to drive when we can get from A to B without thinking. Or, we can only really speak a foreign language fluently when we do not have to think about the grammar anymore, because it is all there, in our unconscious. And we achieve those things by repetition!

14 **It needs repetition until a habit is created.** This is how all learning takes place. Repeat, repeat, repeat – until the learning has been 'written' into our neurology. Neuroplasticity, the mechanism of re-wiring the brain, is activated through repetition in order to create new connections between our nerve cells, our neurons.

In his third best-selling book *Outliers: The Story of Success*, the Canadian journalist Malcolm Gladwell, (also author of *Blink: The Power of Thinking Without Thinking)*, he repeatedly mentions the '10,000-Hour Rule'. The rule emphasizes the key ingredient to achieving world-class expertise in any skill is: practicing the correct way, for approximately 10,000 hours.

15 **It is a highly moral being.** This relates to the morality we were taught and that we accepted. What motivates us is not always the same as what motivates others. We might not always agree with what drives others, but that does not necessarily make it wrong. We all have a specific set of 'rules' that we live our life by, which form our opinions about what it is to be beautiful, or successful, or kind, or correct, and so on.

The last six directives about our unconscious are very interesting, so hang in there, because these ones can change our mindset and goal-setting in profound ways.

16 **It is programmed to continuously seek more and more.** People *like* progress – it is how the world moves forward, and there's always more to discover. And your unconscious mind likes progress too. When it hears the phrases to do less or to stop doing something, it may not necessarily like them.

The prime directives I describe next come into play in goal setting (Ch.28), along with the concept of Well-Formed Outcomes and moving forward. Here's more about what your unconscious does.

17 **It enjoys serving and needs clear orders to follow.** This takes us back to the metaphor of our ship, our captain and our crew. The unconscious is not supposed to *give* instructions – it relies on getting them from our conscious mind, just like a child relying on the instructions of its parents. The unconscious is happy to follow instructions because otherwise it feels a bit lost and disoriented – the same way a child behaves without its parents' guidance.

18 **It works on the principle of least effort.** Your unconscious will always take shortcuts. In a way, this is innovative and efficient. It is designed to follow the path of least resistance and effort. Think about it: would not you prefer to produce the same amount of work in three hours rather than eight? The unconscious is not pro-struggle or pro-obstacles. It loves finding the quickest solution, which is why making goals specific is vital. The more details and clear directions the unconscious receives, the faster it can work on delivering the end result.

19 **It takes everything personally.** When someone mentions eating salmon to us, we automatically think about the last time we ate

salmon or ask ourselves whether we like salmon. In other words, we focus on our own personal experience of salmon. Carl Jung held the premise that what we like or dislike about other people is, in fact, related to things we like or do not like about ourselves.

This theory gave birth to Tad James' NLP concept of 'perception is projection' (Ch.5) and inspired me to write my book *Perception Projection: 9 Principles How To Empower Your Team.*

20 **It does not process negatives directly.** On the first day of my NLP Practitioner course, I was asked to close my eyes and – no matter what happened – *not* to think of a pink elephant with big blue ears. When I closed my eyes, I tried hard to follow those instructions, but despite my best efforts all I could think about was a pink elephant with blue ears.

Think of how many 'not wanted' words we utter every day. When we say 'I do not want stress' what our crew actually hears is 'stress' with the result that we focus on stress, which in turn results in, yup, you have guessed it, more stress! And this is crucial when it comes to goal setting!

And finally, there is one more game-changer dimension to our unconscious mind.

21 **It is symbolic.** Your unconscious uses and responds to symbols. What is a symbol? Well, if our eyes can see it, or our ears can hear it, then it's a symbol. That makes it a direct 'order' to our crew, which it consciously focuses on. Recognising and harnessing the power of symbols has been significant for enhancing my own life, my work and that of my clients. Therefore, I will expand on this concept in greater detail in the next section. More in Ch.20.

By now, you know a little bit more about your unconscious, and how it relates to your conscious, your memories, emotions and habits. This learning will at some level make you understand yourself and others a little bit better and hopefully get you excited about your immense potential.

The Importance Of Symbols

Generally, a symbol is a mark or character used to represent an object or a process. We have universal symbols like the sign of peace, the smiley face and the heart shape. Symbols exist at country level like flags, culture level like the lotus flower symbolising the holy seat of Buddha and there are symbols specific to governments, professions, sports and so many other aspects of life. Individuals get represented by a symbol: our signature.

Fig. 1: Positive symbols that lift our heart.

In our unconscious, the term is even broader. Everything and everyone, you could argue is a symbol.

Pictures, paintings, sculptures, artefacts, television series, movies, theatre plays, cultural and national celebrations and advertisements are all symbols. Words, stories, books, newspapers, songs and emojis are also symbols. They all influence the way we think and behave, as well as our choices in much deeper level and in more ways we ever thought they would.

The things surrounding you in your home serve as subliminal reminders of who you are.

Denise Linn, healer & writer.

A horror movie will fill our unconscious with quite different images than a comedy. Therefore, our crew will get a different 'internal vision' and mission. And remember, what we feed it with, it focuses on.

People are symbols too! Surround yourself by people whose qualities you want and who inspire you. The people we live with and choose to spend our time with are the ones whose characteristics and behaviour we start to develop.

As children, our parents and teachers were the most important symbols in our life. During childhood, we were like sponges and 'blindly' followed the ways of our parents. We all know that we have become like our parents in many ways, or sometimes we do the exact opposite of what they did, because we no longer accept their ways. In either case, the point of reference is our parents – our first symbols.

Symbols influence our goals and reflect our values and emotions. Pay attention to them in your everyday life, and who and what you choose to have around you! Make symbolism work for you. Let me explain with some examples:

- **Yourself:** The expression on our face is a symbol to us and to others. When people think of you, how do they remember you? Smiling and happy, most of the time, or frowning and sad? Our smile is a powerful symbol for peace and kindness. Look at the pictures of yourself around your home. What is your expression? Does it translate to confidence and happiness?

- **Your significant others:** Whether you are single or in a relationship, be aware of what you look at every day in your bedroom. I have heard that clients have paintings of World War II in their bedrooms – from my experience, couples looking at this type of image do not make it easy on themselves to enjoy loving relationships. Symbols are powerful and carry meaning and vision. How much better would it be to have pictures of you and your partner looking connected and happy together?

- **Your family:** Think about the family pictures in your home. Are there pictures of your children with their friends in their bedrooms? Pictures of great memories and holidays? Pictures where the children hold awards or are at a favourite concert? Go around the house, be aware, and plan accordingly.

- **Animals:** If nature and animals are important to you, surround yourself with pictures of trees and animals. Buy nature books for your shelves and take pictures while hiking, which you can then enjoy looking at in your living room. Or if you can, take a leap of faith and open your home to animals. The more you take care of them, the more they take care of you.

Until one has loved an animal, a part of one's soul remains unawakened.

Anatole France, poet.

- **Art:** Art is a medium of expression. When in turmoil, we sometimes create or buy art pieces that represent our state of mind at that moment. That does not mean we should keep looking at them every day – this instructs our crew to stay in an *unresourceful* state. Conversely, art can be uplifting and meaningful. It is up to us to decide what to look at consciously and unconsciously every day.

- **Work:** What are your work objectives? What are your targets for your business? What are your company's values? What is the position you dream of getting? What is the salary you want? Place representations of all of those answers where you can see them easily – on your walls, your laptop, and your desk.

When I enter an office, I take note of what symbols are there. I quickly form an idea of what they look at every day and how the people working there become 'programmed'. Are the year's results celebrated? Are there pictures of team outings? Is there a framed display of the company's values?

Symbolism inspired Florence and I to have this book filled with pictures of defining moments in our NLP journey and whilst writing this book. We came up with icons and drawings that bring to you the NLP concepts and teachings more holistically, speaking to all of your senses. We want to 'talk to you' through language and also through pictures, shapes and colours.

Ships Created by NLP Course Participants – No Two Alike!

One of the biggest honours of my life has been to witness hundreds of people that I have worked with drawing their own 'ships' on the second day of the NLP Practitioner course. Continuing the metaphor of the conscious-unconscious, this idea to symbolise our very own being with *a ship* came to me. I offered some important guidelines how to go about it and choosing the timing this is done during the course is equally crucial. For the most part though, it was an open invitation for the participants to draw their 'ship', meaning 'themselves'.

Drawing our 'ship' is a profound experience. Full of symbolism and streaming out of the depths of our spirits and souls, capturing our 'ship' on paper reveals our emotions, thoughts and outlook on our own selves. I have seen cruise ships, naval ships, pirate ships, submarines, and spaceships – you name it! They are all packed with symbolism, reflective of each person's personality, their emotional state and the voyages they have been on. With their permission, and with great joy, I am sharing some of them with you (Fig. 2).

Irena Parpoula | Avito D. Ruina Jr. | Melina Danakaki

Fig. 2: Ships drawn by participants during various Life Spheres NLP Courses.

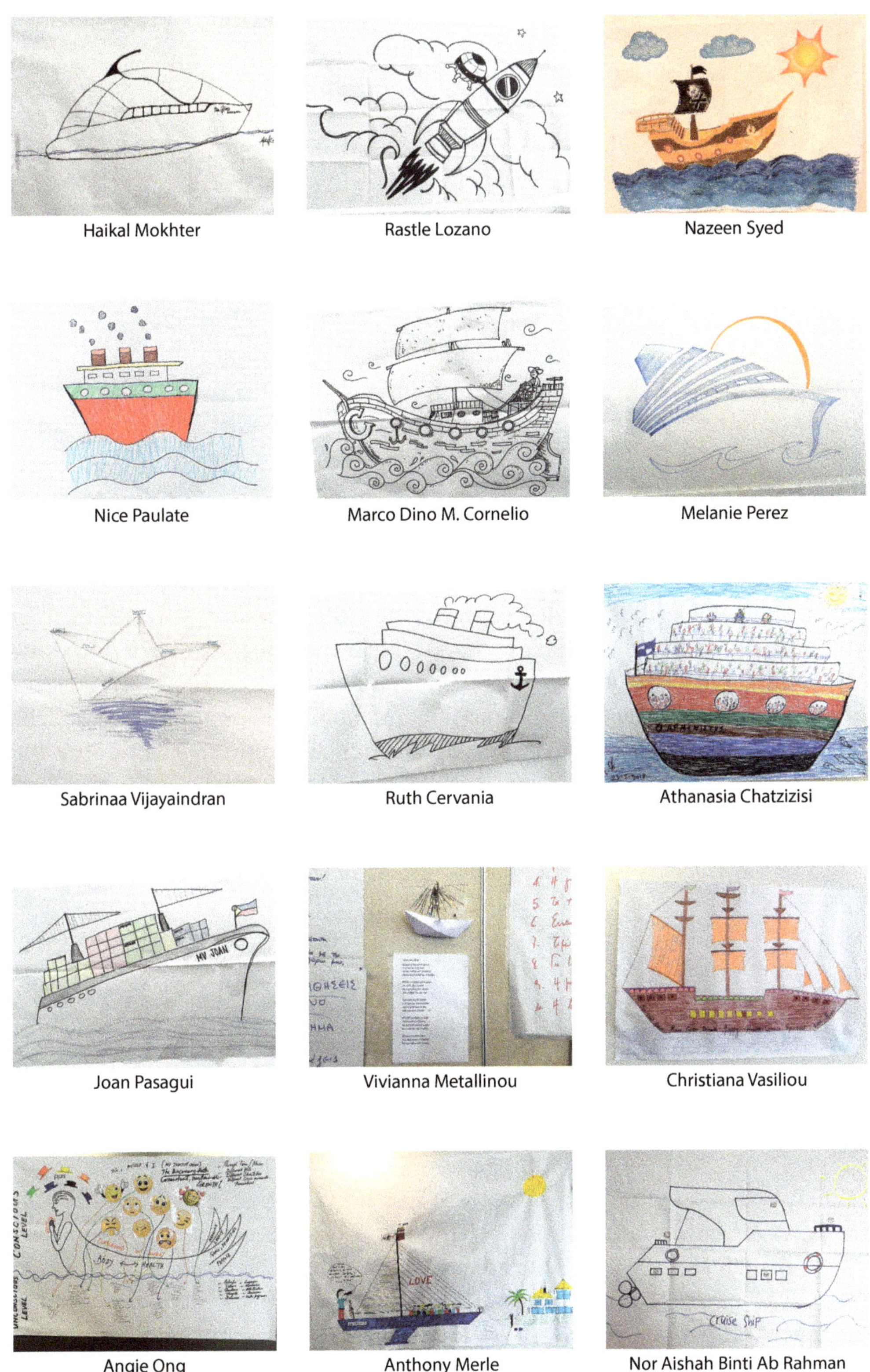

Haikal Mokhter | Rastle Lozano | Nazeen Syed

Nice Paulate | Marco Dino M. Cornelio | Melanie Perez

Sabrinaa Vijayaindran | Ruth Cervania | Athanasia Chatzizisi

Joan Pasagui | Vivianna Metallinou | Christiana Vasiliou

Angie Ong | Anthony Merle | Nor Aishah Binti Ab Rahman

Fig. 2: Ships drawn by participants during various Life Spheres NLP Courses.

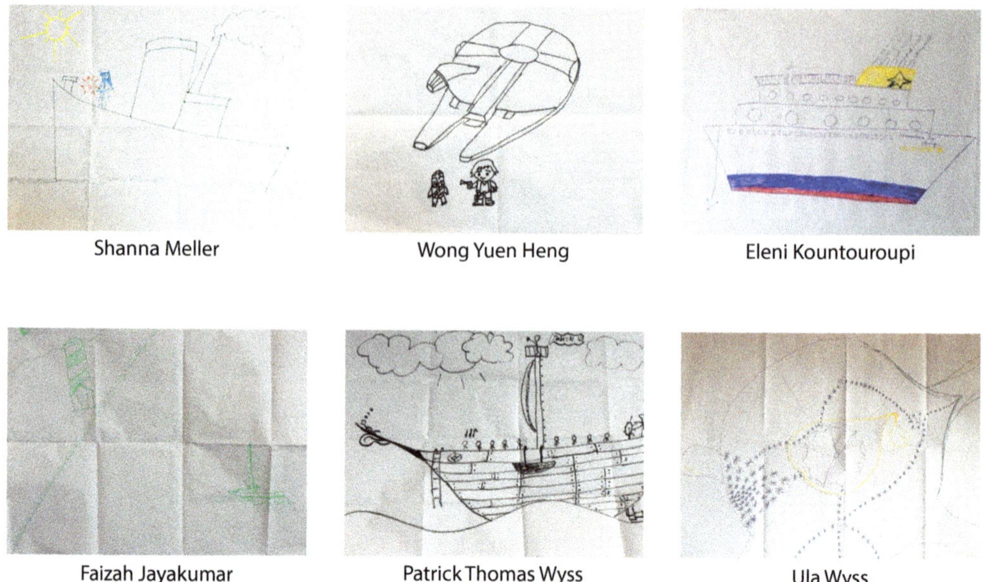

Shanna Meller — Wong Yuen Heng — Eleni Kountouroupi

Faizah Jayakumar — Patrick Thomas Wyss — Ula Wyss

Fig. 2: Ships drawn by participants during various Life Spheres NLP Courses.

During one NLP Practitioner course, I had the pleasure of working with one of the participants, Ramani who, on his own initiative, decided to draw a **second** ship on the last day of the course. Ramani experienced a massive transformation during the course and felt compelled to re-draw his ship. His first version of his ship on the second day did not represent any more the way his thinking and emotional world had shifted in a week. His ship had developed in his mind. Nothing stays the same.

Fig. 3: Ramani's two ships, the second and last day of the NLP Practitioner course.

A few words from Ramani himself:

"When I drew my first ship, I had a long-held view that my life was always meant to be hard and the image in my mind was one of having weathered many brutal storms, but still remaining tough and able to chug along regardless of difficulties. Eleni's loving and comfortably uncomfortable guidance throughout the course led to an amazing awakening about the many self-imposed limiting beliefs I carried as a result of past conditioning and life experiences, with a new appreciation that life was indeed all about our own projected perceptions. My second, shiny new ship representation of myself

– before the course even ended – was simply a self-realisation that I can and will make positive transformations to my life by making constant and gradual upgrades to my thinking software."

Everyday Thinking and Doing: Consider This …

As you now know, your unconscious works best with clear instructions, and the power of repetition creates new habits. So here are a few tips to help you install habits that lift up your 'reality', those around you, and the future generations to come.

- Take some time to reflect on your emotions as understanding them and their source helps raise our awareness, bring us closer to our unconscious, release unpleasant emotions from the past and raise our self-esteem:
  - Get your journal! Write down as many emotions as you can. Write them as they come – spontaneously.
  - Write about the times you have felt appreciated, exhilarated and blissful.
  - Express your frustration about things that happened ten, twenty, thirty or forty years ago. If you cry, it's fine! Empty out!
  - Write about your achievements and the moments you have felt the happiest and most proud.
- Take a moment and reflect on your symbols. Be aware about what these are for you and what you look at every day. Whatever we see, hear, taste and feel with our senses finds its way into our mind. That means, it is better for us to place ourselves in an environment that moves us forward and holds images and sounds we like and that benefit us.
  - Look around you and check what pictures, paintings and objects you have, for example in your bedroom, your office, or living room.
  - Who chose them?
  - Observe them in detail. What could possibly be the message they carry for your unconscious?
  - Do you need to re-decorate some parts of your home? Make a list!
- Take your time with these exercises. Re-read this chapter if you need to. It contains so much valuable information and it takes a while to absorb it all. When you are ready, turn the page and dive into the chapter about processing information through the NLP Communication Model.

NLP Communication Model …

… processing incoming information via our senses

By Florence

Illusion is the first of all pleasures.

Voltaire, French writer, historian, and philosopher.

My great nephew William loves his building bricks and at the age of four he presented me with his representation of my home (**Fig. 1**). It had my husband Pat and I on the roof, apparently putting out the washing to dry. Then it seems I fell off the roof, but Pat came to my rescue and I was all better after he applied a sticking plaster!

Fig.1: William and my 'home'!

It's odd to get such a graphic illustration of how a young child sees your life and home. Yet in another way it's a perfect illustration of how we interpret what we see in our own way and according to our own life experiences. We don't dry our washing on the roof, indeed I have never been on our roof. If I fell off it, something more than a plaster would be needed. And, to my knowledge, my husband rarely pegs out the washing (and never when William has been around!). Yet in William's mind and 'map' all of these things were plausible – they are his view of reality!

So What Is Reality?

Let's just look at this idea of 'reality' for the moment. Here are some conversations I have experienced:

- A delegate on a course once said to me mischievously: "But of course in the real world, Florence ...". And I replied (with a twinkle in my eye): "What makes you think the world I inhabit is not real?" He laughed and admitted he hadn't thought about it that way.
- Another person introduced himself by saying: "I'm the kind of person who tells it like it is – and other people don't like it". I thanked him and said:

"Well, how you see it, certainly." He looked at me quizzically and we smiled at each other.

- On another occasion, the staff in a hotel I was staying in kept bringing tea and coffee at quite random times rather than what (as I thought) had been agreed. My frustration was building up and I only just stopped myself from saying out loud: "What are they thinking?". When I checked things out, they had been given the wrong information.

The point is we all see the world through the prism of our own experiences and what we think is going on… and they are unique to us. Even though we may have siblings brought up in the same household, we will have different experiences within our family life as well as throughout our lives. From our beginnings, our world is being shaped by the emotional states and the circumstances our parents are in when we come into the family. Our position in the family: eldest, middle child or the baby of the family impacts on our experience and the expectations placed on us from the earliest time in our lives. When we leave home, we are likely to live in different places, go to different places on holiday, have our own relationships and have a whole myriad of different life experiences – for each person their 'map' of the world is different. After all that, and even though there will be some things that we agree on, it is highly unlikely that we all see everything the same way. If we consider that our siblings have the same roots as us – imagine the differences from people we encounter from different families, different areas, different parts of the world. How much more differently are they likely to see things from the way we do? To use a favourite expression of mine, we might be tempted to think other people are "wired up to the lights" (mad!) in the attitudes they take and the choices they make.

As mentioned in the first chapter, one of the underpinning theories of NLP is a branch of philosophy called constructivism. A central assumption of this is that people uniquely create their own realities or models of the world based on their life experiences. We internally order our experiences into organised patterns or structures. Simply put, we each experience the world in our own unique way, and it can be a big mistake in our relationships to assume others see things in the same way that we do. In NLP we summarise this with the presuppositions (see Ch.9 – these are in effect resourceful beliefs), namely:

- Everyone has a different map of the world.
- The map is not the territory. *

*This phrase was originally coined by Polish–American scientist and philosopher, Alfred Korzybski in 1933 and is a metaphorical illustration of the difference between belief and reality. I.e. how we see it is not necessarily how it is.

In other words, how we see things is not necessarily how it *is* ... how we see things is simply our internal representation of a person or a situation.

Once we're thrown off our habitual paths, we think all is lost, but it's only here that the new and the good begins.

Leo Tolstoy, Russian writer.

A very common example of this is when we listen to people debating a topic. Whichever point of view we favour at the outset, when another person puts forward their view in a compelling (and respectful) way, we may not necessarily change our view, but we may understand more clearly why they hold theirs.

So how do our experiences influence us and how we see the world around us? To answer that question, we need to look at the way the brain processes the information it receives.

The Origins Of The NLP Communication Model

I was giving my address over the phone one day and the reaction of the person on the other end of the line illustrated how the brain processes information and the influence of their 'map'. My house name is Orchard Syke (*syke* being a Cumbrian word for a stream). Orchard is a familiar word, but syke is not (if you don't live in Cumbria that is!) So, the person kept calling it 'sky' because it was the closest word she could think of. Eventually I had to spell it out for her. When I gave her the next line – Unthank – she groaned, and I had to spell that too. This person was from another part of the country and the words I was using were alien to her. One of the ways we make sense of new information is to fit it with what we know already, so she found it hard to process what I was telling her. This is a common experience for me when giving my address (and of course I also struggle when hearing unfamiliar words!).

So, to look at how the brain filters incoming information let's look at the model developed by Tad James and Wyatt Woodsmall, based on the work of Richard Bandler and John Grinder, and is illustrated in **Fig. 2.**

Originally it was estimated that we have over two million bits of information coming into our brains every second, far more than our conscious mind can process. More recent research suggests this figure could be as great as eleven million (according to Timothy Wilson, professor of psychology at the University of Virginia and author of the book *Strangers to Ourselves: Discovering the Adaptive Unconscious*).

Consequently, the brain acts as a sort of reducing valve; by the time something comes into our conscious mind, the unconscious has refined it and given it

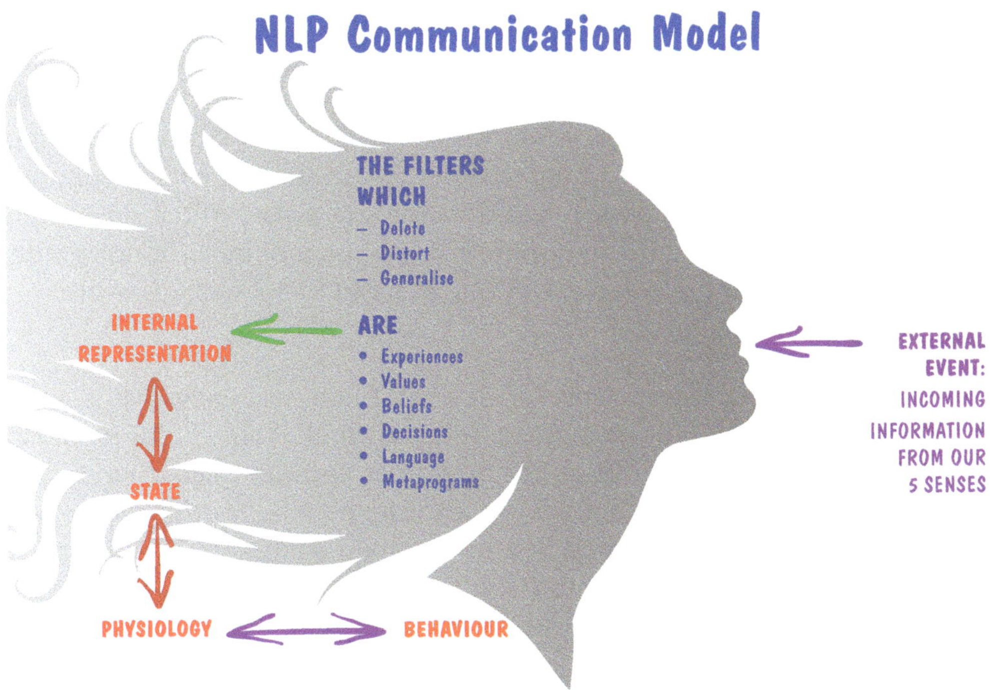

Fig. 2: The NLP Communication Model.

a meaning – in effect it creates its own view of the 'territory'. In NLP this is referred to as our *internal representation,* in other words the thought or ideas we hold in our head about someone or something that we have experienced. Noam Chomsky (sometimes referred to as 'the father of modern linguistics') explained that the brain filters the incoming information in a three-part process of deletion, distortion and generalisation – let's look at these parts more closely.

Deletion

The unconscious mind selects what is brought into our conscious awareness and what is left in the background. We become aware of this process when people draw things to our attention that we hadn't noticed before. You may have experienced this, for example, when you are interested in a specific type of car: you start to see these cars more and more on the roads or in car parks; or when a holiday destination you hadn't considered before keeps cropping up in magazines, television programmes or conversations. Those things were always there, but your unconscious mind did not consider them worthy of your interest, so they were deleted – at least, as far as our conscious mind is concerned.

An experiment that demonstrates the effect of '*deletion*' was conducted as a result of a New York policeman who was convicted of collusion with his colleagues. The police officers had been found guilty of beating up a suspect, and their colleague, who was chasing a felon past the scene, denied that he had seen anything. The court did not believe him. Subsequently an experiment was set up in a park to recreate the scene. This time the 'chasers' – unsuspecting members of the public – were simply told to chase another person running in front of them. At one point, a mock beating was staged to the side of the path they were running on. The experiment was run a number of times with different chasers, and more than 60% of them failed to notice the brawl!

Distortion

Our brain also fits new experiences with what it knows already, that is, with patterns of thinking already established. When we look at clouds, for example, we start to see shapes – our brain is fitting their abstract shapes into forms it already knows. This is really useful in learning because it helps us use our current knowledge to understand new information coming in; if someone is already proficient with a number of software packages, that knowledge will help them get to grips with one that is new to them.

Distortion can cause us problems when we 'bend' what we hear to fit with an already existing internal pattern, such as hearing an unfamiliar word like 'syke' and turning it into 'sky'. Another example, one of my own experiences, is that when someone gives me directions in an area I have some familiarity with, I find myself fitting what they are saying into my mental map of the area. I bend what they are saying to fit my pre-held pattern. (And it's not just humans that I treat in this way – I have done the same thing with the sat-nav in my car!) Unsurprisingly, this often results in me getting lost!

So *distortion* is an essential part of our learning experience and helps us make links between existing knowledge and new knowledge. Distortion can have much less helpful consequences for us, though, when we 'bend' the information coming in to our brain to reinforce negative patterns of thinking about ourselves or others.

Generalisation

The third filter is generalisation: this involves taking an 'instance' and making a general rule from it. This is really useful in our everyday lives because it means we do not have to re-learn basic things every day. So when we get in the car in the morning we just assume that we, and everyone else, will drive on the left-hand side of the road (if we are in the UK). Or, having read a number of books from one particular author, we tend to assume that because we like their style, we will like any new book they publish.

While valuable in many respects, generalisation can also create problems too. It means we can reapply a certain pattern of thinking to other situations, often without question. For example, if I mention performance appraisals to people,

I often see a range of facial expressions that are followed, more often than not, by derisory comments. These people's opinions of appraisals are based on their previous bad experiences, and this colours their views of the whole process. This can also work the other way around of course: a previous good experience can lead to an assumption that all appraisals are like this.

This three-part filtering process is common to all of us, it is essential to manage the flow of incoming information and is happening unconsciously. The result of this process, however, is to narrow and 'customise' our band of what we regard as reality. In conscious awareness, most people can only handle a relatively few pieces of information at any one time. The actual number is subject to debate, but just try going shopping for, say ten items, without a written list and notice what happens!

A way to think of this process is to imagine that the 11 million pieces of information coming into us, (mentioned earlier), is like a beam of light being shone on a screen. Our brain, and more specifically our internal representation of what we are experiencing, is like that movie screen. As we cannot handle that volume of information, our brain filters it – so the majority of what is coming in is deleted or altered. This is like a filter being passed between the light and the screen. So what gets through the filter and gets projected on to the screen of our mind is our unique 'internal representation' of the world around us. This is illustrated in **Fig. 3** where the filter, in this case a flower, alters what is reflected onto the movie screen of our mind i.e. our internal representation.

Fig. 3: The 'Movie Screen' Of Our Mind.

And part and parcel of this filtration process is that we apply our own values and level of significance to what we perceive, and hence our interpretation of events. In other words, our individual internal filters act like the flower filter and determine what gets projected onto our internal screen; which will therefore be significantly different to what other people experience in the same moment.

Moreover, because this process is happening unconsciously, we may not even be aware that how we perceive things is just that – our own perception – and is not necessarily correct. So when people say that they 'tell it like it is', they seem unaware that it is more accurate to add the words 'to me'.

In fact, our views of the world are so heavily 'interpreted' that when we recount a conversation or incident, around 80% or more is in effect 'made up' by our brain. Every time we recall an event or conversation, our brain networks change in ways that can alter our recall of it later. As a result, the more times we retrieve the information, the further away the facts are from the original event.

As a trainer I was dismayed by this at first. But now, when anyone gets anything of what I have said, I get such a thrill! It stops me thinking that just because I think I've set out something clearly, people will understand what I meant them to. My impact as a trainer, therefore, depends on staying aware – and not assuming. I wonder how I am doing with my explanation to you so far?

The Conscious Versus The Unconscious – Who Is In Charge?

In spite of our self-awareness… and many of us spend a lot of time working on it… it is estimated that over 90% of our behaviour is driven not by our conscious, but our unconscious mind. (See Chapter 2). The scholar, artist and author Bob Samples reflected on how Einstein saw the unconscious as a sacred gift and the conscious as a faithful servant; and quipped that in modern life we now worship the servant and degrade the gift!

This was understood by ancient civilisations but it only began to be really understood in modern times in the twentieth century. The unconscious mind has been likened to a five-year-old child seeing things in a simplistic way, needing direction and eager to please. As Eleni points out in the previous chapter, when we have a goal of some kind, the conscious mind sets the direction – like the captain of a ship. But it is the integration and the communication between the conscious and the unconscious – the captain and the crew working together – which has the power to get us there (or not, as the case may be). How the unconscious part of our brains filters information coming in greatly determines how we react and what we show to the outside world.

How Does Our '*State*' Affect Our Impact On Others?

When you look again at the NLP Communication Model, you can see that the filtering process creates our own internal representation of the information coming in to us. Part of how information is filtered relates to the beliefs and values we hold, and this affects the interpretation we make of that information.

This interpretation, in turn, affects our emotional *state*. (In this context, state refers to the mental and physical processes we are experiencing moment to moment.) So, if the way in which someone speaks to us seems disrespectful – because of what they said, or how they said it – then the state could be one of anger. For example, someone might speak to us using language or a turn of phrase that reminds us of someone else with whom we had a bad relationship. Our interpretation, therefore, is affected by that association in our mind.

And this chain reaction continues, because our state affects our internal physiology. The body responds to anger as an emergency signal and our muscles tense, our breathing rate increases, and our heart rate increases. This reaction is triggered unconsciously, and we are into a physiological response to anger before our conscious mind can rationalise the situation.

Of course, what is happening on the inside shows on the outside and our emotional state can impact on other people around us – even before we say anything. Someone once said to me: "Florence, when I'm angry with someone there is no way they can tell". Well he may be right in as much as some people display their emotions more readily than others, but as this process is largely unconscious, the greater likelihood is that there will be some external indication of our state – of which we may be unaware. Just like any other animal, humans are likely to pick up such signals at some level. At the very least, when we start to speak, our choice of words and tone of voice can give plenty of information about our emotional state to others.

Then, of course, the whole process starts to happen for those who are on the 'receiving end' of our state; they start to interpret our behaviour as it impacts on them, and our original intention may be lost as the reaction of one draws in the other. An NLP practitioner friend of mine, when working with groups, starts by asking the question: "What is it like to be on the receiving end of you?". Many members of her audience start to think of the answer to that (possibly chilling) question for the first time. It's quite a thought, isn't it?

Does it Have to be This Way?

In short … no! We can intervene in several key areas and make a change in this process. We can:

- Update our filters by revising our values and beliefs – in effect 'reframing'* our views of ourselves and others to take a more resourceful attitude.
- Changing the messages to our unconscious by becoming aware of and changing our language.
- Becoming aware of and taking control of how we are presenting ourselves physically to others i.e. our body language.

We *can* change our story, and indeed we can write any story we want (remember the exercise I did on the plane?) When we choose to change the filters that aren't working for us, our reality changes too. For example you may have a colleague or a family member whose motives you question – consider what else might be behind their behaviour that may have a more positive connotation. How would thinking in this way improve your relationship with them? There may be times too when the person we are having negative thoughts about is ourselves – perhaps before we take a meeting or give a presentation. In these situations what thoughts do we have about ourselves and the reaction of our audience? What could more helpful thoughts or attitudes give us?

As well as what we may do *intentionally*, of course, our brain also continues (unconsciously) to re-filter the experiences in our lives over time. The result of this is that we naturally review, re-assess and re-interpret events. Very often our view of a situation or a person can shift. This is sometimes described variously as taking a longer view, maturing, or even mellowing. Whatever we call it, clearly our 'filters' are not fixed, but are modified as we progress through life, as we experience new things, learn new things, and meet new people. And as our filters change, information passing through, or being re-filtered, is interpreted differently.

So read on. As you progress through this book we will look at ways in which NLP can help you to take more control of this process, by making changes about how you think about yourself and others, and how you view the situations you find yourself in.

Robert Dilts, author, trainer and co-founder of NLP University, says what brought him into the world of NLP was observing that when people make changes, they usually moved from a fixed perspective to be able to see multiple perspectives.

---

*The term reframing is used in NLP when we give an alternative meaning to or interpretation of an event (Ch.23).

Everyday Thinking And Doing: Consider this …

You can start becoming more aware of how we 'filter' the world around us now by doing this short exercise:

- Have a look around the room or area where you are reading this – notice what stands out to you? Then consider what it is that drew your attention to those objects or areas?
    - It may be for example flowers, animals or pictures of loved ones that draw your attention because of the positive significance they hold for you.
    - Conversely so, it may be a messy area, a piece of unfinished work or something that looks out of place that has the opposite effect.
- Now close your eyes for a moment and when you reopen them notice the number of objects that are coloured red. Had you noticed them before you applied the 'red filter'?
- Now deliberately take your attention to an area around you that you hadn't focussed on before during this exercise e.g. items on a shelf, the bark of a tree, a light fitting etc. When you focus on it what do you notice now that you hadn't before?
- Consider applying this type of thinking to yourself – as human beings we are often quite self-critical, so instead take time to notice:
    - Three good qualities about yourself that you don't usually notice or acknowledge?
    - What difference would it make for you to notice these more regularly?

NLP Pillars of Success …

… the foundations of NLP thinking and doing

By Eleni

Concentrate all your thoughts upon the work at hand. The sun's rays do not burn until brought to a focus.

Alexander Graham Bell, inventor and scientist.

Fig. 1: Pillars Parthenon inspired!

First there were three, then there were four, then five, then six, then some more – the NLP Pillars of Success! They are the foundations of NLP thinking and doing. NLP has developed over the years and so have the pillars. While having three was a great start in the early days of NLP, more were required to reflect how NLP evolved and to meet the demands of our increasingly diverse world.

So, let me offer six pillars, not necessarily strictly abiding by any former list, yet fully leaning into the NLP wisdom of decades, and hopefully giving you a snapshot of how these pillars can turn our everyday reality into to a more fulfilling and joyful experience. As you will experience, these themes run throughout this book.

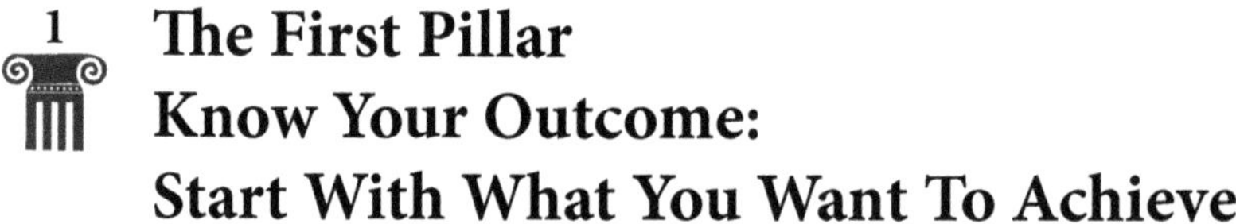

1 The First Pillar Know Your Outcome: Start With What You Want To Achieve

No matter what book or website about NLP you find yourself looking at, they all share one common pillar, namely that NLP is *results-oriented*. It paves the way to get you from where you are now to where you want to be, from the present state to your desired state.

More often than we'd like to admit, we spend a lot of time thinking about what we *do not* want; it's when we focus on what we *do* want that things start changing and going in the right direction for us. Reflecting on what we want, combined with our enthusiasm and certainty, makes achieving our goals easier and contributes to growth and learning.

People want to move forward, and NLP makes this possible through its win-win mentality and focus on well-formed outcomes. The term 'well-formed' means well-defined. It's about setting goals by not only being specific and clear about them, but also taking into consideration other variables such as any possible internal conflicts or resistance. It takes a person with vision to see far ahead and create a path that will lead to the result they want, while still being prepared to deal with any potential hurdles along the way.

There will be more about goal setting, well-formed outcomes and living our dreams later, in Ch.28 to be precise – the last chapter of this book – but of course that will only be a temporary ending, more likely it will be the beginning for you!

The Second Pillar
Sensory Acuity: Maintain Awareness Of What Is Happening Around You And Within You

Our senses are the readers of the world around us. By being more observant, we become sharper at noticing and collecting information that we'd otherwise miss. The more we pick up about the world around us (and within us), the more we spot opportunities for what we want to achieve. We start to recognise different emotional states more effectively and develop a deeper level of understanding about people and behaviours.

Most of us were not taught in school, or at home, how to deal with our emotions. Their importance in our lives and relationships was not highlighted like it is nowadays. Today, we have all the necessary knowledge to understand our emotions far better and to manage them effectively.

Finding the right words to define our emotional state frees us from the chains that keep us captive in unwanted patterns. When expressed, any feeling serves its purpose and we become freer. Instead of living in silence about things that have hurt us, even for decades, we have a choice – to put a name on 'what's going on' inside us, to share it, to communicate it and to empty out.

This is when we can start talking about emotional and social intelligence. It's when we hone our skills to see more closely, hear more actively, and regularly practice noticing more, that we become more in tune with our own needs and wants. We get to know ourselves better and become more efficient in what we are out to achieve.

The tools and techniques that help us manage our emotions are one of NLP's major contributions to the world. It helps close any gaps we may have experienced during our education in our formative years.

We'll look at emotions in more detail throughout this book, particularly in the chapters on submodalities, anchoring and timeline.

3 The Third Pillar
Rapport: Create A Climate Of Trust And Understanding Quickly

Rapport usually happens naturally with our friends and people in our family because of our common backgrounds, culture, interests and goals. It does not necessarily happen with everyone, but if there is common ground then through the years it creates a bond. This is why we develop deep levels of trust and understanding with certain people.

The key to NLP is that it asks how we can build similar relationships with people we have not necessarily spent many years with. How can we establish rapport with people we have just met? Among the many NLP tools, there's always the underlying principle of being interested in others, and genuinely wanting to learn more about them – their feelings and their way of thinking.

4 The Fourth Pillar
Behavioural Flexibility: Be Prepared To Change What You Are Doing If It Is Not Working

Behavioural flexibility means taking a decision to learn from *any* situation, no matter how uncomfortable it is. Just like going to the gym, it involves a certain level of discomfort, because it's meant to work on our muscles and our body's flexibility. It takes courage and consistency every day to find ways to be flexible and adapt to a new reality.

The good news is that once we practise these things, the uncomfortable bits become more comfortable. And we discover that the fruits of our labours are triple-fold! Outside the gym, one question we may ask ourselves is: how often and how consistently do we change our ways of thinking and doing?

When we decide to consider other points of view, we expand our thinking. And as a result, we have more choices about how we move forward with our plans.

The plasticity of our brain may be one of the key factors that makes us able to develop as a species everywhere and anywhere. It may also still be one of the most underestimated ingredients of success. It is when we step out of 'our way' of seeing things, that we interact with others more easily and efficiently in order to get better results.

5 The Fifth Pillar
Psychology And Physiology of Excellence: Elicit The Patterns Of Excellent Behaviour

In the previous chapter, Florence introduced the NLP Communication Model which demonstrates that beliefs and values lead to thoughts, and these in turn affect emotional states and physiology, and ultimately our behaviour. They are all linked.

When we adopt positive physiology, emotionally we feel better and our behaviour has more chances to produce the results we hope for. Furthermore, when we successfully manage our emotions, our physiology and non-verbal communication improves.

This management of beliefs and emotions is a skill – a skill we can learn and get better at. We can all learn to adopt emotional states and body language that gets us better results. And we can all model win–win behaviours by working and mastering our beliefs.

This leads us to the wonders of 'modelling excellence'. This is the NLP pillar in which everything comes together. Typically, it embodies the doctrine "If one person can do it, anyone can do it", which helps us dig into the beliefs, values, language, body language and internal strategies of someone whose behaviours and results we would like to reproduce in ourselves.

6 The Sixth Pillar
Take Action: Take The Steps And Put The Effort In To Accomplish What Your Desire To Be/Have/Do

From all the incredible quotes I collected when I first created my company Life Spheres, I was looking for one that encapsulated the essence of my vision and message to the world. I focused in on this one, by *Napoleon Hill: **Action is the measure of intelligence.*** He captured my thoughts in a concise and powerful manner, and which becomes more relevant to me every year that passes.

"Just do it!" is the world-famous slogan of the sports brand NIKE. It appeals to many of us. It's all about going after your dreams by taking steps and showing your crew, as the leader–captain you want to be, that you mean business. It's about going after what you want.

The obstacles we encounter on our journey are proof that we can and have progressed, and it's by sheer determination and total conviction that we overcome them and get closer to what fills our heart.

Action can also mean *in-action*, if it's a consciously made decision not to do something. There are times in our lives when we have just got to let go and let things flow. But as long as this is part of a bigger plan and it helps us achieve our dreams, then it's fine. But we *must* have a clear agenda, and take the necessary steps, and be ready to adjust along the way!

Athens, One Day, One Chance

Having my wallet snatched from my bag back home a month previously, I had to also replace all my banking cards that were issued by banks in Europe, including one in Greece. Together with my family, we were passing through Athens and I had just twenty-four hours to ensure I got a replacement for my stolen Greek debit card.

Agitated and in a hurry, I entered a branch of my bank in the centre of Athens, hoping the issue would not take long to resolve. We also wanted to get to the Acropolis later that day for our annual family picture. A not-so smiley clerk came up to us and I explained my problem to him. He asked me for my Greek passport, and I realised I was traveling on my Dutch one! I offered to show him an electronic version of my Greek passport – not good enough.

To have my credentials checked, I would have to go to the Consulate and get official proof of my Greek passport and who I was. And I had to do all that before boarding the plane back home to Malaysia. Otherwise, I'd have to wait for another whole year until my next holiday abroad. I left the bank in a foul mood. I could see the man's point, but how could he not see mine?

The NLP pillars came to my rescue! I simply focused on getting the job done – because *I wanted results.* My senses allowed me to be aware of my irritation, but they kept playing the wrong tape over and over in my head. I had hoped for some flexibility from the man in the bank, but in reality, it was easier for me to tap into *my own flexibility options* and to *take action*!

Clearly, I had failed to build *rapport* with this man. His non-smiley face had gotten to me from the very first second, and my husband and I had entered the bank in a bad mood. I missed out making a success of the interaction, but I realised there were more branches of my bank in the city! Ten minutes later, I was in another branch with two clear things in mind: to build rapport, and to control my tone of voice. Nobody owes me anything, after all, and in the main they do want to help.

Deploying my sweetest smile, I soon found myself sitting in the bank manager's office, explaining calmly how I saw the bank's reason for wanting to see my passport and was hoping for a miracle. Sure enough the director offered me the following option: they could call an employee in the branch in my home-town of Thessaloniki, who knew me and who could easily identify me over the phone. In the meantime, I asked the bank manger about his holiday which had been on the same island as ours. We had a lot to talk about!

I was the epitome of *physiological and psychological excellence* at that moment (and my husband did a great job too!). By the end of the morning, I was formally identified. We made some new friends, and I even forgot about the card that had vexed me so much. When they handed the new one over to me, I smiled and thought about the lessons I had just learnt.

Everyday Thinking And Doing: Consider This ...

So, here are a couple of ways to hone some new skills:

- What results do you want to have? What is meaningful for you to create?
- During a twenty-four-hour period, observe who you naturally get along with and with whom you face certain resistance.
- Who do you feel you can count on?
- Next time something upsets you, write down on a piece of paper all that you feel and think about the situation around this unpleasant feeling – without any censorship – then throw the paper away. See how more aware you feel of what caused the frustration and note what you might have learnt from it.
- Consider the last time you demonstrated great levels of flexibility. Did it make a positive difference in your life, and that of others?

Perception Is Projection …

… recognising our own behaviour in others

By Eleni

The playwright William Shakespeare said:

We see the world, not as it is, but as we are.

Similarly, Stephen Covey, the American author and businessman, beautifully added:

Or, as we are conditioned to see it.

My Mother's Genius

Let me share one of the biggest lessons of my life ... taught to me by who else but my mother. When I was a child, I would sometimes catch her looking downcast or apparently not knowing how to enjoy her day. Problems of all sorts were weighing on her shoulders and I felt helpless. I wished that she wanted to change and to feel happier.

Then one day, my mother said: "Eleni, you want me to change. You want my feelings to change and for me to be happier, right?" I nodded in agreement. "Then, Eleni, why not start with yourself? Why don't you change your need for me to change? Then, your life will be easier".

Perception Is Projection

Remember how The NLP Communication Model works (Ch.3) and how we see things through our own filters? Florence used the metaphor of a projector and screen to explain how we filter information coming **in** to us. But this works both ways, so, switch this around and imagine you are watching a movie on a large screen and the projector is now your own brain. What you ***project*** to the outside world is a perception from within.

The essence of 'perception is projection' is that our reality is in fact our own mind's projection to the outside world, and this projection will be fed back to us by others and so create new perceptions. We see things more as we are rather than as they are, just like William Shakespeare stated.

When we change our internal world, our projections change as well. Our world is reflected on the world out there and fed back to us. Knowing this helps us realise that in order for things to change, we have got to change ourselves — our beliefs; the way we see things inside. After all, we create a mirror of who we are inside.

When we think about a particular thing or concept like moving to a new house or starting a new sport, we tend to see it everywhere! And everyone seems to be talking about it! That is because our brain acts like a search engine, and when we 'type something in' our brain starts retrieving relevant information.

What does this mean? Well, it's the basis of 'perception is projection'. When we concentrate on 'loveliness', our internal encyclopaedia looks for 'loveliness' everywhere. Our mind gets instructions to fill up with 'loveliness'.

Remember the Prime Directives of the Unconscious in Ch.2 and the one where we 'take everything personally'? If we hear people talking about cars, we think about our own car. It's how the mind works, and it associates notions from the outside world with our own model of the world. Again, this is the basis of 'perception is projection'.

Perception Is Projection In Action

Have there ever been times in your life when you met somebody and thought, "Such an arrogant person!", or "They're quite opinionated – I'm glad I'm not like that!" I'm guessing, like most of us, that you have.

By taking a good look at a situation and what has been triggered inside you, you might come to the realisation that it is you who is behaving arrogantly and or being opinionated – not necessarily during your interaction with that same person but in another context in your life, or perhaps even within yourself. Frankly, simply having the thought that someone is arrogant means that we think we're better than them at some level. Therefore, are we not being arrogant ourselves?

The idea is that what we see in others we *only* see because, at that moment, it's a prominent part within us. *If you spot it, you got it!* And the very fact that we deny this quality means that we deny a part of ourselves, as if, or because, we're ashamed of it at some level. This alerts us to accept that part of ourselves, to deal with it and give it its place.

What others do or how they act is *their* choice, and how we perceive their actions is *our* choice. Which begs the question: "Would it not be useful to make sure we are giving the other person a fair chance and to take a good look within ourselves, instead of jumping to make a judgement?" We then might conclude that, since the only information we have about other people is what we project on them ourselves, there is hardly any benefit in judging or trying to change them. Because we cannot change others, the ultimate choice is to empower ourselves.

In a nutshell, understanding 'perception is projection' can provide a powerful tool and foster habits that we can employ when we encounter resistance or a lack of rapport in our relationships.

Thus, instead of making futile attempts to 'make others change', we can invest our time in working on ourselves and find more answers and solutions for ourselves, a strategy that simultaneously contributes positively to everyone around us as well as ourselves.

Take a moment to think: 'How will discovering your own unconscious, your set of beliefs and values, help you? How will concentrating more on you and what you can do, provide you with far more life options?'

'Perception is projection' is not today's news. Its message has been recognised, discussed and lectured on for centuries. It gives us the responsibility and empowerment to change what we do not like in our current situation by projecting a new scenario. Of course, that's not always as easy as it sounds, but it is an encouraging thought which provides us with the power of 'choice'.

Let him who would move the world first move himself.

Socrates, classical Greek philosopher.

My Favourite 'Perception Is Projection' Story

One of my favourite stories arises from when I was running my first Master Practitioner course in Malaysia. I was fully engrossed in a presentation by one of the delegates, focusing on her profound sharing, grace, and choice of words, and being grateful I was there to witness that moment, when I noticed that she was wearing a silver chain, and – oh my god – gold sandals! I felt an unsettling sensation in my body, and my previous state of euphoria was disrupted by a sort of bump. I silently questioned what happened in that moment and noticed that it related to my beliefs around fashion, elegance and colour matching – they had been challenged!

You see, I come from Thessaloniki in Greece, and back in the day, and because of the way I was raised, combining silver and gold colours was a real *faux pas* – my reaction was instant and came straight from some unconscious ingrained belief from the distant past! Within just a couple of minutes I 'recovered' – I am an NLP trainer, after all, and you would expect that, right? So I quickly re-focused on the speaker and the inspiring parts of her presentation.

During the break, I headed to the women's restroom. As I washed my hands, I looked in the mirror and a moment of panic turned into a moment of intense laughter. My mind was running 'perception is projection' consciously and unconsciously, and presented me with some interesting facts! I was wearing a gold chain and silver earrings! A dreadful sight! I'd forgotten to take my chain off that morning because I was rushing. And, so, here it was: the only reason I'd noticed the delegate's 'mismatch according to me' was because I had done it myself. I quickly took the chain off (correcting the 'problem'), smiled to myself and made my way back to the training room.

The delegates were still chatting, so I went to congratulate Flavie on her presentation and I noticed that in fact her chain was not just silver, but silver mixed with gold round circles, a lovely design I could not fully see from where I had been seated previously. Now that I had taken off my own chain and somehow corrected the 'issue' that had clearly only been in my head, the 'issue' about her seemed to disappear (not that there ever was an issue – just one I thought existed).

Although this story might seem trivial, I learnt a massive amount from it, and in my opinion, it's funny stories like this that have the most juice!

For the next few years, I shared this story hundreds of times, and each time it touched new parts of me and new dimensions of my mindset. Who said you cannot combine silver with gold anyway? And what other 'realities' or 'opposing ideas' was I not willing to combine?

This story is still providing me with new learning curves, and I'm convinced that I'll hear from you because it means something to you, too.

It's not what you look at that matters,
it's what you see.

Henry David Thoreau, poet & philosopher.

Perceiving Others: Mirror Neurons At Work!

Some relatively recent discoveries in neuroscience give us another insight into what is happening in our interactions with others. A specific class of brain cells called *mirror neurons* make the whole discussion around how we perceive others even more interesting.

Professor of human physiology Dr Giacomo Rizzolatti and his team from the University of Parma, noticed something peculiar while testing monkey brains: the *same neurons fired* when a.) a monkey performed an action AND b.) when it watched another monkey performing the same action. Or put another way, the brain activity in a monkey eating a banana was the same as when the monkey was watching another monkey eating a banana.

The mirror neurons are also found in humans and some scientists consider them as one of the most important findings of neuroscience in the last decade. Have you noticed if you are watching a contact sport or motor racing for example, that you wince and move when you see a crunching tackle or a crash? That is those mirror neurons at work.

What could this possibly mean?

Mirror neurons open the door to the fact that whatever we observe and are part of, we develop the same neurology in our brain, which brings us to the fact that when we notice it, to some extent we experience it. This highlights the idea of how connected we all are and how we influence each other. Hence, in personal development books, we often come across the suggestion to surround ourselves by positive people.

It all becomes a bit like the egg and the chicken, not sure which one was first; our own projection upon others or theirs upon us? In any case, mirror neurons also highlight the importance of being aware and managing our own filters first as they do not only have an impact in our lives but also our environment and the world.

Part of this interaction between us all is our ability to feel **empathy**. Speaking of this giant concept, empathy, I believe we all have work to do. You see, too little or too much can create havoc. Empathy probably belongs in the top three most important qualities of any successful leader and at the same time, when unable to manage it, we can find ourselves continuously feeling the pain and despair of others, making us freeze and not able to think clear and act.

From my personal research, I have come across many people who do not come across as empathetic but who surprisingly had developed illnesses and misfortunes similar to those of others around them. Empathy is a lot more than what meets the eye and sometimes, even when a person cannot express empathy, compassion or convince others about how much he/she cares, there are undeniable unconscious processes that prove their empathy. I am also wondering to what extent when we cannot express empathy with words, and be there for people as they would probably wish we were, we unconsciously choose to empathise by reproducing the same level of discomfort they experienced? In a nutshell, empathy is a valuable attribute we all possess and we have got to manage it.

Responsibility Versus Blame

'Perception is projection' clearly redirects responsibility about what is happening to us … to us. We are responsible for our life, since we are the projectors … and the protectors of it all. The power of the concept, though, is that such responsibility means empowerment – not blame of any kind.

In NLP terms, it represents the power of choice and continuous learning. It prompts us to stop listening to our own excuses and focus on our results instead. When we take 100% responsibility for our reality, a way is opened for us to be more adaptable and flexible. That does not mean we take away the responsibility of others or accept everyone's and anyone's offensive actions. Absolutely not. It's just that we primarily focus on the only person we can change, which is ourselves. When we take control of our life and do all we can to create the reality we want for ourselves, we stop feeling the victim, stop feeling like we are at the receiving end of other people's decisions without any power of our own.

In NLP, we often talk about being at Cause or at Effect which is essentially the same concept: do we live **at Cause**, do we explore how we could have possibly 'caused' or 'created' a situation or **at Effect**, meaning blaming and as a result feeling powerless to change the situation.

This distinction between *responsibility* and *blame* helped me understand better some of my unhelpful thought processes. These two words could not be more different in meaning, but until I had that realisation, I thought they were exactly the same thing.

In the past, when I failed at something I blamed myself. I considered my failures to be a result of a moment of weak or bad judgement which got me into an unfavourable position, with negative consequences for me and sometimes others. At times I would really beat myself up mentally. I could not see failure as a stepping stone to learning, only as an unfortunate event that should have never happened in the first place.

Taking responsibility for ourselves is the exact opposite of this. Taking responsibility means building a true friendship with yourself, and offering care, tenderness and forgiveness to your crew and captain. It takes wisdom – and a bit of humour! Taking responsibility means: "I know I can turn things around" and "I know I failed, and I'll probably fail again because it's all part of learning, but I also know that while I learn, I progress, and I'm the one who can turn things around".

This is a power-house of a concept. It takes confidence and it builds strong self-esteem. But by taking it on board, we learn to value ourselves more and fully embrace the journey.

Once we stop wasting time blaming others, and get on with what we can do, then we move things forward. Taking 100% responsibility is definitely not 'taking the blame' and definitely not 'leaving the responsibility' to someone else. In any relationship, it's about having 100% responsibility for person A and 100% responsibility for person B.

Take a good look in the mirror!

Often, throughout the years, I asked course participants to take a good look in the mirror and tell us about their experience the next day. Each and everyone of them had different sensations, thoughts and emotions. Some could not do it at all, maybe it was something to ponder on and consider in the future. I have been looking deep into my eyes many times for the last decade; consciously connecting with myself in deeper levels. When you do this, you are likely to find that your body, heart and soul react, and during the day, you will find you get messages from your crew.

It was only while writing this book that I ran into one of my now 'next to my bed' books of Louise Hay, *Mirror Work*. Louise Hay is a motivational author. She has been a source of support and inspiration to me when I was diagnosed with ovarian cancer. Louise Hay overcame the same challenge in a time that seemed almost impossible to beat it. Her mantra that we are the power and authority in our mind, I still carry with me every day.

The *Mirror Work* book is a small pocket size book with a 21-days suggested positive affirmations to repeat out loud while you look into the mirror in the morning. When you look deep into your eyes and express statements like 'I love you' and 'I am sorry', you can help build the most important relationship in your life: your relationship with yourself.

Imagine the sense of responsibility we exhibit when we take on such a task as an individual to raise our awareness, our self-esteem and peace of mind. Imagine making this as part of our morning ritual; imagine if everyone would do this; just imagine! I like to think of it as a fundamental step to world peace!

Everyday Thinking And Doing: Consider This …

Let us see how we can understand other people's behaviour through our change of focus:

- Write down two traits that irritate, upset or drive you crazy about someone else. Try to write three or four sentences about each, unless you have more time and want to add more. Don't overthink your words and write without censoring yourself! Just let the pen write for you.
- After five days, check if there are any common themes among the things you've written about. Can you spot a pattern? A specific situation that is reoccurring? Then take a big breath and see how the words, the symbols, the scenarios of what you wrote might possibly apply to you in a different context.
- Think about some action of a particular person that irritated you or upset you. Have you ever taken a similar action in a different context?
- Think about a habit you really don't like. Could it be that you used to have it yourself? Could it be that you still have it sometimes now?

Part 2
Believe It!

It's the view of Richard Bandler Co-Creator of NLP, that our greatest limitations exist not in the things we think we can't do, but in the things that we haven't even thought of doing !

So exploring the power of our beliefs and values allows us to become aware of which ones help us, which ones limit us, and which ones really empower us!

NLP Neurological Levels …

… the different levels at which we think and process information

By Eleni

The mystery of human existence lies not in just staying alive, but in finding something to live for.

Fyodor Dostoyevsky, author of 'The Brothers Karamazov.'

On the first day of any NLP course I run, I ask the delegates "What is your *purpose*?". As expected, some have thought about it, while others are surprised by the question. Some have an answer already or just need a moment to think about it, while others have no idea. But no matter which category they are in, they start thinking about it then.

As an assignment, when they go back home in the evening, I ask them to reflect on who they are. Despite some strange looks and jokes, the next day they always have some insights: "I am a husband/wife/mother/father and citizen of the world", or "I am someone who will achieve great things", or "I am my parents' son", "I am a lawyer", "I am vegan", and so on. This is all about how they *identify* themselves.

During the second day, I ask them what it is that drives them to get up in the morning. What is it that motivates them to go through the same routine every day? What is important to them? Some want to be happy, successful, fulfilled, healthy and much more. And as they acknowledge that, they are in fact discovering their *values*.

The following day, we take a good look at their self-talk and the statements they make about themselves, others and the world; in short, what they *believe* in. "I deserve to be happy!" or "I am not good enough for this job", or "Dogs are loyal", and so on. All our opinions and points of view that form our picture of the world.

Then, comes my favourite part: "What are you good at?". Often, it takes a moment for them to start writing a list of their talents and qualities. They might start with "good at cooking" or "always lending a helping hand" or "calm in stressful situations" and so on. The more they write, the more they discover *skills* they had not thought about in a long time.

Next comes their *behaviour*; their actions. What are they busy with every day? This can be an overwhelming question which can take them in many directions. Questions like "What do you do?" or "How do you handle a situation?" often generate responses like "I do the same things every day", "I do not do enough", "I keep busy".

Finally, I ask them about their *environment*. "Which one?" they ask, and I let them decide for themselves. "Nature?", "My city?", "My home?", "The people that surround me?". I leave it up to them to write and explore.

The above questions were inspired by the Neurological Levels, a straight forward and enlightening model by Robert Dilts, Master Trainer in NLP and author of *The Encyclopedia of Systemic NLP and NLP New Coding*. You can find a more detailed explanation of these in his article *The Brief History of Logical Levels*.Robert Dilts was inspired by Gregory Bateson's concept of *Logical Levels of Learning and Change*, a mechanism formulated in the behavioural sciences.

The following questions are a way of breaking down an experience and then working on it to facilitate change. They make a difference when we face a problem and we want to decide at which level to make a change. Do we change our environment, behaviour, skills, beliefs, identity or purpose?

I summarise them here:

- **Purpose/spirit:** What is my purpose? What do I want to accomplish?
- **Identity:** Who am I? How do I define myself?
- **Beliefs and values:** What do I believe in and what is important to me?
- **Skills and capabilities:** What am I good at?
- **Behaviour:** What are my actions?
- **Environment:** Where and when do I operate? Who am I surrounded by?

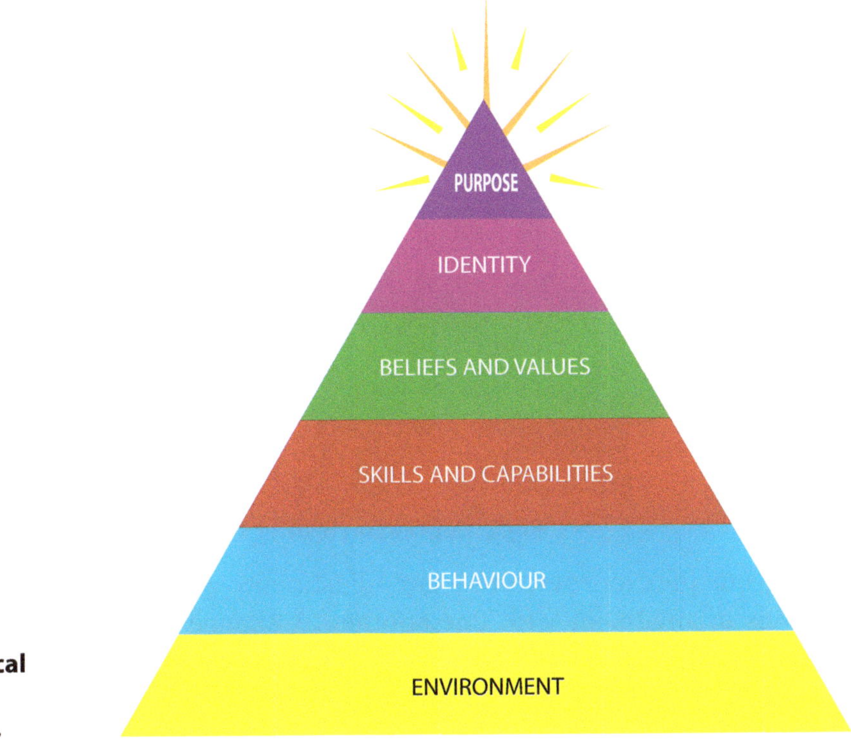

Fig.1: The Neurological Levels of Behaviour.

In short, do we 'walk our talk'? Do we follow thoughts and actions to get us to the legacy we long to leave behind? Do we stay on course with the desired destination of our ship? How often do we check with our binoculars to see how close or far we are from what we want to visit, experience and create in our lifetime? How connected are we every day with purposefully living our dream?

Fig.2: Captain on his/her ship.

During our life's journey, there are adjustments which can be made to get all levels in alignment with one another. A change at a higher level surely influences the levels below. In fact, the higher the level the change takes place at, the bigger the impact. A change at a lower level may or may not affect the levels above. Remember again the NLP Communication Model (Ch.3) and how beliefs and values are linked to behaviour?

Of the valuable insights the Neurological Levels offer us, I am going to focus here on two major ones that I think we come across often in our everyday understanding of things.

Progress In All Spheres Of Life

When we reflect on the questions set out in the previous section, we get a wealth of information about ourselves. This reflection also enables us to make the connection between the answers we provide.

The most difficult thing is the decision to act; the rest is merely tenacity. The fears are paper tigers.

You can do anything you decide to do.

Amelia Earhart, American aviation pioneer.

If, for example, our purpose is to become a pilot, but we do not believe we are good enough to learn how to fly (belief) because we consider ourselves to be someone without opportunities (identity) who doesn't take any action to learn to fly (behaviour), then we have a mismatch – a misalignment.

Either we change our purpose to become a pilot or beliefs about our ability to learn to fly, or our behaviour by *actually* getting busy and learning how to fly. Automatically, our perception shifts one way or the other. We move forward! When the levels (the answers to the questions) are aligned, we progress, and life unfolds smoothly. Alignment means a 'state of agreement' between our neurological levels.

If we want to create a legacy as someone who touched people's lives and contributed to this world with our positive actions (purpose), but we consider ourselves shy (identity) and we do not reach out to find out about others (behaviour), we clearly end up working against different parts of us. There is an internal conflict.

The Neurological Levels make it clear what our choices are and where the point for improvement lies. They are a great framework to work with to identify conflict and to help us work towards a resolution either by re-evaluating our beliefs or changing at another level. We become aware there is an adjustment to be made and we have a clearer picture and understanding of where we need to start taking a closer look.

Progress In Our Day-To-Day Communication

The Neurological Levels model helps us with our communication with others and our internal conversations. Here are some examples of when confusion between levels creates potentially negative consequences for our well-being, self-esteem and relationships with others, and how to bring back the order and clarity.

> "You are not a good boy (identity level), because you did not do your homework (behaviour level)". This statement does not address the boy's

behaviour, it makes a conclusion about his identity – think about the conclusions this boy will make about himself that will affect him for the rest of his life.

Instead, suggestions like the following help put things into perspective: "Doing your homework helps you learn better what you do at school and it will make you feel so much more confident in class. Please make sure you do it tomorrow."

Here's a similar example in a working environment:

"How can you *be* so irresponsible (identity level), and not show up on time for the appointment with the client (behaviour level)?" This is again making an inappropriate link in the levels.

Instead, consider this: "What you *did* was not responsible. Being on time for the appointment is the first good impression and it is important."

Can you hear and feel the difference and the impact? The verb 'did' (behaviour) sheds a completely different light when compared with the verb 'be' (identity). What's more, it's a more credible statement, as being late for an appointment (behaviour) cannot possibly define a person's entire character as being irresponsible (identity). It does not have to be the verb 'to do' specifically, as long as it is any verb describing the behaviour and not the identity.

Our choice of language gives away the neurological level we operate from. Even the subtlest difference between word choices, can make a difference in meaning and experience.

Here are a couple more examples from my personal file.

- "My wallet was snatched (behaviour). How could I be so stupid? (identity)". This is what I exclaimed to myself, a couple of weeks before writing this chapter. The first day, I blamed myself and felt miserable until I decided to stop as it was not helpful.

  So, I changed my behaviour level instead by (a) not carrying all my bank cards with me every day, and (b) avoiding a specific crossing in the city which had become a trap for such thefts. I looked at the behaviour that cost me dearly and responded with a change in my behaviour – and as a result, I protected myself from poorly chosen statements about my identity.

- Twenty years ago, when I quit smoking (behaviour), I stopped hanging out at the smoker's corner at work (environment) which meant spending less time with many of my good friends as well as key people at work. Understanding the impact of my newly-acquired non-smoker status prompted me to seek new ways to regain the benefits of being a smoker; the company cafeteria was also full of people to connect with as was the games room!

Were You An 'Easy' Or A 'Difficult' Child?

As a kid, I must have heard the following comment thousands of times: "He/she is difficult" or "He/she is easy". It might have been about a child or an adult. Nearly everyone I knew, spoke in terms of describing people's character as a fixed aspect of them.

I also noticed that many of my friends happened to be the 'easy child' or the 'difficult child'. What then would follow, was a lot of evidence to justify how this difficult person failed again or was naughty or jealous or had bad grades or was a bad friend. I was of course inclined to avoid 'difficult', 'ungrateful', 'jealous' people. I looked out for 'happy', 'nice', 'well-mannered' people to hang out with.

Why would I ever associate with people who were naughty or jealous? Or difficult people who you could not trust?

What puzzled me though was that at times, I was also difficult, jealous, emotional, and I had lied on several occasions. Of course, this was not something I wanted to talk about, as my parents were clear that I was a *good* child.

Being labelled a 'good' or a 'bad' child can create serious problems. A child who is perceived as bad or difficult will almost certainly react to this identity and eventually might unconsciously choose to 'prove' that he/she *is* bad. A self-fulfilling prophecy, based on the parents' perception of the child.

While in turn, the so-called 'good' child will try to keep up with their reputation and dread making any mistakes for fear of ending up as a bad child as well. The consequences for both labels can be quite severe.

When I was introduced to the Neurological Levels, everything fell into place.

Just because I have lied once, it does not make me a liar! If I have told a hundred lies, it still does not make me a liar. There is a distinction between identity and behaviour. Behaviour does not define the whole person. This is one of the NLP presuppositions (Ch.9):

A person's behaviour is not who they are.

If at any time, my beliefs held me back, it does not mean they define me, either. There is a constant need for alignment and discussion amongst the levels, and they are and remain separate entities that influence one another.

Olga To The Rescue!

Back in Greece, when I was a teenager you had to choose the direction you wanted to go in your studies, a year or two before finishing high school. There were four main orientations: A was for Engineering, B for Medical, C for Philosophy and Languages, and D for Economics. As both my parents were engineers (identity) and mathematics was always a huge source of awards and praise (skills) for me as I studied diligently (and liked it), I naturally went for orientation A.

A few weeks into the final year, when we still had a chance to switch orientation, my physics teacher handed me back a test in which I had scored 9 out of 20. It left me speechless.

My good friend Olga, also the daughter of an engineer, whispered in my ear that today was the last day that we could still switch orientation. The bell rang, and I sprinted to the principal's office who was astonished to hear me say I wanted to change my orientation.

So, because my skill in physics was putting my 'purpose' of following the footsteps of my parents as engineers severely in jeopardy, I decided to use my skills in Maths for a *purpose* similar to engineering – namely, economics. This way, I was still aligned with my purpose, as well as my identity as the daughter of engineers, and I could still be good at maths, which was important to me (*values)*.

I did succeed in the exams and my friend Olga, having given me one of the soundest pieces of advice I've ever had, was a few points short. She eventually changed orientation from A to D the following year, succeeded, and then joined me in Economic Studies.

Similarly, when I moved to Amsterdam to work for Hewlett Packard, they were looking to train technical engineers, and once again my identity as 'daughter of engineers' kicked in! My *skills* in technical issues and languages – my French – also served me well. That was a job which at that moment meant that all my levels were perfectly aligned!

The environment was multi-cultural and served another part of my identity which was to be open-minded, to travel and find out about the world. Things that my father had instilled in me and which were quite important to me (values).

Additionally, part of my life's *purpose* was to have a career and be financially independent (also instilled by both my parents) and these were also served fully!

As a result, *my actions* everyday were in perfect alignment: investing time and effort into learning the software and hardware for my job while helping clients resolve technical issues.

Design Your Life

The best way to predict the future is to create it.

Abraham Lincoln, American President.

The word 'purpose' has French origins and is a 'proposal'. It captures the idea of 'living by design' – to create anything starts with a concept and a design. Be *your life's* designer. Change the design if you want to. Evaluate, re-define, align and enjoy more. Repeat. The process makes our needs and wants clearer to us; it offers us the freedom to go after our definition of success and discover the tools and ways to achieve it. Finding our purpose is key – knowing what we are here for. Making our purpose clear, helps us live every day to the fullest.

"What about living in the moment and going with the flow?", I hear you ask. Well, if this is also a conscious choice made by you, it will serve as a purpose for a while. But living without purpose for a long time, we will eventually feel lost and probably follow other people's purposes and idea of living. We will then get frustrated and not get what we want. It will be hard to make decisions.

And yes, I am the first one to say that no matter what your purpose is, do not take yourself too seriously. An important ingredient for pursuing our dream is to enjoy the ride while doing so. As someone once said, "There are a million ways to surf, and as long as you're smiling, you're doing it right."

Duke Kahanamoku, the Australian father of modern surfing, as well as Phil Edwards, the first person to ride the Hawaiian pipeline, both believed that the best surfer out there, is the one having the most fun. In fact, when we do not enjoy the process, it's probably a sign that we need to rethink our purpose and re-align our neurological levels.

Angels fly because they take themselves lightly.

Arianna Huffington, Greek-American author, businesswoman & founder of the Huffington Post.

Everyday Thinking and Doing: Consider This ...

This is the moment you have all been waiting for!

- Take a deep breath, take a pen, and put down in words your life's purpose in your journal. There, you have it now!

  We can safely state we know how to do something, when we regularly practice this new habit and it becomes installed in our unconscious. New and upgraded habits in our communication are essential for our progress in every domain.

Here are a few ideas to help you get into the habit of asking yourself the Neurological Level questions every day, as part of your daily routine:

- Each week choose a problem you face. Then go through all the questions of the neurological levels corresponding to each level and provide answers relating to each level. Feel free to create similar ones for the specific problem you choose and answer them too. Take this example of a specific problem: "I do not get along with my boss".
    - **Purpose/spirit:** What is my purpose in my relationship with my boss?
    - **Identity:** Who am I when I'm around my boss?"
    - **Beliefs and values:** What do I believe about my boss and what is important to me in this relationship?
    - **Skills and capabilities:** What skills are helpful to get along with my boss?
    - **Behaviour:** What is my behaviour towards my boss like?
    - **Environment:** Where and when do I spend time with my boss?
- Once you have the answers, you will see how one level supports the others. Where's the alignment – and where's the misalignment?
- Reflect on what levels have the biggest influence on the other levels for this specific problem. For example, does environment play a major role on your identity and beliefs?
- Consider what steps you can take to bring alignment into your answers on neurological levels.

Chapter 7

What Drives You? Your Values …

… finding where our priorities and motivation lie

By Eleni

Two things fill the mind with ever new and increasing admiration and awe, the more often and steadily we reflect upon them: the starry heavens above me and the moral law within me.

Immanuel Kant, philosopher.

I must have shared this story a thousand times. It's about one of my life-changing moments and here it is once more, in black and white. I chose it because it captures the moment that my values and subsequently my purpose (as discussed in the last chapter) changed radically. From being fully motivated, being certified in software applications and mastering the world of information technology, I found a different calling.

It was 2005. A cold November evening in Amsterdam. While I prepared spaghetti, my visiting friend Amanda was sharing her impressions of a presentation she'd been to the previous day about life coaching. Busy with the sauce and not paying her full attention, I asked her if it was about football. Patiently, and ignoring my absentmindedness, she explained that this type of coaching was not specific to sport but was about life: how with specific types of questions, a coach can help you understand more about the decisions you make, and more importantly, your beliefs.

Initially, I listened because, well, because she's a good friend and I like to keep up with her news. As she continued, I was caught between wanting to hear more on the one hand and on the other hand, a voice in my head was telling me this was not for me. After all, I was already quite a self-motivated person and my life was full of goals and fun anyway. In the end, my curiosity won, and inspired by Amanda's excitement, I booked a short session with a life coach to find out more.

What followed were the best invested fifteen minutes of my life.

It took just a few questions from the coach and I literally changed the page in my own life story book – right there and then. The questions he asked were different from those I'd normally ask myself. Even though I did most of the talking, the fact that I was asked to identify my beliefs in a structured way, created shifts inside me and made me see a new dimension to events that I'd previously been unaware of.

I found myself talking to someone with a curious mind. Someone who was genuinely interested in the reasoning behind my actions. He listened attentively and that smoothed the way and created the space I needed for self-exploration and self-discovery.

He asked me to draw a circle and split it in to different sections, each section representing an important area in my life. I wrote the obvious ones like health, relationships and family, and then added hobbies.

A second later, I added another category I called 'hobbies' and then another one and another one until I had drawn thirteen different categories, all called 'hobbies'! In my mind, all these 'hobbies' categories served different parts of who I was – some were about me, like meditation, research and reading. Some I shared with friends like cycling and cooking. Some I enjoyed as part of a team, like playing chess or with my husband, like dancing and traveling.

The coach then asked me to give a number from 0 to 10 to each hobby, representing where I felt I *was*, compared to where I would *like* to be. The perfect score would be 10 out of 10. To my surprise, I scored most of my items and hobbies quite low and what followed was a complete revelation to me.

There it was, right in front of me. Clear as day. I simply did not have enough of those things that were important to me in my daily life. And up until this point, I had been waiting for … what? For a miracle? For tomorrow? For another time? I do not know what I had been waiting for.

It had taken just fifteen minutes to completely change my outlook on life and my level of self-awareness.

I thanked the coach and stared at my 'wheel of life'. I could hardly sleep that night and just days later, I signed up for my first Coaching Certification course. And the rest is history. After I started to step outside my comfort zone and safety net, I found myself on a journey of continuous growth.

I have designed so many different life wheels through the years and I have had the privilege and honour to see thousands of other people's wheels. I still find it one of the most effective tools in self-awareness. It opened the way to life coaching for me in a way that played a pivotal role in who I am today.

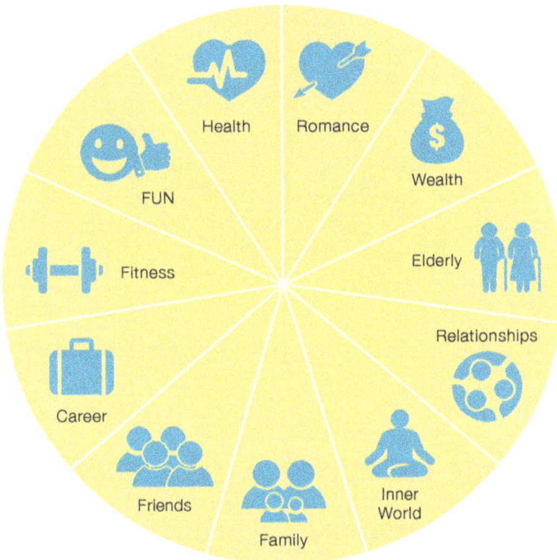

Fig. 1: Example of a wheel of life.

Then, from life coaching, I got to find out about NLP, to change career and to find a higher calling. Of course, you already know about that first NLP day, just a couple of years later!

VALUES = what is important to us, qualities we value, principles that drive our motivation and decisions.

Your Values = Your Motivation = Your Drive

Kindness, joy, celebration, connection, acknowledgement, freedom, serenity, expansion, gratitude, innovation, consistency, results, loyalty, fun – these are some of the values that make up my wheel of life nowadays. They are examples of values that drive my thoughts, emotions, behaviour and actions every day. The reasons I do what I do! We might not always be consciously aware of our values, but they are there. Our compass is programmed to follow them to get to our destination.

Fig. 2: Our Compass points to our Values.

Values: The Eternal Internal And External Negotiation

At any given moment, there is an internal negotiation going on among several of our values, all of which are asking for our attention. Our crew members are voicing different parts of us, and that includes our values. When it comes to our decision making, one value may take precedence over the other, depending on the context and various other factors. (For more on this, see Ch. 16 on Parts Integration).

Our choices and reactions will vary at different times, sometimes they are flexible, and sometimes they are unshakeable (such as always putting your child's well-being above everything else). Just because one value has taken priority in a specific situation, does not mean that another value is not important to us, or part of what drives us. It just took a back seat on this occasion.

When we think about what our own values are, we might not even include health in our top ten because we first brainstorm what *matters* to us. But if health becomes an issue, then it may enter the list – and even move up into first place. This might be because values are relative, so they get influenced by the situations we find ourselves in.

Despite our best intentions, we sometimes part ways with someone when one of our core values has been disrespected in our relationship with them. This happens more at an unconscious level as our values are so deeply ingrained within us.

I have come to realise that the friends I thought I had 'lost' or who had in some way hurt me, had not been lost, and never meant to hurt me. Our values had just shifted. And because of that, we had become strangers to one another.

As a young adult, I always held birthdays sacred. I noted down all the birthdays of my family and friends on my calendar and I would make sure I honoured their day with at least a phone call, a visit, even a surprise. Then, my own birthday would come, and not all my friends would remember. I found excuses for them, but I still felt deeply hurt inside when they would forget.

Over the years, my circle of friends has become spread all over the globe and my priorities have changed. Birthdays are still important to me, but I do not always call or email. For my own birthday, I have come to understand that when they do not call me, it really is not the end of the world – or the friendship!

Our values and decision-making mechanisms are connected unconsciously and their inner workings have a lot to do with who we keep in our life and who we connect with more easily (or not).

What I also noticed over the decades is how every time I start a conversation with anyone (in a café, on a road, with a friend's friend, with anyone), there is at least *one* idea, *one* item that we both feel passionate about, and that *one* thing is enough to carry the relationship. I make a note to focus on finding this common ground with as many people as possible.

Here below a couple more lessons I have learnt about the values that motivate me:

Whatever it seems – it is not what it necessarily is, or the full story

What I think drives me is not always the first thing that comes to my mind. I have to put in work and time to really find out what is under the surface. Values that are important consciously, can be relatively unimportant unconsciously (and vice versa). This was made clear by the findings of Professor Joel Weinberger from the Derner Institute of Advanced Psychological Studies at Adelphi University, and Chip Walker from Y&R Advertising in the spring of 2013, where the main part of the study they conducted (carried out in three countries – US, China and Brazil), concerned conscious and unconscious values.

When asked about their three top life values, the majority of participants consciously listed higher-order values, such as caring for others, finding meaning in life, and choosing their own path. When researchers tapped into their unconscious thought waves to identify their top values, they concluded that their core unconscious values were quite different from their conscious ones. They were more basic and included security, sexual fulfilment, and adherence to tradition.

Whatever it is – it is not what it will always be, or what it will become

What drove my twenty-year-old self is not the same as what drove my thirty-year-old or my forty-year-old self. My motivation changed. Some of my needs and wants remained the same, but changed in intensity. Some are not important at all anymore. As I change, and the world around me changes, I follow a different direction, always with my own very personal compass.

What drives me has very little to do with what drove my parents, my teachers, my friends and even my now close family members. Sometimes, our parents have a vision for us to become a lawyer or a doctor and we may follow that vision, because we lack our own vision at that moment or we do it out of loyalty to them. It's important to realise *whose* vision we are following in life and take responsibility for our choices based on our own heart's song.

The book *Values and the Evolution of Consciousness* by Adriana James is based on the work of Clare W. Graves. It focuses on societies and how collective society values shift. What our collective values, society values, world aspirations were last century, are not what they are now –or even last decade. And they will not be the same in future centuries, decades – or even next year. Time and space are crucial factors that define minor and major shifts in values, and the world changes as a result.

Everyday Thinking And Doing: Consider This …

I hope you are now a bit intrigued, maybe excited too, and ready to write down what is important to you in life, by creating your own 'wheel of life'. I shared an example earlier, just to give you an idea. What yours looks like is up to you. Just let it come from within as you start to create it.

- Sit quietly and draw a circle just like the one in Fig.3 and reflect on what areas you need to have present in your life and do well. What makes you smile from ear to ear? Write them all down as they come.
- Once you have finished, go and get yourself a cup of tea and take a second look at what you have put down. Start a dialogue with yourself and enjoy taking time to become more aware of what is important to you.

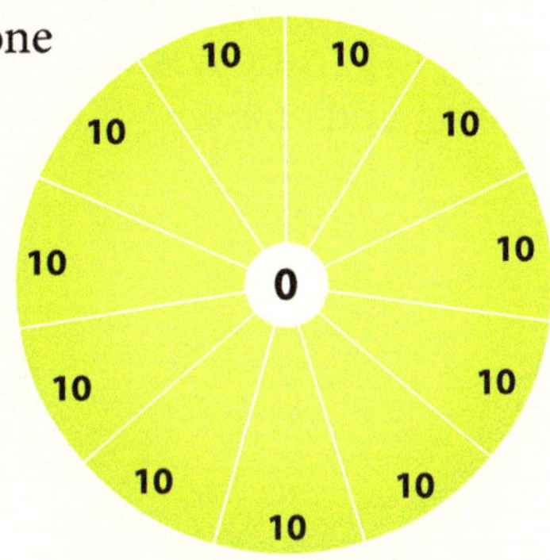

Fig. 3: Empty wheel of life.

- Give each area a score, just as an indication of where you are compared to where you would ideally like to be. If health scores 5 out of 10 for example, what would make it a 10?
- Reflect on your scores. Do you take your health for granted? Do you ask a lot from yourself regarding your health? Are health and fitness the same or different for you? What's the story behind the score you have given?
- Have fun with the process and remember … nothing is written in stone! You can always design a new wheel of life tomorrow and follow either the similarities or the differences of your previous wheels. Do not over-think it! Go with your unconscious. You are benchmarking right now, and there are no right or wrong answers.

Just like the wheel of life you created, you can also draw ones that only relate to your career, relationships and other areas, by splitting the wheel in to what is important to you in this specific sphere of life.

A slightly different approach

The second wheel of life exercise is a little less conventional and perhaps more aspirational. The one below is an example of mine, and it includes various concepts I want to explore and develop, so that I can improve my skill set and help others.

The point I want you to understand from this exercise is that you can take the basic idea of the wheel of life and expand on it. Open your mind and let it guide you, using the wheel of life in whatever way works best for you.

The wheel of life tool is fluid and flexible and when you are clear what its purpose is, you can work with it regularly. You can personalise it, and even experiment with it, checking in from time to time to see how you're doing and enjoying the amazing results.

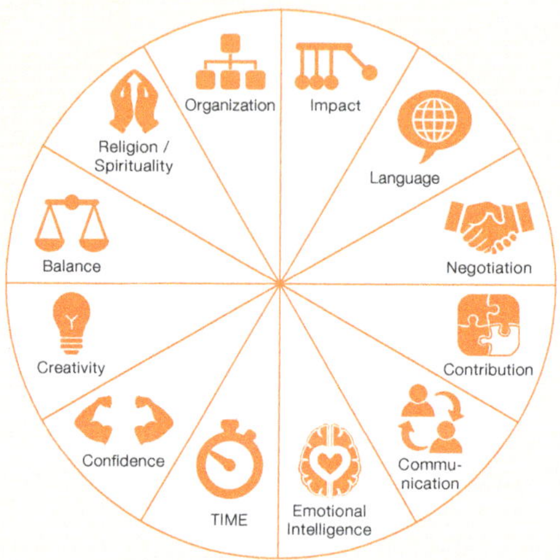

Fig. 4: A different kind of wheel of life.

Beliefs We Live By …

… discovering what we tell ourselves and hold to be true

By Eleni

There are no facts, only interpretations.

Frederick Nietzsche, philosopher.

In the place I was raised, and at the time I was raised, lots of people believed that it was cool to 'work hard and play hard'. In fact, I still come across this saying on advertising boards, and it makes me sad. Holding this belief made me excel at school but at the same time I sacrificed sleep and consumed massive quantities of alcohol and junk food during my teenage years.

Some of the positive attributes of this expression are self-explanatory: I was quite successful in many areas with a good ability to focus and concentrate. On the negative side, I totally disconnected from my body: I neglected its need for moderation and love. I suffered from serious illnesses and lost confidence in my own powers and in the future.

Then, I re-defined 'cool'! And as a result, my life became a whole lot cooler. I now believe it is cool to connect with my body, mind and soul; it is cool to grow spiritually; and I will go a long way to protect my body and work on my dreams and ambitions at the same time.

Most importantly of all, what is cool is now *my* decision and *mine* alone. In short, I have created a new set of beliefs for myself.

What Do You Believe?

Our values are what is *important* to us – while our beliefs are how we think everything works. If our values are our compass, then our beliefs are the ship's engine. Our values show us the way, and our engines make it happen.

Beliefs are ideas or generalisations about the world based on our experiences. Beliefs are thoughts that we keep thinking and hold as our truth. They affect our decisions, behaviour, perception of the world and they direct our approach to life.

Beliefs influence who we are. They can limit, empower, inspire, console or defeat us. For example, one belief I had, was about me being a 'hard worker'. Some people believe that they are not good enough or deserving of success, while others believe they have great talents and skills.

Beliefs have structures, specific functions, and are attached to internal strategies. We cannot have a clear idea of what works for us and what can be improved, until we open the door and look within the unconscious at our beliefs. The largest part of the thousands of beliefs we run on, was created in one way or another during childhood: parents, school, society, socioeconomic conditions, climate, war or peace, religion, politics, and much more. They have all played their part in the formation of our individual beliefs.

> BELIEFS = thoughts and statements we hold as true about ourselves and others.

If, as a child, we were part of a family where we could express ourselves and felt heard by our parents, we tend to grow up believing in the power of sharing and being supported. On the other hand, if we were told to go to our room every time we got angry about something, we tend to believe that asking for help when we are frustrated is not an option. In fact, we tend to think we have got to figure out a solution alone.

If, years later, we then sit as a team member in a meeting, and one of our colleagues gets emotional, we will be prompted to react to their behaviour according to the beliefs that we grew up with. This means either that we will think that our colleague should have controlled his/her temper, or we will do our best to support them. Similarly, all the other people at the meeting will have a different belief about his/her behaviour, and they will all react differently and uniquely depending on those beliefs.

How we react to specific situations is the result of all the millions of beliefs that we hold, operating together and deciding what experiences and emotions will play out at that moment.

Is It Worth Revisiting Our Beliefs?

Considering that our beliefs make us who we are, it seems a good idea to open our minds and become aware of which beliefs have shaped our behaviour and how we have managed our life so far in accordance with those beliefs. Would it not help to re-evaluate those beliefs from twenty, thirty or forty years back, and update them?

We tend to keep an eye on the latest fashions, gadgets, car models or phones, and we are definitely not happy about settling for a twenty-year-old computer. So, what about our mind then? How do we upgrade it, consciously and methodically? The answer is that we have to take a close look at the beliefs that create our reality every day, and then we need to keep the beliefs that still get us results, update some of our other beliefs, and throw away some.

The key to this process is, on the one hand, to remain thankful for the wealth of powerful beliefs we inherited and respect our mind's status quo; and on the other hand, we should open up our mind to innovation. This is about combining tradition and transformation within one person, promoting a culture where each one of us wants to move forward and take new paths, while remaining thankful for what got us safely here today.

Types Of Beliefs

Seeing the different types of beliefs we hold helps us understand their purpose and their role in our behaviour and results – and it starts an internal dialogue around each belief, putting it under a microscope and analysing it.

For example, we could classify the statements we repeat inside our head and also share with others – our beliefs – into three main categories:

- **Empowering:** Some beliefs like "I deserve to be happy" move us forward and prompt us to take action towards being happier and more fulfilled.
- **Limiting:** Other beliefs will be a constant obstacle, not letting us get what we want ("I don't have a college degree, so I can't get a well-paid job"). Unconsciously playing this tape over and over again creates repetitive self-sabotage, so we just will not apply for those high-paid jobs. And even if we do, it's likely that we will look for evidence to 'fail' the interview or create a series of obstacles to stopping us from getting the job.
- **Empowering and limiting at the same time:** The common belief that 'to succeed in life you have got to work hard', empowers us and limits us at the same time.

  On one hand, it moves us to create and take the actions necessary; on the other, we might get stuck in 'doing' and forget about 'being' and 'enjoying'. We can all think of examples where days pass by and we forget to *live* our life because we are so caught up in 'getting things done'. But what's the point of working hard if life passes you by?

Challenging the assumption that work needs to be hard can shed light on new ways of organising work. In Sweden, companies have started shifting to a six-hour working day, aiming for happier employees and increased productivity. There's more and more evidence that it's better to work *efficiently* rather than *hard*.

When I was a child, we went to school six days out of seven, and that's still the case in a few countries even now. The amount of homework we had to do was five times more than the average of most developed countries nowadays – countries that have better socio-economical and educational results.

In short: a belief is just a belief. When it gets us results, it serves its purpose – so keep it! But when you do not get the results you want, change the belief or upgrade it until you do!

By believing passionately in something that still does not exist, we create it. The non-existent is whatever we have not sufficiently desired.

Franz Kafka, novelist.

For example: "I am fifty. I am too old to change career". Is this limiting or empowering for you? If you want to change career because it makes you unhappy, this belief is clearly limiting. If you are happy to stay where you are, even though it sounds like a complaint, it highlights a 'secondary gain', as it is called, meaning that we express it as a limiting belief, but in fact we keep it for a reason; there is a certain 'gain' for us as changing our reality can be too uncomfortable or require too much energy we are not prepared to put in.

When we realize the secondary gains, we free ourselves from playing over and over 'old stories'. We become aware of our reasons to keep certain beliefs and we realize that when there is no more secondary gain, we do have a choice to change our stories.

How can we change a limiting belief into an empowering one?

There are different ways you can go about it. For example, we can change "I can do nothing" to "I can do anything".

"I cannot stop smoking" might need you to think a bit longer. You can turn it into "I can stop smoking" as a side step, but eventually you will need to work out how you can say it in an even more positive way. Remember our crew? Well, they will not be picking up a clear message with "I can stop smoking". What they will hear is 'smoking' – and remember what happens when you type a term into the search engine of your unconscious? It will start scouring the world for 'smoking' and suddenly smoking will be everywhere.

There are many ways, depending on the context, to turn this limiting belief to an empowering one. We could say "I manage my stress ecologically" or "I manage my feelings effectively while keeping my body healthy". We get empowered when we find an alternative to dealing with negative emotions.

As we have already found out, beliefs are created by an event, a look, or a word. They enter our head because of a situation, or they are part of our culture and religion. They come to us through many different channels. Nonetheless, no matter how they got there, they did so through repetition and habit.

- **Repetition:** Beliefs enter our head during the 'imprint period' (Ch.2) by way of massive repetition. Equally, for us to imprint the new beliefs that we now want, we do it the same way: by repetition. It takes consistency and a systematic feed of the ideas we want to focus on to 'imprint' a new belief.
- **Habit:** Through repetition, the beliefs become our 'new-thinking habit', and by getting into the habit of re-evaluating our beliefs, we work on a

continuous internal process of focusing on those beliefs and optimising them.

Working on our beliefs takes time, effort and commitment.

- Firstly, when re-evaluating our beliefs we need to accept our limiting beliefs and acknowledge the learnings they have for us, then go on and change them.

  Acceptance: About some limiting beliefs that might persist, beliefs like the ones below help us bring balance and acceptance within. This is a good moment to also say that we will always have limiting beliefs. We are human and we keep growing. Limiting beliefs are stepping stones to help us get where we want, they carry their own wisdom:

  "Limiting beliefs carry gifts and lessons."

  "I am not the one with the least nor the most limiting beliefs."

- Secondly, we have to have beliefs that remind us about the benefits of this re-evaluation and help us practice it regularly even when we get de-motivated, so it becomes a habit:

  - **Empowering beliefs to support the process:**

    "I believe 100% in the process of re-evaluating my beliefs and having the power to develop and upgrade my mindset."

    "I believe changing my mind and beliefs is possible."

  - **Self-belief and self-worth:** Should doubt and uncertainty sneak in, and we do not see the fruit of our labours, we need to find what we need to think to remain focused.

    "No matter what the circumstances or obstacles, I believe in my power to transform my life."

    "No matter the set-backs, my resolve always prevails."

We can learn something new anytime we believe we can.

Virginia Satir, family therapist.

Belief Trees

Beliefs create beliefs. You could say that there are invisible belief trees inside us, all of which include beliefs on different branches. At the bottom branches, we have more 'general' beliefs that influence us in identity level and in most areas of our life. The middle branches are less 'general', often opinions about certain patterns in our life and the upper branches hold statements about a specific situation.

Let us imagine a limiting beliefs tree like in Fig.1. A belief such as "I am not good enough" will have a negative impact on every area of our life. "When I speak my mind, I often get in trouble" describes our opinion about a pattern we noticed in our communication. "I have to compromise again to get moving with the project" is a limiting belief, about a specific situation. They are all related though.

At the bottom branches of the limiting belief tree (left and right), we can often find two beliefs we all share when things do not go our way: "I'm not good enough" and "I'm not loved enough".

A tree full of limitation will be bare and in suffering because their otherwise powerful tiny seeds, the acorns will be annoyed, unsatisfied and grumpy. The tree representing our mindset will not flourish and the acorns representing our beliefs will feel helpless. As a result, the squirrel used as a metaphor for our whole being, will be hungry, reluctant to go near the acorns and deprived of energy and playfulness. Worse still, squirrels take acorns away and spread them, potentially propagating more limiting belief trees.

Fig.1: A Limiting Beliefs Tree.

On the other hand, when we imagine an empowering belief tree, our acorns – beliefs – smile from ear to ear!

"I love myself" is a great foundation for more happy acorns! That belief can give birth to beliefs such as "I deserve a good job", and "I deserve a bonus for this project".

At the bottom of an empowering belief tree, there are unconscious statements running like "I am enough", "I am deserving" and "I am loved".

Fig. 2: An Empowering Beliefs Tree.

Happy, content acorns give a squirrel energy, too! I remember reading somewhere that acorns are also blessings. In that sense, these small but powerful nuts can lead to big and great outcomes. We bless our mind and body with statements that move us to the directions we want, our empowering beliefs.

Full of smiley acorns, the squirrels wander about, play and go from one place to the other. They enjoy life!

In reality, the limiting and empowering trees co-exist within us. Identifying our beliefs, their impact and the relationships between them, helps us re-write our story.

So now seems the right time to share another of my favourite moments. In fact, this one is so powerful that it actually kept me alive! It is from a column I wrote ten years ago and it is a timely and powerful reminder of what is possible.

Beliefs Save Lives!

I'm sitting on my sofa. It's nine o'clock in the evening. The kids are asleep. My husband is next to me holding my hand as he meditates. A few days ago, we heard that I've got cancer. This is the second time, but the odds of overcoming it this time are slim. Stage four. Multiple organs affected.

Since we heard the diagnosis, we meditated every minute we could, after the day's blood tests and doctor's visits. I breathed in deeply to allow the oxygen to enter every cell in my body to heal it. I visualised, like this:

My body is a skyscraper full of invaders. My mission is to get them out. I bring in thousands of policemen to help out; strong, descent, well-trained, hard-working policemen. They have started on the top floors, chasing everyone away. I have asked them to avoid guns, no more harm, just get them out. I can hear their firm voices through the loud speakers. When a floor is double-checked and free again, they carefully move on to the next floor, working their way down slowly but surely. The invaders are many, but they are running scared and they have no real power.

I am talking on the phone at ten in the morning. One of my dearest NLP mentors, Carol Talbot, is on the other end of the line – supportive, available, offering help without asking anything back. I tell her about my visualisation.

She asks "Why policemen?". I have no answer.

"Who else?" she asks. And then, "What about fairies?".

"Fairies?"

The same night, I see fairies. They are lovely. Magic wands and miracle dust replace the loud speakers and shouting. Fairies change to whatever form they want and have the power to appear or disappear whenever it pleases them. With their supernatural powers and noble nature, they fill my body with their beautiful melodies, their innocent giggles reassure me. The whole process feels lighter and effortless. They grant me wish after wish. Sleep comes more easily, but the fairies continue while I am out of consciousness.

It was then I realised how strict I still was with myself. My beliefs around recovery were about policemen and guns. That was the moment I trusted my life for the first time to believing in fairies! This is when the end of the beginning and my road to recovery really started. My blood results became more promising!

One year later. The fairies never leave my sight. The kids are being naughty, playing with their food. Just when my mouth is about to open with some kind of order, a fairy appears inside my head. I get it; it starts making sense. Fairies have had an impact on my body and my perception of life. I am not the same. I like my 'fairy period' better. Past strategies have given way to new, softer, more trusting ones. "Ach, they're just kids – wonderful kids", I think to myself and join in the fun. I lift some pasta and create my own macaroni moustache. The kids giggle. A fairy passes by and winks at me. Bliss!

Everyday Thinking and Doing: Consider This ...

Recognising beliefs that get us results, upgrading beliefs to make them even more empowering, letting go of beliefs that hold us back, listening to beliefs of others, reflecting and changing beliefs are all processes that lead to change. To regularly revisit these processes consciously, re-evaluate and re-construct them where necessary in the unconscious is what life is about. Let's do it!

How can we change our beliefs?

- Identify and write down your beliefs – any kind of belief in any area of your life.
- Reflect on how you got this belief.
- Who else has the same belief and who not?
- Decide where it adds to your life, and where it stops you in your tracks.
- How could you make it more empowering?

Chapter 9

NLP Presuppositions …

… the resourceful beliefs of NLP

By Eleni

Reality is merely an illusion,
albeit a very persistent one.

Albert Einstein, physicist .

We are what we believe. Our results are the product of what we believe. Beliefs help us fly, discover new heights, and they keep us chained in dark dungeons. Now you know you have a say in what you believe. It is your canvas to paint. Your song to write. This is the year that the movie *Bohemian Rhapsody* was released, and listening to that song once more in the movie theatre, it was right there –the first verse of the Queen song that touched millions of hearts with the line "Is this the real life? Or is it just fantasy?" Freddie Mercury grasped the essence of the ultimate choice we've all been given, to make our fantasy reality. It is up to us to have a ball!

NLP gives us tools and techniques to help us renovate our mind's household. What NLP also does is propose a list of beliefs that helps programme our mind to help us achieve the results we want. These beliefs have been adopted by pioneers who have used them and integrated them into their everyday life. Time and time again, these particular beliefs, when engrained in the unconscious mind, bring greater understanding of ourselves and others, increasing our levels of tolerance and our options when it comes to moving forward.

You will also hear these referred to as the NLP Presuppositions or Beliefs of Excellence or Empowering Beliefs proposed by NLP. They are beliefs or presuppositions that help make a difference to people's lives – for the better – so they can reach higher standards in character and life experience. They are *suggestions*, which means they do not claim to be true or universal. They are simply statements that were inspired by great minds like Gregory Bateson, Virginia Satir and Milton H. Erickson, and have been proven to deliver phenomenal results in most areas of life.

They can serve as your ship's engine, just like any other empowering beliefs you choose to navigate life with. Full of altruism, they are the core of NLP's philosophy and they are expressed in different ways in different publications. There are many and here I will briefly touch on eighteen of them.

NLP Presuppositions Or Beliefs Of Excellence

1. The map is not the territory – everyone has their own model of the world

This statement was coined by Alfred Korzybski, a Polish-American independent scholar who developed *general* semantics (as opposed to plain semantics*). His argument was that we are limited by our own nervous system and our language and therefore we cannot have direct access to one global 'reality', because our own idea of reality is filtered through our brain's unique responses.

As you already now know, we all have a unique perception of the world and how things work. This unique perception serves as our map with which we navigate through life. At no moment in time, do we have all the information available about every single thing in life. Each one of us has a specific map of the world, and the world changes all the time. Everyone has a different upbringing and we view the world in our own unique way. Different people = different maps.

When we operate from such a belief, we become more flexible and understanding. Such a mindset helps us realise that the way we experience an event is not how everyone else experiences it. This helps us to refrain from judging or second-guessing others, and it helps us to become more tolerant and understanding of the motives and actions of others.

2. Respect other people's maps of the world

People react positively when their model or map of the world is respected. Adopting this belief helps us be more tolerant, as well as curious, about other people's way of thinking and behaviour. While we can and should hold on to our own uniqueness, keeping an open mind, accepting and respecting others' perception of the world, brings us closer together.

3. There is no failure – only feedback

With strong roots in cybernetics and echoing Gregory Bateson's teachings, this one is definitely a life-changer. To learn, grow and therefore change, you have to *practise*. Growth comes with patience and perseverance. Before we could walk, we had to stumble and fall many times, and that was part of the process. All pioneers in the world, all the great ones, had to fall many times before they rose to excellence. Michael Jordan, an NBA – the National Basketball Association – hero and an idol for millions of people, could actually be considered a total failure – yet we all know his is one of the greatest success stories.

* Semantics is about the meaning of words, while *general* semantics is about connecting words and experiences.

4. The meaning of your communication is in the response and feedback you get

How often have you found yourself saying "Oh, but that's not what I meant – you didn't understand what I was trying to say". When we hold this belief, it is not that people do not understand; it is that we did not communicate clearly. So we work towards making ourselves understood more clearly next time round; thus we develop and improve our communication and start to become more adaptable.

> ***The message sent is not always the message received.***
>
> *Virginia Satir, author and therapist.*

5. Every behaviour has an (unconscious) positive intention

This is another Virginia Satir quote. We all have a different set of ethics and values but behind all of our actions (no matter how hurtful they might be to ourselves or others) lies a higher intention that forces us to do something. We have our own reasons and beliefs that give us the conviction (often unconsciously) that our action is the best choice we have at that specific moment, sometimes for lack of a better and more ecological alternative (ecological meaning a way in which everyone's space is respected).

When we understand and believe this 'positive intention' belief, it creates a layer of understanding of ourselves at a deeper level and helps us grow spiritually. We take a step back and take a closer look about the underlying reasons of a behaviour we are not necessarily proud of.

This is not to condone bad behaviour, not by a long shot. It has more to do with forgiveness and acceptance and the fact that deep down, everyone longs for connection. Even in extreme scenarios of appalling crimes, it helps us realize that even the people who committed them, they thought this was their best shot at feeling *significant*, an important human need.

Children and adults alike do their best to connect and sometimes, when everything else fails for both to feel significant, they draw negative attention on them, by horrible actions. Even then, the intention is a deep need to love and be loved.

6. A person's behaviour is not who they are

We have all been in a situation in which we wished we could take back something we said or did. And chances are, we'll be in similar situations again in the future. It's a journey, and no matter how noble our character and values are, our behaviour does not always reflect this. Remembering this means that forgiving ourselves and others is a much easier process. Take the example of the boy who is not good because he did not do his homework (Ch.6). Just because people do or do not do something, it does not make them good or bad. Their behaviour does not determine who they are as a person. It says a lot about them, but it does not even come close to explaining them as a whole.

7. The most important information about a person is how they behave

This belief might seem to contradict the previous one but in fact, it is complementary. Even though a person is so much more than their behaviour, and their behaviour is also context dependent, their behaviour still remains the most important and crucial part of how others perceive them. Holding such a belief, helps us find more resourceful ways to behave and re-visit the beliefs and values behind our behaviour.

8. The person with the most flexibility will have the most influence

By making changes in our behaviour and being flexible about things, we break patterns and create new strategies that can lead us to greater possibilities. If we can visit and understand other people's maps of the world, we can add to our own skills. For example, when our children urge us to do things that we would not naturally do, if we're open to their ideas and do them, we very often find that a resistant part within us opens up, thus adding a new dimension to our personality or skillset.

9. Resistance is a sign of a lack of rapport

How can we ever get our message across when we do not have any rapport with someone? It is a priority to build a climate of trust and understanding with people first, then seek to convey our message. When there is resistance, it signifies a lack of trust and understanding at some level. This creates an opportunity to grow and improve our communication.

10. People have all the resources they need

Holding this powerful belief gives us the wings we need to fly to higher levels when it comes to our skills, talents, behaviour and connection within ourselves, and with others. Focus on the word 'within'. You've got the potential – according to this belief – and by believing in your potential, you will start to tap into it! This is not about *external* resources like cars, education or background. NLP is about *internal* resources – resources such as confidence, creativity, diversity and respect. We all have these and we can always choose where and how we invest our energy.

11. Everyone is doing the best they can with the resources they have available

The resources we talk about here again are the 'internal ones'; like patience, confidence, understanding, vitality and hope. This one reminds us that depending on how we feel, we can tap into different parts of ourselves and behave differently. But there will be days when we do not seem able to focus or forgive or imagine. Life happens, and we all do our best under the circumstances that prevail at any given time. Consequently, when we are faced with mistakes or the unresourceful behaviour of others, this belief helps us be more tolerant towards pretty much everyone and everything.

12. If it's possible for one person, it's possible for others

An old-fashioned way of thinking is that some people are blessed with unique skills and talents that we do not necessarily share. We all have the ability both to learn those skills from others and to teach our own skills to others. If, for example, someone can make a great omelette, we can learn from him how to make an omelette by just focusing on that one skill. We will not necessarily acquire his other character and communication traits. When we want to get better at making omelettes, we can learn from the skill he excels at only. This is an example of a model of excellence.

Finding models of excellence to learn from is key to our continuous progress and it's the very essence of NLP. When you know what it is that you want to achieve or create, find someone who has already done it successfully and copy them. Look to understand and adopt their beliefs, values and behaviour in order to get the same results as they did.

I regularly talk to clients who do their best to 're-invent the wheel', wasting valuable time for themselves and others. Holding a specific role in a company, or even as a parent, they work harder than they have to trying to figure out how to go about things without asking those who have already dealt with similar situations. Worried about losing face, they suffer, and they learn far less than they could.

Modelling (adopting or copying the beliefs, values and behaviour of others see Ch. 27) is about finding out how to do something. It can be applied to every single area of our life. It's also a great self-confidence booster and helps us to connect with others. When we ask people about what they do well and how they do it, people recognise our strength in reaching out to them and appreciate the implied positive feedback. It's a way in which to 'honour' them, and we honour ourselves by not expecting that we should automatically know everything.

13. If something isn't working, do something different

Same beliefs, same behaviours, same strategies produce the *same* results. Different beliefs, different behaviours and different strategies lead to different results. Repeating the same actions that you know did not work before is like hitting your head against a wall and then watching it bleed. When we want something different, we've got to take a different approach. It's that simple.

Einstein is credited with saying that true madness is doing the same thing and expecting a different result. Yet as human beings we often repeat a strategy that has not worked for us in the past. In a more resourceful state we recognise this and the need to make changes to get a different outcome.

14. Having a choice is better than not having a choice

This one is about the power of choice. When we feel that we have choices, we feel more empowered. The more choices we have, the freer we are and the more influence we have. If we're looking for a job, the more interviews we go to or jobs we apply for, the more chance we have of getting a job we love. The more friends we have, the more supported, applauded and comforted we're likely to feel. It's also about being flexible – the more choices we have in the way we think and act, the more maps we can connect to, and the more we can expand our imagination, ideas and opportunities at all levels. In effect we become our choices.

15. We cannot not communicate.

If you spend any time around an animal, you know that everything about our way of being communicates something to them: a look, a stance, a voice tone and all this to creatures who only understand a limited number of words. How we are, even when we are silent gives a message that others interpret.... rightly or wrongly.

The non-verbal communication is by far the bigger piece of the pie in our communication. When we internalize this belief, we pay far more attention in our gestures and facial expressions. Our smile or frown speaks tons about our state!

16. The mind and body are part of the same system.

Its seems obvious when you think about it, that we are one complete system. So when change occurs in one part of a system there is likely a corresponding change in the other. What we are thinking about is reflected in our body language. Similarly, how and where we are sitting or standing, and over what period of time impacts on our thinking e.g. sitting still puzzling over a problem is likely to be reflected in 'stuckness' in our thinking.

17. Memory and imagination are wired on the same circuits.

Sports people are a great example of how they 'programme' themselves for success. The champion boxer Muhammed Ali rehearsed each fight in his mind over and over creating what he called his 'future history' – in effect in his mind he thought the fight was won before he got into the ring ! The unconscious cannot easily distinguish between the two which makes using the imagination a powerful method for achieving real change.

18. Experience has a structure. our thoughts and memories have a pattern to them. Changing that will change our experience.

In Ch.3 NLP Communication Model, (yes, again!), the brain is described as acting like a reducing valve, narrowing the field of our attention and making generalisations. The result of this is we have 'patterns' in the way we think about others, ourselves and situations, and what we choose to remember. On the other hand when we choose to focus on different things, then our experiences change and with them our state changes too.

The above proposed NLP beliefs of excellence are suggestions for your own mindset. Try them out, see what kind of results they get you. The great minds that blessed and influenced the founders of NLP, were known for their altruism, empathy, behavioural flexibility and emotional intelligence.

Re-Baptising Failure

The greatest mistake we can make is allowing the guilt of what we haven't yet achieved consume us.

Orly Wahba, author of 'Kindness Boomerang: How to save the world (and yourself) through 365 daily acts'.

Now you understand some of the fundamental NLP presuppositions, it's time to take a closer look at failure, which is possibly one of the most misunderstood notions. Would you hold it against a toddler who keeps falling over as they start to learn to walk? No, of course not. Because falling over is an essential part of the toddler's learning process. In other words, rather than failing, we're learning.

NLP Presuppositions do marvels helping us deal with failure. When you accept that everyone has a different outlook on life (their map), that failure is only feedback and part of the learning process and that everyone is doing the best they can with the resources they have available, it sheds a new light on what we consider to be a failure. As one lovely workshop participant exclaimed: "We can re-baptise failure and call it 'small success' if we want to". How? By using powerful words, and changing a word's definition to break barriers. Recognising failure as something different, as something positive, has a significant impact on how we perceive and do things.

When I reconsidered what failure was for me, I noticed that I felt lighter and was not so bothered about some of my wrong-doings. Even those mistakes, often trivial or unimportant to others, had tortured me for days, months and years.

What is also interesting is that some people may be quite forgiving of others and will advise their colleagues or friends to stop beating themselves up about something, but those same people become rigid and unforgiving when their friends or colleagues fail in ways they did not expect.

The NLP approach to failure helps here, by teaching us to embrace all failure, consciously and unconsciously, and allow people to fail in all sorts of ways.

Twenty years ago, I remember being in floods of tears after a chess tournament where my loss had cost my team's win. A moment of miscalculation had turned the whole match to the advantage of my opponent, and we lost. This understandably created a massive pain point for me.

My friend Simon, a source of inspiration to me and a chess buddy for years shared a similar experience: "Eleni, it's painful when you've worked so hard on your game strategy. You find yourself perfectly positioned, just minutes away from a big win, and then you make that fatal move that costs you the match". Pausing for a minute or two, he added: "The best chess players are the ones who recover faster than anyone after a wrong move or painful loss. That's what makes the difference. How quickly you can overcome a shattering loss and get back in the game the next day. That's what it's about. How you handle disappointment defines your chess game, and your life, in every way".

Simon's words made me naturally think of many great minds. One of them: Thomas Edison who experimented with creating a lightbulb, experienced hundreds of failures. But he remained positive and determined and described his defeats as the feedback he needed to get him to the next stage. He considered all his failures to be part of his learning curve.

I have not failed. I have found ten thousand ways that won't work.

Thomas Edison, inventor and businessman.

Today, we are not that unlike Edison as we make our way through life: experimenting with new relationships, communicating, building habits and learning new skills. If we can all adopt Edison's approach to the many failures we will have along the way on our personal journey, then what an inspirational and educational journey it will become!

At the end of the day, each and every one of us has a different definition of failure and even that definition changes for us with time and in different contexts. Defining the word failure in a negative way will most certainly lead to many -isms, like perfectionism, extremism, fanatism, racism and sexism. Think about what this means for our world! Embracing failure as a natural step towards our goals, though, helps us stay committed and get to where we set sail, unfazed. The more comfortable we become accepting failure, the easier and faster we move towards success!

Pre-Suppositions And Programming Ourselves For Success

Time for success, now! Focusing on what we want to succeed in transforms us, whether we want to expand our sense of forgiveness, notice more beauty in others, or achieve a personal goal. Once we minimize the time lost feeling sorry for our failures, we nicely re-focus on the end result! One could argue that feeling at ease with our failures is one of the greatest successes of all.

And once again, success is subjective and defies one single definition. What I often say to my son when we play chess is: "Make sure that no matter if you lose or win, you behave with grace." This is also success.

Once you start to incorporate the NLP presuppositions into your everyday life, and you start to gain deeper levers of understanding of yourself and others, you begin to communicate better and establish greater levels of rapport. You start to open yourself up to an exciting array of new opportunities and experiences – opportunities in respect of relationships, work and spiritual growth. And surely, the ability to do all that, simply by using your own internal resources, has to be one of the greatest successes of all!

Furthermore, success is often associated with career goals and wealth accumulation. I am the first one to aim for career and cashflow successes. Achieving in your career goals and meeting your financial goals gives us power as it does freedom. When we have done so based on confidence and not trying to prove something (insecurity), we can again bless our own crew and many others' crews with many more opportunities.

AND, a capital AND, next to the above definitions of success, there are many others, like living in a fit body, mastering negotiation or be there for someone who needs to hear words of hope. I think the below poem by poet Bessie Anderson Stanley, called 'Success' opens up the way to many more meanings of what success is:

He has achieved success who has lived well, laughed often,
and loved much; who has enjoyed the trust of pure women,
the respect of intelligent men and the love of little children;
who has filled his niche and accomplished his task;
who has left the world better than he found it, whether by
an improved poppy, a perfect poem or a rescued soul;
who has never lacked appreciation of Earth's beauty
or failed to express it; who has always looked for
the best in others and given them the best he had;
whose life was an inspiration;
whose memory a benediction.

Everyday Thinking and Doing: Consider This …

Take time to find out what role the NLP presuppositions already have in your life and how they can help you even more in achieving your goals more easily and effortlessly.

- Which of the presuppositions do you not feel comfortable adopting? What is stopping you from including them in your new mindset?
- Which of the presuppositions would you like to believe more, and how would it help you improve right now?
- What do you consider to be the major successes and failures in your life?
- Which of the presuppositions would help you see your failures through a different lens?
- Which presuppositions have you already been running on, and which have already helped you with your results?

Part 3

Tune Up ... Tune In

Feeling that we are worthwhile can only really happen, according to Author and Family Therapist Virginia Satir, when our differences are respected and we are in an open communicative environment.

Tuning in to ourselves and other people deepens understanding and builds rapport; we learn the importance of acuity and to pay attention to little details to build effective relationships and be our best.

Chapter 10

The Intention Impact Conundrum …

… recognising our impact on others and how tuning in to ourselves and others can help

By Florence

The life of every man is a diary in which he means to write one story, and writes another.

J.M. Barrie, Scottish writer and creator of Peter Pan.

What Is The Intention Impact Conundrum?

The 'conundrum' is neatly summed up by J.M. Barrie in the quote above i.e. we do not necessarily make the impact that we originally intended. We are aware of the intentions behind our own actions, but others around us only feel the impact of our actions. We, in turn, judge others on their actions, without knowing their intentions.

In much of the work I have done with groups and individuals over the years, (as well as dealing with my own challenges, of course), issues relating to relationships often come down to this conundrum. I seem to have a lot of conversations about the gulf that exists between our *intentions* and our *impact*, and helping others (and myself) to reduce or bridge that gap. My previous book *The Intention Impact Conundrum* was the result. I'm going to reference some of its key elements in this chapter, by way of an introduction to this part of the book – Tune Up … Tune In. Eleni and I chose this heading because it relates to our recognition of the aforementioned 'gulf', and what that does to our effectiveness and happiness; the heading underlines the importance of 'tuning in' to others, as well as being self-aware.

The metaphor I use in my book is that of a person inside a house who only sees the world through their windows. They do not see what others see, nor are they fully aware of what is inside other people's houses. And they may not even be fully aware of their own house – there may be other 'rooms' that they haven't visited.

The other people that we interact with are, of course, all in their own 'houses' too!

Fig. 1: We see the world through our own windows.

How Did We End Up Here?
And How Do We Move Forward?

In Part Two of this book, Eleni addressed the fact that we are a product of our upbringing, with our experiences and behaviours driven by the beliefs and values that we acquired along the way. The problem is that this is our own map of the world, and we may not be fully aware of the beliefs and attitudes that drive us, or how these are experienced by others. Sometimes, as Eleni points out in Ch. 5 Perception is Projection, we see the behaviour of others and we judge it, apparently unaware that what we see in others is likely to be a reflection of ourselves.

While you were busy judging others, you left your closet open and a lot of skeletons fell out.

Unknown.

A useful place to start unravelling the 'conundrum', and thus improve our personal and work relationships, is to take personal responsibility. When we put ourselves '*at cause*' in this way, we can look at what *we* can do, rather than expecting someone else to take the lead. Every chapter of this book (as I hope you have found already) has something that can help you – whether it's a concept, or an activity, or simply a different way of looking at ourselves and the world around us. The focus here is on how we develop our sensory acuity to be more aware of ourselves and others, and how to use this awareness to build our relationships and transform how those looking into our 'house' perceive us.

How Do I Need To Be To Achieve This?

In my book I refer to the author and speaker Jack Canfield's formula:

E + R = O

Which translates as: ***E****vent or* ***E****xperience + Our* ***R****eaction =* ***O****utcome.*

In other words: it is what happens to us, and subsequently how we choose to react to that event, that creates the outcome. The event or experience in itself does not create the outcome in any situation.

We often have little control over the things or the people that 'happen' to us, in the short term at least. The key point is that what we *choose* to do, or *choose not* to do, is crucial – it is the main variable that we do have control over. Hence my strong belief that what happens is 'in my hands'.

But making choices is not always that straightforward. On occasion, I have been unaware of the blocks that I've put in my own way. In thinking that I couldn't do something, I thought I was being *realistic* – not realising that I was in fact limiting myself (as Eleni points out in Ch. 8 Beliefs We Live By).

Walk on air against your better judgement.

Inscription on the headstone of Seamus Heaney,
from his poem 'The Gravel Walks'.

Remember my metaphor about being inside a house, looking out? Not knowing how we are viewed from the outside? Sometimes we are so familiar with the furnishings around us in our house, that we don't always see when it is time to refurbish or update them until we look at them through someone else's eyes. A friend recently told me that she only noticed how scuffed her skirting boards were when she showed someone pictures of her children and saw the skirting boards in the background!

Our mindsets can be like this: life and circumstances change, and our thinking and thus our approach may need to be 'refurbished' too. The psychologist Carol Dweck studies why people succeed, and how to foster success – and specifically the mindsets that get them there. She poses the question how it would be if we saw our abilities as develop-able, rather than being a fixed trait in ourselves - and the possibilities this could open for us.

Dweck has identified two mindsets: a 'fixed' mindset and a 'growth' mindset. Those of us with a 'fixed' mindset limit ourselves by seeing our intelligence and capabilities as set in stone; those of us with a 'growth' mindset believe that our intelligence and capabilities are things that we can grow and develop. Put simply, she considers that our ability to grow is determined by what we believe, and that what we believe is a choice.

First of all, though, we have to actually recognise when we are doing something that might be holding us back *before* we can choose to change it.

How Can I recognise 'fixed' and 'growth' mindsets in myself?

Consider your level of agreement with each the following statements in turn:

- You are who you are and that cannot be changed.
- We are all capable of change if we want to.
- You can change some things but basically you stay largely the same.
- We can always make change and develop aspects of ourselves.

If you agree with the first and third statements, this suggests you have a 'fixed' mindset, whereby you believe that that is just how you are, and you cannot do much about it. If you agree with the second and fourth statements, this suggests you have a 'growth' mindset, whereby you believe that you have potential to learn and grow.

For those of us with a 'fixed' mindset, Dweck suggests we always try to prove ourselves and get worried about being wrong and making mistakes. When we have a 'growth' mindset, we see mistakes not as failing, but as learning. This is the same idea as the Discovery Frame referred to in Ch.23; when we set a course or a meeting within a Discovery Frame, the objective is to create a safe space for learning in which it is okay to make mistakes, rather than be the best or get an exercise right first time (a theme we both return to through this book). Often the people that make the most mistakes get the most learning – as long as they're in an environment where they feel 'safe' to do so. In everyday life, growth-mindsetters permit themselves to accept that to struggle and make mistakes are part of the learning process, and they balance this by recognising that they have responsibility for the mistakes they make and for learning from them. They can extend this to other people also, thus creating create a 'safe' space for them to grow.

Saying this, having a growth mindset does not necessarily mean someone can be the next Einstein or Mozart simply by having the right attitude. What it means is that our *potential* is both unknown and unknowable, and believing that we can learn and grow is essential for tapping into it. A recent delegate on one of my NLP Business Practitioner courses captured the concept of the growth mindset and its power perfectly when she said: "I really believe now 'I have all the resources I need' and it has changed everything. I didn't know that before!"

'Tuning In' To Handle The Intention Impact Conundrum

The truth was a mirror in the hands of God.
It fell and broke into pieces. Everybody took a piece of it,
and they looked at it and thought they had the truth.

Rumi, 13th-century Persian Sunni Muslim poet.

In the remaining chapters in this part of the book, the focus is on becoming aware of preferences with respect to how we take in information and how we express ourselves – and how different that might be from the point of view of others around us. By paying attention to others, as well as being self-aware, we can tune-in far more effectively.

The aim is to be *congruent* – the best version of ourselves that we can be –

and to strengthen our rapport with others making our interactions with them more effective. In other words, to narrow the gulf between our impact and our intention!

Everyday Thinking and Doing: Consider This …

You will be taken through a number of exercises in the following chapters, to build your awareness of yourself and of others. But for now, a useful start is to consider your own mindset.

1. From the descriptions given in this chapter, which mindset do you identify with most strongly?
2. Consider also whether there is a difference between your work life and your personal life.
3. If you think you may have a fixed mindset lurking in some aspect of your life, consider what your first step might be to change it, or what question you might ask yourself that may get you thinking differently?

Chapter 11

Representational Systems …

… becoming aware of preferred senses in ourselves and others

By Florence

The Chameleon and The Leopard

By Hayley Finmore

Once upon a time, deep in the lush and leafy rainforest, lived a chameleon. This chameleon had an amazing ability to transform his emerald green scales to match not only his rich and exotic surroundings, but also the colours and patterns of those around him. His ability had earned him much fame and he had long felt accepted by his fellow animals. Lately the chameleon had become a little weary of his technicolour talent; he realised that he was starting to forget how brightly his own emerald green scales had shone.

And so one morning, the chameleon set out on a journey into the heart of the rainforest, in the hope that he could recover his now unfamiliar self. He walked for hours and hours. Eventually he reached a clearing in the rainforest, in the middle of which was a giant tree covered in a myriad of rainbow-coloured leaves. The chameleon was mesmerised. Laying down at the foot of the tree, he stared at the colourful canopy above him until he fell asleep.

A short while later he was suddenly awakened from his sleep by a heavy thump on his tail. Standing in front of him was a tall and magnificent leopard.

"I'm sooo terrrribly sorrrry," purred the leopard. "I didn't see you lying there. You are almost invisible". The chameleon realised that he was camouflaged against the bark of the tree, so he consciously reverted to his emerald green.

"That's quite a talent you have there," purred the leopard "But you could have come to great harm".

The chameleon told the leopard about the purpose of his journey. The leopard listened with interest.

Slightly bemused, the leopard exclaimed, "You spend all your time matching with everyone else and we leopards are famed for not changing our spots. I can't imagine what we could do if we were flexible enough to do both!," said the leopard with a wry smile.

Before the chameleon had a chance to respond, the leopard leapt off, out of the clearing. And the last thing the chameleon saw was the flick of the leopard's emerald green tail.

What Are Representational Systems And How Do They Create Our 'Map'?

That beautiful piece of writing has stayed with me since Hayley read it – a few years ago now – as do most of the stories that people have created for one another on my NLP courses. She had written the story for another delegate with the message of achieving a balance between building rapport with others and being yourself. The appeal and stickability of this story (and all good stories) is in its language.

Sensory acuity, (our awareness through our senses), is one of the NLP Pillars of Success (Ch.4) and paying attention to the language of others is essential for building rapport, for modelling, and for influencing other people. As humans, the world around us comes to us via our senses: seeing, hearing, feeling (as in touch or movement), tasting and smelling. In NLP these are referred to, respectively, as the visual, auditory, kinaesthetic, gustatory and olfactory representational systems, respectively. The first three (visual, auditory, kinaesthetic) tend to be our *primary* senses, but there is an additional representational system called 'auditory digital', which is not tied to any particular sense, but deals with logic and self-talk. This is expanded upon later in this chapter.

When I did my NLP Practitioner training, back in 1999, my trainer Sarah selected Genie Z. Laborde's book *Influencing With Integrity* as our pre-course reading. This was as much for its style as its fabulous content. Filled with imaginative illustrations, it is a visual feast, and it is laced with stories and at least one exercise that gets the reader to place their hands on the pages – appealing to their kinaesthetic sense. It is a rich read!

In her book she explains that we don't operate directly in what we think of as the 'real' world. Rather we experience the world through our senses and form perceptions. As we think about these perceptions we turn them into language and give them meaning.

What Laborde is describing is how we 'code' our experiences using our sensory channels and express them in words – that is, the words are *not* the experience itself. This creates what she calls a 'slippage' in our language, and further slippage occurs when we file away our experiences when, in doing so, we delete, distort and generalise (Ch.3). This is how we create and express our 'map of the world' and why it is likely to be quite different from that of other people. This, in turn, determines how we behave.

Over time, we usually develop a *preference* for one representational system, although this can change with different situations. So it is important not to characterise someone as being 'a visual' or 'a kinaesthetic', but to pay attention to how they are speaking in the moment. This is the representational system that they trust the most and is most developed, but the other senses will still be bringing in information, whether consciously or unconsciously. This preference by a person for a particular system may also affect their ability to acquire certain skills, thus people with a strong auditory preference may find it easier to learn to play a musical instrument.

In addition to our *preferred* system, we also have a *lead* representational system that may be different. Our lead system is the sense that we use to retrieve a past experience; once we have brought it into our conscious mind, our preferred system then takes over to recall the details. For example, when I recall the time Eleni and I spent together on the island of Tinos in Greece, a picture of us hugging outside a restaurant pops up – **Fig:1**.

Fig. 1: Eleni and I on the Greek island of Tinos.

Next I remember the warmth of her welcome and the happiness and contentment I felt that day. So in my case, Lead and Preferred are different: my lead is visual, and my preference is kinaesthetic. N.B. In some people they will be the same.

How Can We Recognise The Representational Systems?

In order to take in information through our senses, and store it, and then use it, we have to adjust what Dilts and DeLozier refer to in their book *NLP II The Next Generation* as "our physiological and neurological machinery to direct our sensory information properly". These behaviours are referred to in NLP as 'accessing cues'. So in addition to the language a person uses, we can detect a person's preference in the way they are thinking, by observing their reflex actions. These 'accessing cues' are actually helping them access this particular mode of thinking. We can recognise someone's representational systems by noting/paying attention to the following:

- Eye movements (referred to as 'eye-accessing cues').
- Words or phrases (referred to as 'predicates').
- Breathing.
- Gestures.
- Speed of speaking.

N.B. what follows are the *typical* accessing cues – but it is worth noting that in some people the eye accessing cues are reversed, so rather than jump to conclusions based on eye accessing cues alone, it is safer to pay attention to all the person's cues over a period of time i.e. a process called calibration mentioned later in this chapter.

For each preferred representational system here is what to look out for:

Visual preference and accessing visual information

People exhibiting a visual preference or when accessing visual information:

- ***Eye movements:*** when creating a picture in their head for the first time, like imagining their bedroom walls painted purple (assuming it isn't already!), they look up to their right (**Fig. 2**). When recalling a visual memory (what their bedroom actually looks like) they will look up and to their left. However, some people have this configuration reversed; so while **Fig.2** is typical, it does not apply in every case. Also when someone is recalling a picture that comes to them easily, there is sometimes a forward defocused gaze.

Eyes move up and to their right = visual construct
Eyes move up and to their left = visual recall

Fig. 2: Visual Eye Accessing Cues.

- ***Words or phrases:*** see, picture, colour, clear, hazy, dark, light, vision, 'shed some light on it', 'we don't see eye to eye', 'set out a clear vision', or 'don't colour my thinking.'

- ***Breathing:*** tend to breathe higher in their chest, with breaths that are rapid and shallow.
- ***Gestures:*** tend to use upward gestures with their hands and heads, and squint their eyes.
- ***Speed of speaking***: tend to speak more quickly when they are accessing pictures in their heads as they speak, and the pitch of their voice tends to be higher.

This is believed to be the most preferred representational system in Western cultures, which is partly why many NLP processes relate to visualisation.

Auditory preference and accessing auditory information

People exhibiting an auditory preference or accessing auditory information:

- ***Eye movements:*** when thinking about a sound, eyes move left and right in the direction of their ears (**Fig. 3**). They look to their right for sounds they are creating (e.g. what would their cat sound like if speaking in English), and they look to their left when remembering a sound (e.g. a favourite song).

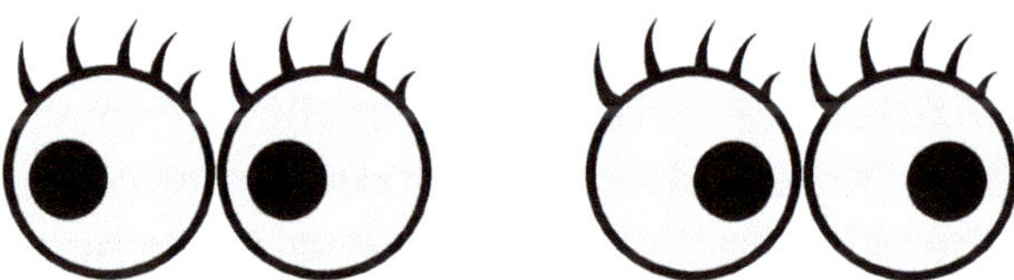

Eyes move lateral right = auditory construct
Eyes move lateral left = auditory recall

Fig. 3: Auditory Eye Accessing Cues.

- ***Words or phrases:*** tune, loud, comment, hear, discord, echo, 'that rings a bell', 'loud and clear', 'he talks a good story' or 'singing from the same hymn sheet'.
- ***Breathing:*** tend to breathe in a way that expands their whole chest area.
- ***Gestures:*** often move rhythmically, touch their ears, or lean their head to one side while listening.
- ***Speed of speaking***: tend to speak more slowly than 'visuals' and often have an internal dialogue going on in which they hear themselves. Their voices tend to be quite melodious, with resonance.

This preference is less common in Western cultures than visual or kinaesthetic.

Kinaesthetic preference and accessing kinaesthetic information

People exhibiting this preference or accessing kinaesthetic information:

- ***Eye movements:*** when thinking kinaesthetically, whether in terms of an internal emotion or an external touch, their eyes move down and to the right (**Fig. 4**).

Eyes move down right = kinaesthetic

Fig. 4: Kinaesthetic Preference Eye Accessing Cues.

- ***Words or phrases:*** feel, move, love, rough, painful, grasp, deep. They use phrases like 'take the rough with the smooth', 'thin-skinned', 'hang on', 'keep your hair on' or 'going off the deep end'.
- ***Breathing:*** tend to breathe deeper and lower in the chest.
- ***Gestures:*** gestures are linked to what they are saying, lower down and towards the body.
- ***Speed of speaking***: voice tone tends to be deeper and even breathy. Their speed of speech is slower than people with visual or auditory preferences, and they make frequent pauses as they check out their feelings about what they are saying.

In Western cultures, this preference is believed to be secondary to visual.

Auditory digital preference and accessing auditory digital information

People exhibiting this preference or accessing purely factual information:

- ***Eye movements:*** when thinking in this mode the eyes move down and to the left (**Fig. 5**).

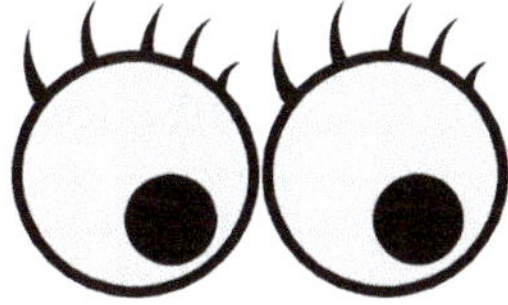

Down left = auditory digital

Fig. 5: Auditory Digital Preference Eye Accessing Cues.

- ***Words or phrases:*** tend to talk with themselves to think and make decisions. Language is devoid of sensory-specific words, instead, using words like: understand, think, logical, indicate, analyse, and phrases like 'due diligence' or 'I sense something is wrong' or 'consider the idea' or 'facilitate the process'. This is the stolid language of many business reports, making a factual but uninspiring read.

- ***Breathing:*** tend to be in lower abdomen
- ***Gestures:*** gestures associated with this type of thinking include placing the hand on the side of the face (the 'telephone position') and often taking notes, otherwise quite reserved.
- ***Speed of speaking***: often it is slow – a characteristic of this mode of thinking is internal dialogue, they may think they have had a conversation with someone when they haven't.

This thinking mode may be how someone processes sensory input or incoming information in a work environment and it may be very important in clearly delivering information to others. It is likely that they may have a strong visual, kinaesthetic or auditory preference in other parts of their life.

What Is The Value In Recognising Another Person's Representational System?

As referred to at the start of this chapter, the more we can pick up *how* someone is speaking to us, rather than simply the content of what they are saying, enabling us to flex how we respond, the more effective we are likely to be as communicators. Noticing the representational system of the person we are speaking to is the first step in speaking in a language that they understand. This builds rapport with them. It is also an essential part of modelling someone's strategy to understand how they are thinking and processing, as described in Ch.27.

At the end of a course I attended as a delegate, we were working in pairs for an exercise that involved discussing our future objectives. My partner was thinking about her future, eyes closed, when I asked: "So how do you see your future then?" This caused her to snap out of her thoughts and reply, rather sharply, "I don't *see* it. I *feel* it!" In that awkward moment, she taught me a lot about the importance of speaking to someone in their own language – their own representational system, or at least in a more neutral way!

When we notice the preferred representational system of the person we are speaking to, and reply in kind, we not only build rapport, but we speak 'their language'. We are more easily understood by that person and can perhaps be more persuasive with them.

Getting someone 'unstuck'

Noticing how someone is speaking can also be a way of helping them to think differently – to get out of 'stuck' thinking. Since 1980s John Grinder, along with Carmen Bostic St. Clair and Judith DeLozier, have been developing what he calls 'New Code NLP' (as explained in their book *Whispering In The Wind).* A starting point when someone is stuck is to 'shake up their map of the world'.

One of the ways of doing this is to notice their representational system, which may be part of what is holding them in their problem state. As Einstein said:

No problem can be solved from the same level of consciousness that created it.

So one way to shift someone's thinking would be to ask them a question that takes them into a different representational system. For example in a coaching context:

> *Coachee*: "I can't see what else I can do in the future."
>
> *Coach*: "What do you feel you would like to do?" or "What could you tell yourself that might help?"

Using rich language

Turn back to Hayley's story at the beginning of this chapter and re-read it. You will notice her use of all three primary representational systems. This is called 'rich' language – the more senses we use when writing and speaking, the richer the experience for our readers or listeners. Here is an excerpt from Martin Luther King's 'I have a dream' speech from 1963. The first sentence alone has three senses, and in the third sentence he even manages to get in a gustatory reference. I think this goes a long way towards explaining the power his speech has more than 50 years on.

But there is something that I must say to my people who stand on the warm threshold which leads into the palace of justice. In the process of gaining our rightful place, we must not be guilty of wrongful deeds. Let us not seek to satisfy our thirst for freedom by drinking from the cup of bitterness and hatred.

Martin Luther King, American Civil Rights Activist, from his speech delivered on the Washington march for Jobs and Freedom 1963.

The 'Charisma' pattern

In their book *Presenting Magically*, Tad James and David Shephard identify the 'Charisma Pattern'. Really great presenters use this at the start of their speeches to draw in all parts of their audience. When presenting to a group, the audience will comprise a whole range of preferred representational systems. If the speech started with the fast-paced speech of people with a visual preference, much of the audience would be left behind. The authors identified a pattern as shown in **Fig. 6.**

Kinaesthetic ⇒ Auditory ⇒ Visual ⇒ Kinaesthetic

Fig. 6: Charisma Pattern.

In practice, this involves speaking slowly to start with, almost hesitantly, using 'feeling' language, to appeal to those with a kinaesthetic preference. Then follows speech that is a little faster, using 'auditory' words, and finally even faster speech that creates pictures with words for those with a visual preference. The speaker then dips back into kinaesthetic language, and with all members of the audience now on board, they carry on using rich language throughout.

Calibrating Another Person's State

Focus on 'how' – Not 'what'

Sensory acuity goes beyond simply noticing another person's representational system. Professor Albert Mehrabian came up with a model of communication that is often quoted. It relates to how we take in and interpret information when another person is present and speaking to us (**Fig. 7**). In this model the way the message is conveyed of how someone is feeling is:

- 7% in the words they use.
- 38% in their tone of voice and emphasis.
- 55% in their facial expressions and body language.

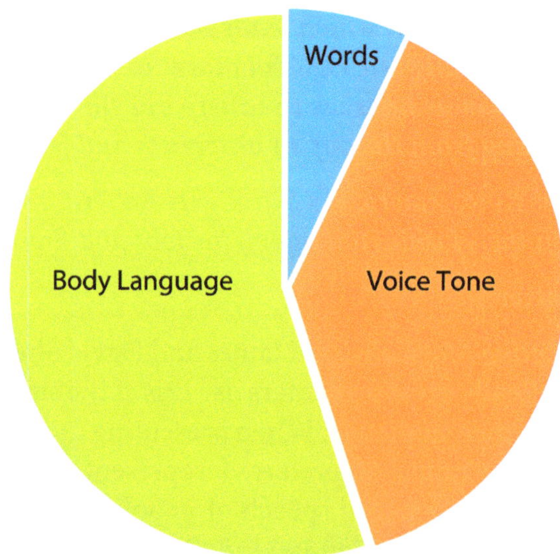

Fig. 7: Albert Mehrabian's Communication Model.

We pick up the words that a person is using in our conscious mind, but our interpretation of their voice tone and body language happens at a largely unconscious level. So when someone says: "I am fine with what you have suggested", and their tone and body language do not match, then they come across as being incongruent and their message causes confusion. When we pay attention to another person in this way, it is referred to in NLP as calibration. It literally means 'measuring' someone's emotional state. What we are looking for is what are termed 'modalities of calibration', not all of which will be apparent on every occasion. These include the:

- Tone and volume of their voice.
- Their posture, stance, seating position, and/or physical balance.
- The facial colour as in blushing, reddening, pallor.
- Eye accessing cues and the degree of dilation of their pupils.
- The tension in their face and forehead muscles.
- The movement of their head.
- The pattern of their breathing (often picked up when they speak).

It is clear that animals do this 'tuning in' very well. It's difficult to fool a dog or a horse about what state you are in, whether you are speaking or not, which is why they are often used on skills development courses these days. When we first got our dog Ferdi, I took him to dog training classes. His behaviour with me was very naughty, while with the trainer he was an angel. Her calibration was superb and she told me, "He knows from your voice and body language that you don't mean it and what you are asking him to do is optional!". Well, that was me told.

And it is apparent to this day that he, and his sister Lola, are calibrating me at every moment – they are very effective teachers and swift givers of feedback!

Fig. 8: Lola and Ferdi assessing my willingness to play!

Everyday Thinking and Doing: Consider This ...

Now time to put all of this to work. Here are some ideas:

- Practice 'tuning in':
  - If you are new to representational systems and calibration, you may be thinking it will be a challenge to notice them during conversations, particularly when it is also important to pay attention to what is being said. A good way to 'tune in' is to allow yourself to notice preferences in situations where you are not directly involved in the conversation, but just listening to others. This might be during a business meeting, in a social context, or even while watching the television.
  - Ask a friend to describe their favourite holiday destination and what they like about it. Then ask them about a work situation or project. In both cases, note when you hear a sensory-specific word in their descriptions. Then feed back to them what you noticed and get them to do the same for you.
- *Review your writing*: Look at things you have written previously – emails, blogs, letters, stories – and notice your own sensory preferences. Is 'rich' language in evidence? Or could the use of 'richer' language have made your writing more compelling?
- *Coaching*: If you coach other people, or have a conversation with a friend who you find to have stuck thinking, notice their representational system and ask a question that takes them into a different one.
- *Presenting*: Next time you are preparing do a speech or presentation, consider how you could use the charisma pattern at the start and rich language throughout.
- *Persuasive business writing*: Look at the documents you produce in your business life. What is the dominant representational system there, and might the content benefit from the use of richer language, to engage your readers?

Chapter 12

Building Rapport …

… what it is, how and why to build it with others

By Florence

We build too many walls and not enough bridges.

Issac Newton, founder of modern classical physics.

What Is Rapport And Why Is It Important?

Some years ago, I was asked to carry out some psychometric testing for a recruitment campaign being carried out by a manufacturing plant. I was invited to do so by the Managing Director whom I knew from another organisation. When I arrived the Human Resources Director was also at the meeting, as you might expect, and it was immediately apparent that he was not happy to see me. The reason became obvious – he (quite rightly) felt that it was his job to engage a consultant to do the testing; it wasn't up to his boss. The meeting did not start well. The room felt cold, and the managing director looked uncomfortable too. The aggrieved HR Director was asking me questions about documents that we hadn't discussed yet, and was not following the sequence I was trying – and failing – to present. I wondered briefly about the merits of having ruby slippers like Dorothy in the Wizard of Oz, to transport me out of that meeting!

On another occasion, I had been invited to meet with the headmistress of a girls' school to discuss development for her team. The moment I met her, I felt discomfort. She was a vision in herringbone tweed and I was in a formal pinstriped trouser suit. I felt awkward and out of place and soon shed my jacket to reveal a more feminine blouse. When we went to lunch, the headmistress walked very briskly and I trotted beside her to keep up. Our conversation over lunch was polite, but with no depth and no connection. I couldn't wait for it to be over.

These are classic examples of what happens when there is no rapport. There is resistance. Conversations do not flow, interest dwindles, and the whole interaction feels strained, sometimes even aggressive. All of this took place in both situations, even though I was invited to be there and was presenting them with a service that they wanted and needed! The discomfort on all sides was palpable. So, rapport in any relationship (business or otherwise) is not something that is 'nice to have' – it is a 'need to have'. It is the surest way to get the best from your interactions with others, or to have any effective interaction at all.

How Do We Build Rapport?

Rapport is a natural process for humans and, indeed, for all sorts of animals. When we have rapport, we can relate to others with trust and understanding.

Fig. 1: Eleni and I 'matching' each other in Thessaloniki.

If you notice how a young child behaves at a monkey enclosure in a zoo, you will see rapport-building in action: children naturally start to imitate the monkeys in order to make a connection with them, and frequently they will get a similar response from the monkeys. So the basis of building rapport is 'matching' and 'mirroring'. Note that this is distinctly different from mimicking, which is often disrespectful and will have the opposite effect. Observe people who are getting on well together and you will notice how much they match and mirror each other through their:

- Body language and gestures.
- Facial expressions.
- Seating position or stance.
- Laughing or drinking patterns (e.g. at the same times).
- Shared interests.
- Shared language, jargon or accent.
- Clothing.
- Breathing patterns.

These are just a few examples. For people in longer-term relationships, the rapport goes deeper, to shared history, beliefs and values, identity, and much, much more.

The very action of starting to write this book is testament to the rapport that existed between Eleni and I at that time. In the course of writing it though, that rapport has been both tested and strengthened by the process, and we could not have done this piece of work without it. We have spent endless hours on Skype and we have met up in Kuala Lumpur, London, Thessaloniki and Toulouse. As we discussed each chapter we have talked at a deeper level than ever before about NLP concepts, our lives, our families, our hopes and dreams.........and squeezed a bit of shopping in too. We hope this book will be transformative for you – we already know it has been transformative for us, as individuals and for our rapport as friends. (Eleni quipped when she read this "If you want to know your friend write a book with her!")

So rapport is something that can start at an apparently superficial level and deepens over a period of time to build stronger and stronger bridges between ourselves and others as Issac Newton referred to at the start of the chapter. This does not mean that people who have rapport will not challenge each other or disagree; in reality, these are relationships in which it is safe and possible to do just that! Which is why they are so valuable in work or development situations. I sometimes refer to these as 'relationships that can take a lot of rain'!

Fig. 2: Max, our cat, rests his paws on Lola's rump, rapport has grown over time...trust and comfort.

Rapport underpins every successful interaction with another individual or group, *and it is an absolute essential before embarking on any NLP process with another person.* If you are running a training course, coaching a colleague or friend, in a meeting, interviewing, giving a presentation, carrying out a medical examination, selling something, painting someone's nails, or talking to your friends and family – you first need to be in rapport for the interaction to go well.

What Is The Process For Building Rapport?

In the previous chapter I talked about sensory acuity, that is, the ability to notice another person's representational system and pick up clues from their voice tone and body language. These are the building blocks of rapport. There is an expression: 'Find out where someone is coming from and go and meet them there'. So rapport starts with taking personal responsibility for the relationship. The process is well illustrated by someone who does this consistently and with ease – my friend Claire, who is a beautician that does my nails.

She always greets me and her other clients with a smile. (Have you noticed a smile is so often the shortest route to rapport?). She asks questions about their day and listens to their answers. She starts to 'tune in' to what is going on for them and adds to what they say without taking over their issue or the conversation. And if someone is relating a problem to her, she can offer an alternative way of looking at the situation without being dismissive of how they see it. She meets dozens of people each week and remembers the details from all their earlier conversations. This shows just how much attention she pays and it bears out her sincerity. Not surprisingly, Claire has a loyal client base – and not simply because she is good at what she does. Her process, and indeed anyone else's, for building rapport is summarised in the figure below (**Fig. 3**). This all comes naturally to us most of the time, but for those times when it doesn't, then this awareness allows us to learn/tap into the skill.

Match/Mirror → Pace → Lead

Fig. 3: The Rapport process.

The starting point is to notice how the person is and then join them there, firstly by getting into physical rapport (e.g. sit in the same way as them). Then ***match*** the pace of your speaking to theirs, as well as your voice tone and your representational system. However, if the person is angry, match their energy rather than their anger; this avoids inflaming the situation. When you continue to match and mirror as the conversation progresses, this is called ***pacing*** and as you do this their unconscious mind will be picking up similarities in what you are saying and what you are doing.

Like the situations I described at the start of this chapter, you may want to lead the other person into a different way of being: calmness, for example, or to be receptive to new information, or so they are prepared to stretch in some way. When you have 'paced' them sufficiently (sometimes it only takes a few minutes) you can start to ***lead*** them, perhaps initially by changing your physical position and then by taking the conversation in a new direction.

A good example of this process in action was told to me by a friend who was a Human Resources Manager. He was dealing with someone who had just been made redundant – a challenging situation for them both. My friend knew the person was coming to his office, so he was already on his feet when the employee stormed in. The employee stalked around the office as he expressed his anger and frustration; my friend walked too, and asked questions, mirroring the energy but *not* the anger (or the language!). After (literally in this case) some pacing, my friend stopped and leant against a filing cabinet. The employee stopped moving and also leant against a piece of furniture – the *leading* had started. After a while, my friend sat down, and the employee followed suit and sat down too. From that point, the conversation could proceed in a useful direction. They were never going to be 'best buddies' because that is not necessarily the point of rapport – but having trust and being able to communicate effectively with another person is.

As Eleni discussed in Ch. 5 'mirror neurons' are a relatively recent discovery in neuroscience. They are believed to play a part in this process, whereby actions of one person fire the 'mirror neurons' in another, thus giving some insight into the intentions and feelings of the other person – the core of rapport.

Putting Rapport-Building To Work

My uncomfortable lunch with the headmistress continued, and as it did, even though we were in physical rapport, the interaction was superficial. I was looking for a deeper rapport with this lady, some other point of commonality on which to build. Just before we had coffee, I found it! It turns out we were both grammar school girls, in fact we were the same age and had been in the same year (at different schools). Finally, the conversation really started to flow. As we walked back to the school she walked at my pace and talked enthusiastically about the work we were planning to do with her team and she asked me if she could be involved. On my next visit to the school I made sure I was dressed in tweed – I was not looking to *lead* them in fashion sense!

Meanwhile, back in the manufacturing plant, without any 'ruby slippers' to hand, I finally noticed what I was doing, how I was speaking, and how different that was to the HR Director. I shifted my seating position to match his and, abandoning my ineffective Mrs Nice approach, I started to present the information in the same way he was speaking to me – polite but to the point, and pointing clearly to the exact document I wanted him to look at. My new directive approach worked and within in a few minutes, the room seemed to thaw out. (Notice here that I built rapport by losing the smiley face!) He became quite jokey with both the Managing Director and myself and then offered me some coffee. The meeting progressed and finished well, The next time I was back in that business it was at the invitation of the HR Director. Our working relationship continued strongly until he took up a post abroad, but I still hear from him every Christmas!

Building rapport isn't always something you need to think about, of course. Often we meet people and the rapport is instant, requiring no conscious intervention. The stories above illustrate what you can do when rapport isn't there, or if something has happened to break it. The key is to be 'at cause' rather than 'at effect' and to take personal responsibility for the relationships that matter to you.

Building Rapport With Groups

Giving a presentation, being at a panel interview, or running a meeting or training course, are all examples of times when you need to build rapport with a group rather than an individual. Once again the principles of matching–mirroring–pacing–leading are the same. Here are some ideas:

 *Make Contact Early*: where possible, have contact with participants beforehand to gauge their attitude, interest level and expectations. This is also starting a connection with them even before you meet formally.

 *Think What Is Happening for Them:* think beforehand about their situation, perhaps how far they have travelled, or what other big events or projects are going on for them. You can then acknowledge these and take them into account in your planning.

 *Greeting Time Before You Start:* create enough time before you begin to greet and have one-to-one conversations with as many of the group as you can. There may be things that come up in conversations that you can appropriately refer to later.

 *Identify Group 'Leaders'*: building rapport with 'leaders' in the group can also affect the wider gathering.

 *Comfortable and Equal Seating*: ensure that the setup and seating arrangements are as comfortable as possible, and that your seating is the equivalent of theirs (e.g. not significantly lower or higher or more luxurious).

 *Develop Group Rapport:* depending on the nature of the meeting, building rapport with the group may be facilitated by them building rapport with each other. This can be anything from a simple, fun introductory exercise in which you can take part, to a longer team-building activity.

 *Attune to Physical Needs of Group:* stay 'in tune' with the groups physical needs by ensuring they take adequate breaks and they do not stay in a fixed position for more than 45 minutes. I often suggest

a 'mini-break' of four minutes to allow people to move around and get comfortable again. (Why four? It is a peculiar time frame that often makes people laugh and they pay more attention to the time.)

Be Accessible: use breaks as an opportunity to continue the individual rapport-building you started before the event. Even those not directly in conversation with you will notice your accessibility.

Everyday Thinking And Doing: Consider This …

At the next meeting or gathering you attend:

1. Take the opportunity to notice the matching and mirroring going on between people who clearly have a good relationship.
2. Pick someone whom you don't already have a rapport with and use the suggestions in this chapter to build it. Notice what changes occur as the rapport builds.
3. When you have built rapport with someone, test it by subtly shifting your physical position or touching your ear or your head and notice if they follow. If they do, you are leading them; if they don't, it indicates that you need to continue pacing for a while longer.
4. Consider what you need to do to strengthen or build a rapport with someone that you think is already good.

Chapter 13

Metaprograms …

… the mental filters through which we process information

By Eleni

What I dream of is an art of balance.

Henri Matisse, painter.

Every day, our brain processes information using specific programmes that direct our decisions. Unconsciously, we run different ones, depending on the situation we find ourselves in, and the sort of decision we are about to make. They are context-related, and they are innate tendencies on how we go about what we delete, generalise and distort from what we perceive through our senses – the main filters of the NLP Communication Model (Ch.3).

Every day, we follow different mental methods as we go about thinking and planning ahead:

- When we are busy with our goals, do we express them in terms of what we want or what we do not want?
- Do we focus more on the end result or the steps that get us there?

Some of us go only to the dentist when one of our teeth hurts; others have their six-month check-up already noted on their agenda. Our individual behaviour in each circumstance is as a result of the specific programmes we run.

At a higher level, we can reflect on ways we habitually approach life, our thinking characteristics, our personality features and our preferences: change or no change, pleasure or pain, sacrifice or not, include or exclude, independent or collaborating, security or adventure, comfortable or uncomfortable? These hard-wired preferences are called metaprograms – another meta-NLP term (don't you love them?).

Is one metaprogram better than another? Nope. There is no right or wrong metaprogram. They all serve different purposes and it's for us to become aware of them and use them in ways that maximise their benefits. And that comes down to awareness, flexibility and balance.

Florence sees metaprograms as our personal palette of colours that can influence what we paint, and make up our perceptions and ways of communication. Naturally, we like some colours more than others and they may come to dominate in some of our paintings. But with more awareness, we start expanding our spectrum of colours, and mixing them to suit each of our paintings better – in effect achieving the 'balance' Matisse refers to. A few examples will hopefully make metaprograms clearer to you! Here are eight of the most common ones:

Proactive–Reactive

As a parent, you take on the role to take care, think about and protect your children. Being proactive helps in doing so. You plan ahead, and proactively get ready to tackle obstacles. This ranges from making sure all their meals are ready for school to handling things when they get bullied. Being proactive is gold and the benefits are undisputable – as most parents will tell you.

But is being proactive *the best and only way* to go about things? Not really – being reactive to situations can have benefits too. Creating the space and the time for your children to fail as safely as possible is a true gift. It's not always easy or straightforward, because our unconscious mostly wants us to prevent them from getting hurt in any way. It takes time and awareness to re-programme our instinctive inclination to catch them before they fall. But falling means failing – and failing teaches lessons!

As a parent, I learnt to give in to natural consequences, meaning the consequences we all have to deal with when we fail and make mistakes. Remember that talking about failure is not the same as experiencing failure, and it is a major part of growing up that requires parents to choose wisely instead of saving a child from an embarrassing moment, to let them experience it, then lend an ear and a shoulder to cry on.

Match–Mismatch

We often compare people and situations with what we already know (our model of the world). Sometimes, we notice what is similar (matching) and sometimes we focus on what is different (mismatching). We might enter a room and feel inclined to go and stand next to someone looking like us or we might start a conversation with the person that we feel we have nothing in common with.

Imagine if you were always the yes man/woman or always surrounded by yes people. That would be a one-way street, leaving us drained. We would not learn as much, either. This is a classic case of too much matching, an extreme scenario. We can all enjoy learning from different points of view. It is believed that there is a very strong preference for matching across populations which can make those who mis-match seem difficult or out of step. In reality, disagreeing or offering a different perspective (mismatching) does not mean we are difficult or peculiar, it is really valuable thinking.

On the other hand, being rigid in our views most of the time, will surely tire the people around us (constantly mismatching). Having discussed this behaviour with those who have a 'mismatching' tendency, it comes down to this: many times, they either feel misunderstood or the need to strive for perfectionism. We can all lock into excessive mismatching when we are not self-aware in our dealings with others. The key here is to raise our awareness and as a result our self-esteem.

A healthy balance between the two (matching and mismatching) is what we want. We can check and re-evaluate this balance based on our outcomes and people's reactions to our behaviour. The balance will help us enjoy behavioural flexibility and more profound relationships.

Towards–Away From

Among the Prime Directives of the Unconscious listed in Ch.2, we learnt about the 'cannot process negatives' directive. When we say "I do not want stress", we concentrate on *stress* and instruct our crew to bring us stress. We feed our mind with images, sounds and feelings that we do not want.

In metaprogrammes, this translates as follows:

"I do not want stress" is Away From – the point of reference is the stress.

"I want peace and energy" is Towards – the point of reference is peace and energy.

Can you see the difference? Our ability to think about what we really *want* is known as the 'Towards' metaprogram. Our ability to think of what we *do not want* is known as the 'Away From'.

When we think 'towards', we are more likely to achieve our goals, but in truth it is not always possible to define the 'other side' of stress, our 'away from'. We can be so blocked that we cannot construct what we would like instead.

During one course, a delegate shared how she did not have a clear vision of what she wanted. After five or ten minutes talking, however, it became clear to her that her choices were based on the fact that she did not want to go back and live in her country. This was an important Away From to focus on to start with, because it was the underlining reasoning behind all her choices.

Big Picture (Big Chunk)–Details (Small Chunk)

A few years back, I was assigned to collect feedback from stakeholders on the general management of a particular company. Along with all the positive feedback, one common area for improvement was mentioned by everyone I spoke to – namely, the manager's inability to look people in the eye. He would look at the ceiling, sometimes for what seemed eternity. Their interpretation of this was that he was deliberately ignoring them, trying to show them who is the boss, leaving them waiting there!

As it turns out, the manager had a visual preference (Ch.11) and when he was reflecting on a question, he would look up to access his visual representations and see things from a helicopter point of view. Putting his hands behind his head as he looked up was his way of taking a good look at his internal images, with the aim of finding valuable insights to offer to the person he was talking to. As a general manager, his natural innate preference was to see the whole picture, the big picture (big chunk), a helicopter's view of things. In contrast, an accountant might have an innate preference for details (small chunk), like the numbers on a spreadsheet.

This is an example of two different roles (general manager and accountant) who have developed different 'preferences' based on their daily tasks. They may have had these preferences before they began their careers, as a result of how they were raised and who they modelled. But the bottom line is that understanding the difference: if someone has the flexibility, whatever their role, to appreciate both the big picture and the details helps makes communication with others flow, it enables them to serve both roles better.

We all function according to these preferences, interchangeably, and without always knowing we are doing so. When I announced a surprise trip to my kids, I used to be somewhat disheartened by their first reaction, wanting to know exactly the when, where and with whom details. My communication was operating from a big picture standpoint – running my self-talk beliefs like "This is a surprise Great news! As a mother I went a long way to arrange this" – but my children were craving the details before they could express any kind of joy. So I learnt to have the details ready and be better prepared if the surprise was not instantly embraced.

Internally or Externally Referenced

Imagine if every time we performed a task, we relied solely on our gut feeling and self-feedback to approve or disapprove of our results. Now imagine the exact opposite, if we went around asking the opinion of everyone and anyone without having a clue about our performance ourselves. Two extremes – both with destructive repercussions.

When we feel we know best (and therefore do not check with others for their opinions), we operate from an internally referenced metaprogram that shuts down feedback from others and leads to our isolation. Conversely, when we constantly seek validation from others before making any decisions, we operate from a strictly externally referenced metaprogram, whereby we literally place our emotional and mental health in the hands of others. Ideally, we should avoid a strong inclination towards one or the other.

Keeping our 'door open' and welcoming feedback enriches our experiences and moves us forward – but so does our self-belief and confidence in our own standpoint. Knowing when to adjust the balance between them in this metaprogram correlates directly with our level of self-esteem and self-worth.

Convincer Pattern

Sometimes we're convinced about something straight away. Other times we need more time. We might need more evidence or experience. Sometimes we make decisions on the spot. Other times, we go asking every single one of our friends about their opinion. Or we think about a decision for days.

In short, do you get convinced 'right away', after 'a number of times', after 'a certain period of time' or is it 'consistency' you focus on?

Buying shoes for me is as easy as it gets in decision making. I know right away when I see a pair I want. This is not the case when I want to buy a house. I love taking my time visiting houses – for months! So, the common factor here is 'buying', but how I go about it is quite different in different contexts, and is influenced by my needs, beliefs, values and overall internal experience. It definitely has to do with the amount of money involved!

Other contexts include deciding about a business partnership, an offer on a product, taking a new position at work, having a child, taking a holiday, opting for surgery, or choosing what movie to watch.

Then there are the decisions to say, "I love you" or "I'm sorry".

The Convincer Pattern also has to do with our preferred representational systems.

We might be more easily convinced that someone is good at what they do after we see them do their job, or hear or read about how good they are at their job.

Associated–Dissociated

This is probably a metaprogram you have not heard of before, and that's understandable! It is part of psychological and NLP terminology (Ch.15). In a nutshell, the experience/feeling of being *within* our own body is referred to as being 'associated', and the experience of feeling *outside* our own body is known as 'dissociated'. The awareness of our 'selves' through all our senses is an associated state. In a dissociated state, we create some distance from those feelings. So let me expand.

Think about a happy memory you have of the past. Something nice from your childhood. And when you recall it, note whether you see it as if you are looking straight from your own eyes, or as if you are looking at a picture with yourself in it.

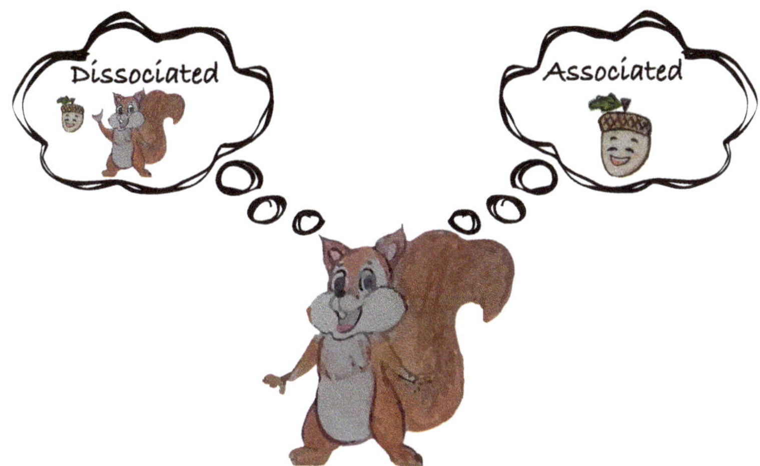

Fig. 1: Dissociated/Associated.

Initially, being associated with positive feelings might seem an obvious preference (as is being dissociated from negative ones). But at times it makes sense to associate with negative feelings, even if only briefly, to acknowledge them and give them space, or to test whether they're still lurking around. It can also be appropriate to dissociate from positive feelings, especially when they're too intense and block us instead of helping us. Consider the examples below and it should all become clearer.

Feeling sadness is a way of expressing our emotions and sharing them. After all, we cannot properly grieve if we do not talk about our sadness. This is a good time to associate with our negative emotions. Who would not want to feel sad when we part ways with someone we care for? Who would not want to feel angry when our rights are being threatened? Once we start acknowledging negative feelings like these and listen to them carefully, the distinction between positive and negative feelings starts to fade (see also Ch. 16 on Parts Integration).

Similarly, we may be over-excited or over-anticipating an event, which might take a toll on us. We have all seen brides and grooms go through tremendous stress in order to have their day as perfect as possible and how this takes a toll on them. I personally can relate to this. After our wedding, it took me a whole week during our honeymoon in Sicily to recover from the self-imposed stress to offer our guests a magical experience. I was exhausted. Luckily, my husband was there to offer his care. Positive stress can be as detrimental as any stress when bad things happen. It can help to become dissociated with these things, to help us enjoy them more, instead of locking ourselves into feelings of 'over-effort' or 'over-joy' that ultimately wear us out or create resistance within ourselves and our environment.

Any form of exaggeration works against balance. The term *toxic positivity* is about a limiting belief that we need to stay positive no matter what. 'Do not give up, try harder!' becomes a mantra for life. Eventually, it hurts us. We need to be able to also know how to give up at times, express our frustrations, write on our journal uncensored. We can still pick up ourselves later. Who needs people around them who are 24/7 positive? We need friends and family who share their vulnerabilities and create room for more authentic experiences.

Past–Now–Future

Think about where you spend most of your time in your head. Is it thinking about the good old days? Or what might happen tomorrow? Or now? This metaprogram is of gigantic significance when it comes to time. After all, time management is life management, so mastering our brains in terms of 'time' thinking can be life changing. A powerful mindset is able to shift easily from the past to the now to the future and enjoy the power of choice.

- Living in the moment makes us enjoy things and helps us to be 'present'.
- Thinking of the past offers us a wealth of resources and lessons we have learnt from.
- Imagining the future opens the doors to our dreams wide open.

Before Sunset

This Past–Now–Future metaprogram makes me think of my favourite movie trilogy: *Before Sunrise*, *Before Sunset* and *Before Midnight*.

Three different movies, shot in three different decades, but with the same two main actors – Ethan Hawke and Julie Delpy. In the first one, *Before Sunrise*, they meet on a train in Vienna and spend a whole day together, and they promise to meet in Paris six months later.

In the second, *Before Sunset*, they are in their thirties, and the young man is in Paris promoting his new book called *This Time*. It is autobiographical, relating to his meeting with the girl on the train ten years before. In the first scene, he is seen presenting to an audience in a bookstore. The book had an ambiguous ending, and he gets asked whether the heroes will meet again or whether they will never see each other again. So he asks them "What do you think? Probably some of you are romantic and think they'll find each other again?" Half of the audience nodded in agreement. He continued, "And some of you are cynics and do not think so." The other half of the audience nodded.

I smiled to myself, thinking directly about metaprograms. Sometimes we see the glass half full, and sometimes we see it half empty. It depends on the context and the particulars of each situation. We all use preferred filters when it comes to our very basic optimistic or pessimistic outlooks on life. With *every movie we watch, every book we read, and every story we hear, our interpretations are subject to our metaprograms.*

Well, in *Before Midnight*, you get the writer's take!

Everyday Thinking and Doing: Consider this …

Looking at different situations and contexts, reflect on and write down your spontaneous answers to the following:

- When do you prefer to work alone? When do you like to work in a group?
- In what situations do you comply? And when do you rebel?
- In what areas in your life do you demonstrate high levels of proactiveness? When are you reactive?
- Where do you get more results: when you're under pressure? Or when there's no pressure?

When you've answered all of these, look at what you have put down on paper and note which preferences come out – which metaprograms. What people, emotions and situations did you write about? What might be your underlying beliefs (limiting or empowering) and values around each of your preferences and metaprograms?

Chapter 14

Being Congruent …

… being the most authentic and effective version of ourselves

By Florence

Apply Within

You once told me
You wanted to find
Yourself in the world -
And I told you to
First apply within,
To discover the world
within you.

You once told me
You wanted to save
The world from all its wars -
And I told you to
First save yourself
From the world,
And all the wars
You put yourself
Through.

Suzy Kassem, poet, writer and philosopher who has graciously consented to us sharing her work.

Why Does Our State Matter?

So far in this part of the book our focus on 'tuning in' has been largely with respect to our relationships with other people. I believe a big part of being totally present for others, and having the most effective relationships with them, relates to the emotional state that we are in. In NLP, the term 'state', refers to the mental and physical processes we are experiencing moment to moment. Being able to control our state affects just about everything we do.

The outcomes a person produces are only as good as the state they are in.

Stephen Gilligan PhD, psychologist, speaking on the Generative Coaching Course, Barcelona 2017.

We have all experienced days when we feel on top of the world. In that state, we seem able to cope with whatever happens with ease and resourcefulness. When we experience the opposite – feeling tired, jet-lagged, unwell, hungry, (or have experienced a setback of some kind), then the smallest issue can seem like a big problem. In other words, the state we are in acts as another kind of filter on our experiences; another factor to add to those set out in previous chapters.

Moreover, what is going on inside us shows on the outside too, in our physiology, as well as in what we say and how we say it. As I explained in earlier (Ch.3), how we present ourselves to others is in turn likely to have an effect on *their* state and, to some degree, on our relationship with them too. Eleni and I live on opposite sides of the world, so our Skype calls are usually early in the morning for me, just a short time after moving from my sleeping state to a waking state! A Skype call with Eleni at that time of day is like a lightning bolt of energy across the miles, and that energy level is infectious, leaving me smiling and upbeat as I carry on with my day.

As certain as that effect is, in practical terms it is even more valuable to be able to manage our own state independently of the events and other people around us. In that way, we can be more in control of our own outcomes and have a positive effect on any situation or another person.

The Humanist Perspective

Our state though can have more far-reaching effects that simply how we get through our day or how effective we may be around others, the picture over time is way bigger than that. Carl Rogers and Abraham Maslow were two hugely influential Humanist psychologists of 20th century. The Humanist approach is that people are basically good, have free will to make choices and have an innate need to make themselves and the world better. Although there were differences in their approach, both Rogers and Maslow believed that human beings needed the right environment to fulfil their potential. Central to this environment is how individuals view and present themselves, and so being congruent is an essential pre-requisite to achieving self-actualisation i.e. fulfilling one's potential. This surely makes knowing about and being in our congruent state an essential?

Where I make an impression it must be by being most myself.

Margaret Fuller, American feminist, poet and author.

How Do I Get Into A Good (Congruent) State?

To be 'congruent' in a general sense means 'to be in agreement'. So in one respect we could be entirely congruent if we were feeling angry, by shouting at someone and slamming doors. Obviously, this type of congruence is not particularly resourceful and is very likely to be damaging to our relationships with others. In NLP, the term congruence has a very specifically positive meaning. It was defined by the psychologist Carl Rogers as a state of awareness, and behaving in a way that is genuine, as opposed to 'incongruence' which suggests denial and putting up a facade.

When we are in a congruent state we are likely to come across in an authentic and trustworthy way with others; presenting a facade can have the opposite effect.

When I was seven years old, I was in my bedroom in the early morning preparing to visit my grandmother who lived about a three-hour drive away. In our family, it was an event that required planning as my father and mother were farmers and there was a lot of work to do in the morning before we could set off. On the day we got up early, donned our best clothes, and all looked forward to it. As I was getting dressed, I was excited about seeing Grandma again. Then I began to think about previous visits and became aware for the first time that Grandma asked me questions through my mother and not directly to me. I started to wonder why that was, as it was not how the grown-ups talked to one another – what was different about me? And then it came to me – quite out of the blue – that I had formed a habit during previous visits of looking at her, and others, shyly through my fringe. I knew straight away what I had to do and remember distinctly my sudden decision to speak to people with my head lifted up and to look them full in the face. When I greeted Grandma later that day that was what I did and I felt for the first time that I was looking at her and she was looking at me, we did not need my mother as an interpreter! It was such a small change, but it not only impacted on my relationships with others, but how I thought about myself. Even at that early stage, and without knowing the word for it, I got the importance of congruence and how I could achieve it.

There are a number of approaches throughout this book that you can apply to help you manage your state and enable you to be whole and genuine. For example, the presuppositions in Ch. 9 focus on shifting your thinking about yourself or other people or a particular situation. And when our thinking changes, so does our physiology. (Eleni looks at how re-integrating our conflicting 'parts' enables us to be congruent also in Ch.16). You will find many more as you read on through the book. In this chapter, however, I want to focus on becoming aware of the instances when we are congruent, and when we are not, and being able to shift our state when we need to. And here's how …

Recognising incongruence

Although this exercise can work well when you do it alone, it is ideal to do it with someone else, because they can make some external observations that you may not pick up on. So, think of a time when you felt out of sorts, frustrated, annoyed or self-doubt. Then associate back into that situation (association is referred to Ch.13). As you do, notice how you are sitting or standing, how you are holding yourself, what gestures (if any) you are making. Notice how you are regarding others around you and their reactions to you.

Recognising congruence

Now repeat the exercise, this time associating into a time when you felt at ease with yourself and others around you: a time when you felt good about yourself and felt able to express yourself freely. Notice what is different in the two circumstances, with respect to:

- The way you are holding yourself.
- How and where you are looking.
- The way you feel.
- The reactions of others.

Hold this congruent position and really notice how it feels in your whole body so that you can easily recognise when you are 'in it'. It is also useful to create your own 'shorthand' or symbols to get into this state by considering: 'When I am like this, I am like ... what?'. This question invites a symbol or a metaphor. Go with whatever pops into your head, rather than trying to work it out cognitively.

Note that we have a number of congruent states. Some may be calm and relaxed, and others more energetic. What they all have in common is the good feeling and being in rapport with oneself.

I was with a coaching client one day, who was struggling with managing some of her team members. When she was in team meetings where those members were present, it was clear (even as she was describing it to me) that she was in an incongruent state: her head and shoulders were slumped, she had little eye contact and her voice tone was dull. So we did an exercise similar to the one above, and when I asked the question: 'When you are like this, you are like ... what?'. She immediately laughed and replied, 'I am like a wedding cake!'. And that was all she needed to think about to bring her physiology, and then her state, back into congruence: head up, shoulders back and relaxed, full eye contact and a lightness and energy in her voice tone. Remember the mind–body link Eleni referred to earlier in Ch.4? The whole point of this is summarised in one of the pre-suppositions of NLP:

The mind and the body are part of the same system.

How we are thinking within clearly comes out in our physiology. And conversely so: how we hold ourselves physiologically affects how we are thinking. Have another look at the sequence in the chapter on the NLP Communication Model (Ch.3). Now try this exercise:

Step 1: Sit with your arms folded in your lap and bend over and look down at your feet. As you hold this position, try to think of cheerful things, and notice how easy (or otherwise) it is to do so.

Step 2: Then stand up and tip your head backwards so you are looking straight up at the ceiling. Put a massive grin on your face. Now, holding that position, and with that wide grin, try thinking about something sad or annoying.

Most people find it more difficult to think of something cheerful in the first position, and just about impossible to maintain a grin in the second and think about something bad.

Getting Into The Congruent 'Habit'

Stephen Gilligan and Robert Dilts in their *Generative Change* work, place a great deal of emphasis on recognising and managing your state. They see this emphasis an essential pre-requisite to effectively handling the challenges of life, as well as being able to generate solutions and bring forth new ideas. Indeed, Eleni and I have noticed the importance of our own congruent state in the writing, and probably even more importantly, the editing of this book. In order to bring our work together and make it flow we have had to be in a good state to give and receive the feedback that has been vital to refine each chapter.

Gilligan and Dilts refer to the unresourceful state with the mnemonic CRASH as described below:

C Contracted (pulling into ourselves, sometimes physically making ourselves smaller).

R Reactive (rather than proactive; often reacting to the behaviour of others without thought of the consequences).

A Analysis/paralysis (turning things over and over in our minds in a way that creates frustration, and no solutions).

S Separated (from others; perhaps marginalising ourselves).

H Hating/hurting/hitting (ourselves or others).

This is a state that they recognise as being unresourceful, rather than 'bad', in that it happens in life when we are tired, out of sorts, or feel criticised – or even when we feel shy or out of our depth as I did in my earlier story about visiting my Grandma. You may recognise some of the elements of CRASH state in my description of myself. It is important that we can recognise that this simply *happens* rather than blame ourselves (which only deepens the CRASH state). In contrast, they use another mnemonic (COACH) to summarise the opposite – a resourceful state that they refer to as the "zone of excellence":

C Centred (balanced and confident).

O Open (to others and what is going on around us; outward looking).

A Attentive (paying attention to others and their ideas, and the situation around us).

C Connected (a feeling of being linked to others and having an affinity with them).

H Holding (the space to choose our response; being aware of how we are feeling and how we feel about feeling that way).

They suggest that what is important is not that you never go into CRASH, but how quickly you can recover from it – if an athlete runs five miles they will be tired, but their recovery will be so much quicker than someone who is not fit. The key is recognising the triggers so that you can be prepared and perhaps 'head off' a CRASH before it happens.

Fig. 1: Walking in The Lake District takes me into my COACH State!

I love walking in The Lake District: the sense of achievement, the peace in my soul, the feeling in my muscles, the air and the views take me into my COACH state, even when I am simply associating back into being there. So when I first did the exercise above to discover my COACH state, I took myself back in my mind to being at the top of a particular fell. I noticed what was happening in that moment in my head, my heart and my gut and allowed myself to make my somatic* gesture – a gesture that symbolises this state for me and serves as an anchor whenever I need it (this will be explained more in Ch.25 Anchoring). I

*A somatic gesture is a gesture of the body (soma) – as distinct from the mind.

have practiced this gesture physically so often now that I can do it in my head, which is particularly useful in situations where making the gesture would look odd to others!

So, find your COACH state to increase your 'state' fitness. As in the earlier exercise in the Recognising Congruence section, think of a time when you were at your best, when you were in the COACH state, from any context in your life. It might relate to being in a meeting, standing at the top of a mountain, having lunch with a friend, or spending time with your pets or family.

As you associate into it, pay attention to what is happening and how that feels now, throughout your body:

- In your mind.
- In your heart.
- In your gut.

Notice in each of these 3 areas of your body, whether there is any shape, colour, or sensation. Then allow yourself to create a gesture that captures that feeling in some way e.g. it may be how you are moving your body or a gesture with your hands. Once again this is just something you allow to happen, rather than think through cognitively. If you have someone with you as you do this exercise, they may notice the gesture before you do.

I did this exercise with a friend of mine who was going to London for an important meeting at Westminster. On the day she was travelling she texted me to say how difficult it was to do her somatic gesture in the toilet of a moving train! I then suggested (in the interests of safety!) that she return to her seat and do the gesture in her mind. It worked beautifully, and she did not have to suffer strange looks from fellow passengers. That is the value of practice: the more often you practise the gesture, and carry it out physically or imagined, it becomes a powerful anchor.

Everyday Thinking And Doing: Consider this …

Now have a go at these exercises for getting to know your triggers:

1. Take some time to review the last two days, whether at home or at work. Notice how your 'state' changed through the events of each day.
2. When have you been at your best, in a congruent or COACH state? What was happening? How were you reacting? What is the metaphor or symbol that takes you into this resourceful state?
3. When have you been incongruent, or in a CRASH state? What was happening? How were you reacting? Think about what you could do differently in a similar situation going forward to avoid a CRASH or recover more quickly.

Part 4
Move Your Mind

Robert Dilts, Developer, Author and Trainer in NLP believes that wisdom comes being able to take multiple perspectives.

So in Part 4 we explore how moving physically enables insights that help us view situations differently, resolve dilemmas and access our resources.

Perceptual Positions …

… seeing situations from different viewpoints

By Florence

Just walk a mile in his moccasins
Before you abuse, criticize and accuse.
If just for one hour, you could find a way
To see through his eyes, instead of your own muse.

Mary T. Lathrap an extract from her poem 'Walk a Mile in His Moccasins'.

What Is It Like Being On The Receiving End Of You?

This is the question I asked in Chapter 3. I borrowed it from a friend of mine who frequently asks this of her delegates at the start of her courses. The truth is that without taking the time to consider this question for ourselves we might not know, and therefore we may be baffled by the reactions of others. We don't see what others see. As a result of 'not knowing', we may have fewer choices as to what we do about it. The following story is taken from my book *The Intention Impact Conundrum.*

I was working with a group of shift managers from a manufacturing business when one of them (whom I will call John) told a story about being involved in a physical fight with a colleague (whom I will call Peter). John was angry about what happened and could not see how else he might have handled the situation with Peter, nor could he see that Peter had any justification for his behaviour. Now, before I started working with this group, one of their senior managers had taken me aside to advise me not to do any of my 'NLP stuff' with them. He assured me that they wouldn't get it, wouldn't buy into it, and – worst of all – weren't up to it! I recognise that his intention was to protect me from embarrassment or disappointment, and yet I also believe it is how things are presented to people that make them easy or difficult to understand.

Anyway, undaunted I asked John to sit as he was sitting when the conversation with his colleague started, and to look across at where his colleague was seated (in effect I was asking him to associate into the situation again). It was immediately apparent that the emotions of that conversation came back, and he was there, in the moment. I asked him to stand up, and made some jokes with his other colleagues, (to break his state*). They had been watching with some amusement. I then asked John to take Peter's sitting position, which was on the other side of the room.

From this new viewpoint, I asked him to re-run the conversation. Almost immediately he looked at me in surprise and exclaimed: "I would have hit me if I had been Peter!". We all laughed (with him), as it was apparent that he acquired

**Breaking state simply means getting yourself out of the mindset you are in, to allow you to take up the next position cleanly – without allowing the thinking from one position to affect the next position.*

a real insight in that short time. I then asked him to take up the position of a 'fly on the wall' and look at the conversation from a more neutral viewpoint. From there he was able to look at the encounter more dispassionately and, as a result, was able to give John (himself) some advice. When we finished the exercise he was in a very different state and far more willing to take responsibility for his own actions, and thus how conversation turned out.

The postscript to this story is that he phoned me a few months later to wish me a happy Christmas and thank me for the course. He added, "And I haven't hit anybody since!". Even then, he was still reflecting on the exercise!

What I had done (without explaining this to John at the time) was to take him through an NLP exercise called Perceptual Positions, with which you may be familiar. From my experience, this is one of the most often used NLP exercises, mainly because of the learning it yields, whether someone else takes you through it, or you do it by yourself.

The Origins Of Perceptual Positions

The exercise I took John through was developed by John Grinder, the co-founder of NLP, and Judith De Lozier, who was involved in the development of NLP in the 1980s. They modelled therapists like Milton Erickson and Virginia Satir and found, quite independently, that these therapists were using similar techniques to get their clients to take up different physical positions in order to get insights into how a situation might be for another person. This is *not* 'mind reading'. We cannot claim to know what another person is thinking. But by taking up someone else's physical posture and moving out of our own space we can get some useful insights as to how things are for them.

My Dad died many years ago. A few months after, my mother and I went to the Donegal coast in the north-west of Ireland for a weekend break. We were walking on a beautiful sandy beach with the Atlantic rollers crashing in at our feet, and belying the beauty around us, our conversation was stilted, as if there was little common understanding between us. I felt this very strongly and started paying attention to what I was doing and what she was doing. I was looking up at the blue sky and out to sea at the waves coming in, but she was walking with her hands in her pockets, looking down at the sand. When I took up her walking posture and eye-line, our conversation started to change – dramatically: in effect, I stepped into her map of the world and met her there (notice the link to rapport here!) When we got to the end of the beach, we sat down on the rocks and talked. I mean we *really* talked, in a way we hadn't before. It turned out I didn't have to 'walk a mile' in order to experience what it was like in my mother's shoes but stepping out of my own was a big part of the process.

Taking 'Perceptual Positions' To Understand What Is Going On

In her book *Smart Moves: Why Learning Is Not All In Your Head*, Dr Carla Hannaford points out how our body plays an essential part in our learning process throughout our lives. So Perceptual Positions is an exercise that uses movement to facilitate learning and new thinking. The basic steps in this exercise (as shown in **Fig. 1**) are:

- Position 1 – My viewpoint.
- Position 2 – The other person's viewpoint.
- Position 3 – The observer viewpoint, the 'fly on the wall'.

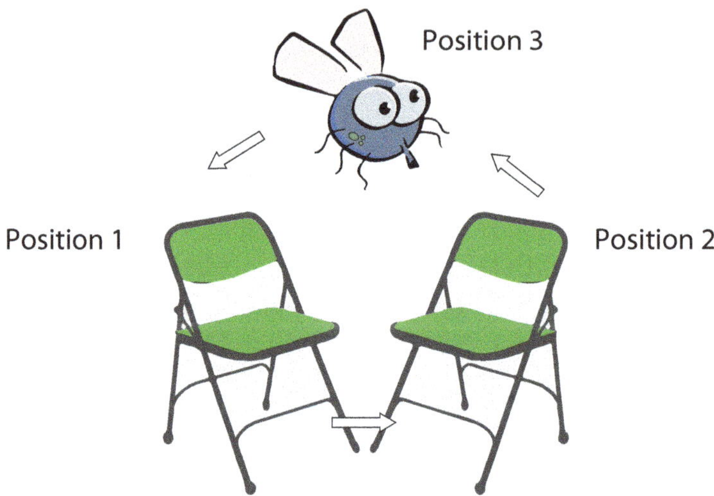

Fig. 1: The steps involved in the Perceptual Positions exercise.

You can successfully take yourself through this exercise or else get someone else to guide you. Whichever option you choose, it is important to do it *kinaesthetically* (physically moving around) because of the strong link between learning and *moving*, and because this process also uses a technique called spatial anchoring. This is when a specific space becomes anchored in our unconscious as having a special meaning or association. This process can be used to:

- Gain some insight on how you are impacting on another person or group.
- Revisit a conversation or situation in which you were not happy with the outcome and want to generate some ideas about what you could do or say differently, to improve the outcome.
- Plan how you could handle a future interaction with another person or group to achieve the impact you want.

If you are using this approach for the first time, it is useful to use a *mildly* unsatisfactory situation. This will allow you to become familiar with the process while avoiding too much emotion. What may surprise you is the level of learning even in these situations.

Everything we hear is an opinion,
not a fact.
Everything we see is a perspective,
not the truth.

Marcus Aurelius, Emperor of Ancient Rome.

Perceptual Positions exercise

To start the process, choose a situation or conversation about which you would value more information. Now follow these steps (for simplicity's sake, I am basing this on a face-to-face conversation between you and another person). First, decide on where positions 1 and 2 will be: if the conversation was seated, place two chairs at the same distance and aspect as they were in the original conversation, (if you were standing, adopt the same positions and relative stances.)

Position 1: YOU

- In your mind take yourself back to the location where the conversation took place, taking up the first position, seated or standing as appropriate, and bring it into the present (associate into it). Notice the layout of the place, and what you are seeing, hearing and feeling before the conversation started. Then look across at the other person and notice how they are positioned, and the look on their face before the conversation starts.
- Run the conversation like a video in your head, noticing your feelings and any physical changes as it progresses. Then break your state by moving out of your position and turn around or take your thoughts to another subject for a moment. Then move into position 2.

Position 2: THE OTHER PERSON

- Take up the seating/standing position of the other person at the point the conversation started (in effect associate into their position). Look across at position 1, and notice your own posture and facial expression, and how it looks from position 2. Notice the feelings engendered as you do so. Notice what you are seeing differently already.
- Run through the conversation again, like a video in your head, noting your feelings from this position and any physical changes as

it progresses. Break your state by moving out of this position, and then turning around or taking your thoughts to another subject for a moment. Then take up Position 3, choose a place where you can see both parties easily and far enough away to be able to take a dispassionate view of the scene.

Position 3: AN OBSERVER (fly on the wall)

- From this neutral position observe both yourself and the other person – body posture; how they are regarding one another (note you are dissociated here).
- Run the conversation like a video again and notice anything different from this viewpoint. From here, you may see things that both parties could have done differently, however the only one you can directly influence is yourself in position 1. (This is also putting you *at cause*).
- Now consider what advice you would give yourself to improve the interaction; it might be your position, or what you say, or how you say it – even who opens the conversation. Give that advice to yourself in position 1 and check that it is accepted. If there is some resistance, or it seems difficult to see how you could have changed the situation, just try to come up with one little thing could have improved the situation, just a tiny bit.
- Then ask: 'Is there any higher learning in this for me?'. This means, is what happened some evidence of a behaviour pattern that you have exhibited in other circumstances? That does not serve you well, or your relationships with others?
- Next, give that advice to yourself in position 1 and check if it is accepted.
- Finally, break your state by moving out of position, then turning around or taking your thoughts to another subject for a moment. Then go back into position 1.

- ***Position 1: YOU (again)***
  - This time take the advice of the observer and re-run the situation once again, noticing what difference these changes create in yourself and the other person.
  - You can end the exercise here, or stand up, break state and go back into position 2 to experience the changes from that viewpoint. You can also go through all the positions again if you want to make further changes.

This exercise can be very revealing and allows us to get more information about someone else's map of the world. You may also notice the link to the pre-supposition that:

Memory and imagination are wired on the same circuits.

This exercise is not simply about generating ideas about what you could have done, it is about programming yourself to handle similar interactions differently in the future, in effect blurring the lines between what you have imagined vividly and your memories. In Ch. 2 Eleni referred to how the unconscious mind operates and, specifically, how it responds to clear instructions and looks to prove us right. This exercise gives the unconscious mind clear instruction about what will work better.

When you take someone else through this process, a 'content-free' approach is useful for re-running the conversations, whilst sharing the observations and learning out loud at each stage with the facilitator. Content-free simply means that the person going through the process runs the conversations in their head rather than out loud. This has several advantages in the exercise, because:

- It is easier and faster than if the person spells out the 'he said/ I said' elements of the conversation.
- The person may not want to relate the details of what was said.
- It helps the person to get and stay associated, and stay in the moment, rather than getting into a conversation with you about what happened.
- Not knowing the content avoids you getting involved in 'solving' the situation.

This approach leaves the person free to share or not. People often do some parts content-free and speak at other times.

Another point to note is that while there is a great deal of learning in the moment with this approach, the effects are likely to be longer-term than you may think. I do work with staff of a call centre and I had the group reflecting on difficult conversations they had had with customers, using this exercise. They all reported that they found the exercise useful, and said they wished that they had handled their interaction better at the time. (It's what the French call *l'esprit d'escalier* – the wit of the staircase i.e. being clever and knowing what to say *after* the event!). A few months later I visited again and one of the team was keen to tell me about something that had happened earlier that week. She had been handling a 'tricky' call. When it was over, one of her colleagues rolled back his chair and gave her feedback, there and then, about how well she had handled the call. She realised in that moment it was 'just like the exercise we did on the course!'. She hadn't remembered the exercise when she was speaking to the customer, but she just handled the situation better and only retrospectively made the connection!

How Else Can I Use This Exercise To Be More Resourceful?

This exercise can have long-lasting effects on how you impact on others, and it is one that you can do on your own or with someone else. And you can add other elements to it, that will help you achieve the outcomes you want and/or expand your field of resources.

Some other useful questions

When you are in the observer position, you may notice that your motivation to solve the issue or to take responsibility for solving it is doubtful (being *willing* to be 'at cause' is not always a given). In these situations, some useful questions to ask yourself are:

- What will happen when I solve this problem?
- What *won't* happen when I solve this problem?
- What will happen if I don't solve this problem?
- What *won't* happen if I don't solve this problem?

The last question exposes any secondary gains; that is, any benefits of doing *nothing* – which could undermine your resolve. (Often the unrecognised benefits of doing nothing can be the unseen blocker of us taking action.)

Other people present

During the interaction being worked on, there may have been other people present. It can be revealing to step into 'their shoes' and see things through their eyes. This can be useful when looking at the original conversation, or for doing an 'ecology check'** on the ideas proposed by your observer. Remember, it is possible to improve your impact on one person in the interaction and unintentionally damage your relationship with another!

Other resourceful positions

Another way of generating ideas, developed by Stephen Gilligan and Robert Dilts in *Generative Coaching*, is to 'step into the shoes' of another person who could be a resource to you – regardless of whether they were present at the original conversation or not. It could be someone who is alive or dead, someone you know personally, or someone you admire from a distance. This position could also be a useful way to check the 'ecology' of what you propose to do.

***Ecology check: This simply means looking at how the changes you are making impact on the other people/processes involved.*

What About Using This Exercise To Plan A Meeting?

When I set up my business, one of the first meetings I had was with a client who I'd met but knew little about. We were meeting to discuss the use of psychometric testing in his company's recruitment process. I wanted to make sure that I handled the meeting effectively and that my impact on him was a positive one. I'd never visited his office, and I knew nothing of the layout, but I knew we would probably be seated for the meeting. So I set some chairs out in my own office and went through how I would open the meeting (in Position 1). Then I moved into his seat (Position 2) and experienced my opening from his viewpoint. The result was dramatic: in his position, I felt overwhelmed by this woman's energy and the amount of information she was giving me! The moving into the observer role (Position 3), the advice was clear – sit back, slow down, and let him open the conversation. It was also clear that when I was in Position 1, I did not know how much the he already knew about psychometrics. Realising this, I made a phone call to check out his own experience of testing. When I actually had the meeting, it was calm, comfortable and *en pointe*.

So, as well as reviewing situations that have already happened, you can use this approach to programme your thinking for meetings or events you are planning, such as:

- A business meeting.
- A difficult conversation.
- An interview.
- A presentation.

The more you experience yourself doing something successfully, the more likely it is to happen!

There is a boundary to men's passions when they act from feelings; but none when they are under the influence of imagination.

Edmund Burke, Anglo-Irish statesman and political theorist.

Everyday Thinking And Doing: Consider This …

- Take some time to try the Perceptual Positions exercise for yourself. Even better, if you know someone with NLP training, get them to take you through it first. They can facilitate the process and allow you to just get on with experiencing it.
- If you are already familiar with Perceptual Positions, then this might be the time to have a go with:

- Asking the question sequence.
- Including the other people present during a situation.
- Exploring other resourceful positions.
- Applying the process to prepare for new situations.

Another way to experience the power of 'moving your position', is to do the following:

1. Look at an object in the room you are in (or wherever you are reading this book). Notice what you can see of it from where you are.
2. How would people in another part of the room (or location) see the object or get up and move to another part of the room.........what do you notice from there?
3. Who would have the 'correct' view? Is there a correct one?
4. If you wanted to know more about that object what would you have to do? Where would you have to move to?

It seems obvious when we are talking about an object that we would need to move our position – and that anyone claiming they have the 'correct' of it view might have an argument on their hands. What if you apply this thinking to a subject on which you have differing views from another person? What would happen if you become more curious about seeing it from their angle? What might happen between you and them if you did?

Parts Integration …

… resolving internal conflicts

By Eleni

The part can never be well unless the whole is well.

Plato, Greek philosopher.

It's the fourth day in our training for trainer's session, and I'm in France, with Florence and Sue Knight, our NLP Trainer, and a gifted group of trainers-to-be. There is a sense of discovery and anticipation, together with lots of sharing, presenting and bonding, everything in full motion and full of emotion.

On that morning, Sue introduced the work of Frank Farrelly, the creator of Provocative Therapy, and asked us to form groups of four and 'play around', provoking each other's thoughts while coaching. Florence and I formed a group together with two other delegates and when my turn was up as a client, Florence took on the task of 'provoking' me on the subject I had chosen – health.

> First, she asked me, "Why health?"
> "Well," I said, "I've had some quite serious issues throughout my life and my health is always my priority."
>
> Florence went ahead and asked how I felt about my intestines.
> "Hmm, they're okay."
>
> "What about your eyes?"
> "Okay, I guess. I do have myopia, but they're okay."
>
> "What about your fingers?"
> "Fine."
>
> "What about your liver and gallbladder?"
> "Hmmm, all okay."
>
> She continued naming every organ she could think of and I felt like I gave each one a grade C.
>
> Then, she asked me: "What about your brain?"
> As soon as I heard the word, I looked up and smiled broadly. I then heard myself say:
> "Aaaa! My brain is exquisite! My brain works beautifully – it's the king of all organs!"

As soon as the words came out of my mouth, I felt my whole body shaking. My three partners in crime looked at me silently giving me all the space in the world. Surely Florence's questions were not the most provocative ones imaginable, and yet the way she went about the task helped me realise that I'd put my brain on a pedestal. And it seemed that I looked down on the performance of all my other organs – no wonder they had kept giving me signals of discomfort and pain through the years.

Fig.1: Us meeting in France for the first time!

An accident during my birth left my whole shoulder in a permanent state of trauma. As a baby, a child, even as a young adult, my mother would constantly repeat to me, "Thank goodness, it wasn't your brain that got injured. Everything else we can fix. You're so lucky your brain is intact. You'll go ahead and do marvellous things with your brain".

It wasn't always easy in gym or dance classes and other children would often ask me, "What's wrong with your arm?" Nonetheless I was full of confidence because I'd been told that my brain made up big time for my shoulder's weakness. Our family always spent more time developing our intellects than our physical fitness. On top of this I was programmed from an early age to believe my brain was 'it', because both my parents had told me so and showed me in hundreds of ways.

My parents had truly done their best with the situation and I hardly ever felt sorry for myself. In fact, the opposite was true, as they made me see the silver lining in what had happened to me. Yet, on that day in France I caught a glimpse of the downside – for my entire life, I'd considered my other body parts to be 'second best'. No wonder they gave me signs through health challenges that my crew were in conflict. I wasn't appreciative enough of them.

That night I invited all my body parts – my legs, my veins, my eyes, my joints, and of course my brain – to have a chat! I talked and talked, and they responded back in ways I could have never foreseen! On the next day, I woke up feeling more alive than ever!

The neuroscientist David Eagleman says in his book *Incognito*:

You have competing populations in the brain – one part that wants to tell you something and one part that does not, and the issue is that we're always cussing at ourselves or getting angry at ourselves or cajoling ourselves ...

What we're seeing here is that there are different parts of the brain that are battling it out. And the way that battle pans out determines our behaviour.

He makes clear how the elements of our complex neural networks constantly fight each other to influence our actions and thoughts, and the things we are attracted to.

In the book *mBraining: Using Your Multiple Brains to do Cool Stuff* by Grant Soosalu and Marvin Oka, there is a wealth of information about how our gut and our heart also seem to have 'neuro-networks' similar to those of the brain.

Connecting the Dots

This is my introduction to a technique that's very close to my heart! Parts Integration is a method for starting a dialogue between our different parts within, and a way to resolve internal conflict. After all, the unconscious wants to be 'a whole unit' (Ch.2)

Often, two parts of us seem to have different opinions on how to go about things. For example, one part wants to stay in your relationship, and one wants to leave. One wants to stay in the company you work for, and one wants to start a new business. One wants to stay single, one to get married. One to have children, one not. One to be sweet, one to be mean. One to relax and one to work. One to be surrounded by people and one to be left alone. One to make money and one to be spiritual. One to travel, one to stay at home. One part wants to move abroad and the other one wants to stay in the place where home has always been; one part wants to start a family and the other wants to travel the world; one wants adventure whereas the other wants security; one likes change and the other one leans more to preserving the status quo.

You get it – constantly faced with crossroads without end. It's called life.

These parts are not necessarily against each other. In fact, more often than not they are going after exactly the same thing, even if they choose a different path to get there. They simply represent different areas in our ship which want to follow their own agendas. Communication between them makes each one's purpose clearer. Bridges of trust and understanding begin to be built and every part feels more listened to and included as a result. For me, it is how I put an end to the feeling of 'conflict' and replaced it with the idea of 'negotiation' instead.

The purpose of the Parts Integration exercise is to help resolve internal conflict and transform our battlefield into a table of negotiation whereby agreements and pacts are made. In my case, my brain was never 'against' my other organs or vice versa. It was a just a series of experiences, together with some strong beliefs, that helped me through a tough situation. And at the same time they also created an unconscious imbalance of how I felt about them all.

How does Parts Integration Work?

There are a number a variations on how to do a Parts Integration and it is likely that if do/have done an NLP Practitioner course you will experience different ways to do this exercise. What I have set out below is one approach and one that I use most frequently:

- Identify two 'parts' of you that are apparently in conflict with each other, as detailed above.
- Once you have identified the two parts, close your eyes, lift your arms in front of you, and visualise each of your hands representing one of the parts.
- Let each part speak for itself for two or three minutes, one at a time.

  When the parts speak, they speak – that means that you don't consciously prepare what they say. Just take a few breaths and let your unconscious and the parts 'come forward'. When you are relaxed and believe in the process and the power of your unonscious, it's astonishing what levels of awareness you can reach.

  Two things are important here: (i) both parts must be allowed an equal time to express their opinions, and (ii) they speak for themselves. When we hear ourselves say "this part wants this …", it's not the *part* speaking, but the captain – our logic. It is when we give the part space, that we hear our voice say "I want …" and this is the part expressing itself from a place we do not normally have access to in our daily 'conscious' life.
- Once they are done talking, ask each part what their higher intention is – their individual purpose.

  Often, we discover that the two parts have very similar purposes. Throughout the integration process, we might find that our lifted hands coming closer together, or stay in the same position, or drift further apart. Depending on how the conversation unfolds, there will be more or less distance between them, but remember that regardless of the outcome, they have talked to each other. They've heard each other. This is a monumental first step and it is progress.
- Have each part offer a gift to the other one.
- Sometimes, the hands come together, and we feel like placing them on our heart. Sometimes, they just want to keep some distance between them, and there is wisdom in this as well. Having witnessed the Parts Integration technique hundreds of times, I am humbled by its positive effect on people's lives, regardless of the final position of the hands.

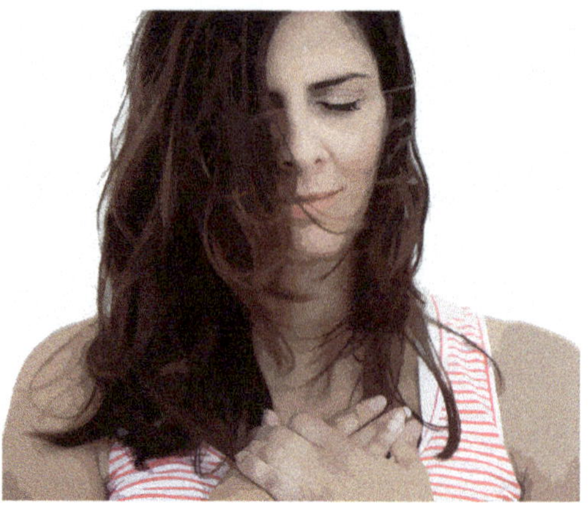

Fig. 2: Kiki & Christina doing Parts Integration on Tinos island, Greece, 2012.

We can find these 'parts' at multiple levels – physical, mental, spiritual and emotional – and they are all inter-connected. If balance is the key to a happy life, we need a patient side to us, as well as an impatient one, a sweet one as well as the firm, a wise one as much as a naughty one, obedient next to revolutionary, good and bad … we need them *all* in order to be a whole.

Each part is unique and even though we might sometimes think that one is right and the other is wrong, the truth is that they're both there to serve a purpose and they both have valuable opinions and their own truth – if they just take time to listen to each other carefully. Each one has its own right to exist inside us.

Here is a short example of a Parts Integration conversation, illustrating how our captain – our conscious – only takes the role of facilitator and invites the parts to connect and share their roles:

> Holding our hands out in front of us, the captain asks each of the parts, "Who are you?".
> "Freedom" says the left hand. "And you?" you say to your right.
> "Security! Nice to meet you!"
>
> We turn to Security: "What are you after?"
> "Stability. Safety," is the answer.
>
> "What will safety do for you?"
> "Give me the chance to relax, make plans for the future, ensure good sleep and a calm mind."
>
> "And what will this do for you?"
> "Provide me with a nice life – a long life, lived well, enjoying people I love for longer."
>
> "And what will this do for you?"
> "Give me a nice warm feeling. *A happy life. A successful one.*"

"What about Freedom?" as your attention shifts to right hand. "What does Freedom want?"
"Excitement! To conquer the world, take risks, expand, try new things, be free to explore."

"And what will that give you?"
"The satisfaction that I made the most out of life, honouring a burning need inside me to connect with as many people as possible, far away, to express my naughty adventurous side – and have fun!"

"And what is the highest intention of that?"
"It gives me a nice feeling of living life to the fullest. *A happy life. A successful one.*"

"Would the Security part like to offer a gift to Freedom?"

"Yes, wisdom!"

"Would the Freedom part like to offer a gift to Security?"

"Yes, wings!"

As you notice, both parts concluded that their purpose was to have a happy and successful life. In just few minutes, and with lots of open mindedness from the captain, the two parts reached a sort of consensus even though they seemed like opposite poles just minutes before.

When going through Parts Integration, make sure you are relaxed, in light trance and remember again that the ones who speak are the parts, not the captain. Close your eyes and let the parts present themselves while the captain enjoys his/her tea. Even though you use your voice, what is said clearly indicates who speaks.

Do Parts Integration regularly just like any team building event. Create the space and the time for the parts to get to know each other. When we feel anxious, it is a parallel of us going to a party we do not know anyone and worry about finding someone to chat or the impression we are going to make. Similarly, when we do not take the time to get to know our parts and bring them together, naturally there is anxiety. Do not seek that there is an immediate resolution, trust that by regularly talking, the parts figure out ways forward that the logical Captain cannot even begin to grasp.

Parts Integration moves us towards more congruence and alignment. It also helps when it's combined with a Perception is Projection mindset. When we realise that any of our external conflicts with others are a mirror of our internal parts having their backs turned to each other, it creates a chance to reflect and get more in 'sync' within.

The 'hands' exercise you just found out about helps with reconciliation.

Just like two friends, two neighbours, or family members who have had a misunderstanding and refuse to talk to each other because of pride, ego, shame or hurt; in the same way different dimensions inside us stay away from each other and create gaps and fractures – that is, until we get them to 'come together' and talk it over. They might share a cup of tea, relax and find out that what really unites them is their common goal, which is more powerful than any differences in how they pursue it.

Therefore, each time I get a conversation going within, I am working towards a solution with people around me. When I can't find any common ground and I feel stuck and drained with 'difficult' behaviours, I turn even more to my within, and check which 'difficult' parts within me haven't talked to each other for a while.

I believe that each time we keep communicating internally, we come one day closer to world peace.

Family Constellations

Another life-changing experience for me was my certification as a Family Constellation facilitator. This is not part of NLP but it shares the same principles represented by Perceptual Positions and Parts Integration. Perceptual Positions is about inviting someone outside of us to chat; in Parts Integrations, the invited are all our own crew. Family Constellation involves both approaches and beyond.

Family Constellation practices drew inspiration from Virginia Satir, the American therapist and 'mother' of family therapy who used to treat issues among family members by inviting them all at the same time to share their emotions and see each other's standpoints. Sometimes, though, a member was unable to get to the session, so Virginia would find someone else to 'stand in' for them so they were represented anyway. Interestingly, the person who stood in to represent the absent family member would have the thoughts and emotions of that family member.

In nature we never see anything isolated, but everything in connection with something else which is before it, beside it, under it and over it.

Johann Wolfgang von Goethe, writer and statesman.

In Family Constellations, there is a belief that we are all connected regardless of space or time. Despite the name of the technique, the people participating in these sessions are often not 'family'. The groups consist of people who have never met each other before. One by one, they take turns to 'look at' a particular issue or situation by asking the other members of the group to represent their own family members, who are not present, and who might be still be alive or have passed on.

Bert Hellinger was the founder of this method, who studied and treated families for more than fifty years. He observed that many of us unconsciously take on destructive familial patterns of anxiety, depression, anger, guilt, loneliness, alcoholism and physical illness – all as a way of *belonging* to our families.

Bonded by deep love, children often sacrifice their own best interests in an attempt to ease the suffering of a parent or other family members. Family Constellations allow us to break these patterns so that we can live healthier, happier, more fulfilled lives. With just one moment of insight, a new life course can be set in motion, and the result can be life-changing! The Family Constellation method has the power to shift generations from suffering to hope.

Family Constellations need to be run in the presence of a certified facilitator, who will moderate proceedings and make sure everyone is safe physically, mentally and emotionally throughout the process.

Parts Integration and Perceptual Positions are equally experiential, whereby emotions are released and major internal shifts take place, and it makes the world of a difference when you go through these experiences with the guidance of a trainer or coach, especially the first time you do it. Saying this, if you have no mental or emotional illness, chatting with yourself or others in mental set-ups like these can provide deep insights, clearer direction and a better quality of life.

Everyday Thinking and Doing: Consider this …

- Everybody's got a dark side. Which one is/are yours?
- What 'truth' is still painful or highly uncomfortable for you? What parts of yours you seem to have neglected, denied or paid little attention to? What could be the reasons?
- Go and find a nice tree in a park to sit under. Then close your eyes, and invite two of your parts (any ones you like!) and let them have a chat. Notice if one is more talkative than the other. Notice whether the captain – your conscious – seems to take a preference for one part more than the other.

Timeline …

… using our concept of time to access our resources

By Florence

How We Express Time

No man ever steps in the same river twice,
for it's not the same river and he's not the same man.

Heraclitus of Ephesus, pre-Socratic Greek philosopher.

For centuries, humans have been fascinated by time and have looked to express it in various ways. We talk about lines of descent in our families, or tracing Kings and Queens down through the ages. We express time spatially, either with physical gestures or with speech. We say things like: "That was way back" or "I'm looking to the future". We ask questions like: "Where do you see yourself in five years?" or "Will that really matter down the line?". The British comedian Peter Kay makes fun of the gestures people often make when describing time: pointing forward to indicate they are going on holiday in a fortnight, or over their shoulder to indicate they just got back last week. When people talk about traumatic events, they use language like: "I need to move on" or "I need to put it behind me".

One of the metaprograms we can observe in others, or ourselves (as discussed by Eleni in Ch.13), is a 'past–present–future' orientation. My husband finds my 'future' orientation an annoyance, as he hears me talk about what is planned and what we are going to do some time down the line. His orientation is to be very much in the 'present', and not to worry too much about the future. Similarly, I have found myself getting frustrated by friends who talk a lot about what has been in the past, and who seem unable to enjoy the present, or look optimistically to the future. Indeed 'location' is common concept to all three of the main representational systems set out in Ch.11: we can *see* where something is located in relation to us, we can *hear* where a sound is coming from, or whereabouts in our body we *feel* something.

So given how we already think about time, the creators and developers of NLP have looked to use this in order to help people deal with issues in their past that may be affecting their present, or to create a compelling future to work towards.

The Origins Of Timeline

A forerunner to what is now known as 'Timeline' is the 'change personal history' process. This is a process that Bandler and Grinder set out in *Frogs To Princes*. Since the late 1970s, the distinctions of how we represent our experiences through our senses had been part of NLP; when these were combined with people's 'time orientation', the full potential for helping someone to achieve personal change emerged. A key moment in the development of Timeline was a presentation that Steve Andreas made in 1985 called *Just In Time*. The usefulness of this approach impressed many people. Since then, Timeline has grown and developed in different ways, notably with Tad James developing his own approach which he called Timeline Therapy, which I will come back to later in this chapter.

Timeline Is A Metaphor – How Do You See Yours?

The ways in which we describe time, as I set out earlier (e.g. to 'put things behind me'), are metaphors. The concept of a 'timeline' is a metaphor. It doesn't actually exist, but it helps us get our heads around the idea of time. In the 1980s, the categories of some people being 'in time' and some people being 'through time' were introduced as another Metaprogram. (This is another to add to those already set out in Ch. 13, at this point over 60 Metaprograms have been identified!). Understanding how people hold time 'in their heads' is a useful starting point for working with Timeline – they are only generalisations, but very useful nonetheless.

Do this exercise to establish your own Timeline preference. If you find this a little tricky, think about specific events: when you think about last Christmas, what direction does that memory come from? Or when you think about your next birthday in which direction is that? Now:

- Think about your life as a line and then allow your left arm to indicate which direction your future goes in. Hold it there.
- Then consider in which direction your past goes and indicate that with your right arm. Hold it there.
- Compare the position of your arms with those illustrated in **Fig. 1** overleaf, as viewed from above.

When asked to bring up their timeline like this, 'in time' people usually indicate their timeline going through them, with their past behind and their future in front. They are, in effect, *on* or *in* their timeline. They live very much in the moment, can get immersed in activities or conversations, and often (as a result) find that time has passed and they are unaware of it. Time management can be an issue for them. I sit in this category. If I'm out in town by myself, and especially if I go into a bookshop, I play a game with myself to guess the time, without looking at my watch. I am frequently an hour out in my estimate! People in this category also find it easier to 'put things behind them' – as they have to 'turn around' to access their memories.

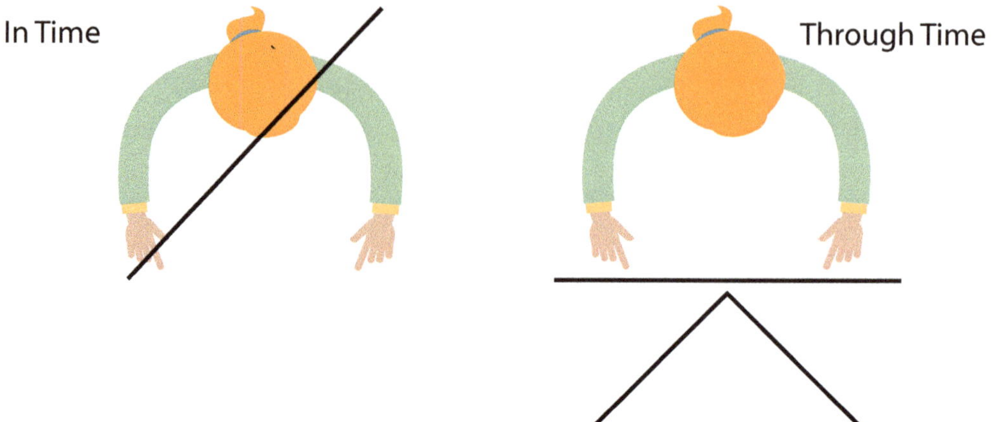

Fig. 1: 'In Time' and 'Through Time' Timelines viewed from above.

For 'through time' people, their timeline is all in front of them. It may be a straight line, or curved or V-shaped. They are usually very aware of the passage of time, with or without a watch. They tend to be quite organised and to make lists, and they like to be on time. Because their timeline, and hence their memories, are in front of them they may find it harder to move on from past issues.

Working, or living, alongside someone with a different concept of time can be baffling – even annoying – so I think it is good to recognise the differences and respect the qualities they hold.

I was running a course on one occasion with a lady whom I now realise was a 'through time' person. Our contrasting approaches to the course made for quite an uncomfortable day – for us both. She complained to me: "Your group always finishes the exercises late!" I replied rather sharply and with incredulity: "But they hadn't finished!" She just looked at me with exasperation. We didn't work together again. Incidentally, the course was on time management! (Oh the irony! I did say back in Ch. 1 that my learning in NLP has been a continual journey?)

Note: I should point out that what I have described here are only the most common timelines. Other people have vertical timelines, or in-time timelines can be reversed, with the past in front and the future behind and indeed they can take any shape.

Are Timeline Memories Real?

My late mother Maura, like loving mothers everywhere, frequently told stories over and over about me and other members of the family – indeed some of them were stories I had told her! So it amused me, (as a mischievous teenager and later on), to notice that when the stories became 'hers' they changed, and became embellished with each telling! They were no longer factually correct, but they all had grains of truth. And as far as Mum was concerned, they were true.

In timeline processes, the client is taken back verbally or physically (i.e. 'walked'*) down their timeline in an associated state to access previous events. This is often the approach where their reaction to those past events may be causing them problems in their present-day life. As noted in the chapter on the NLP Communication Model (Ch.3), our memories of events change over time, and what is being accessed is unlikely to be factually correct. Nonetheless, accessing how someone remembers an event is useful. The reason is that it is not the event *itself* that is the issue, whatever happened in the past cannot be changed in any case, it is the *construct* that we put upon those events that matters. By construct I mean the *decisions* we made about ourselves or others that we carry forward, for good or ill. The brain does not differentiate neurologically between the past, present and future, or whether something is real or imagined; remember the pre-supposition: *memory and imagination are wired on the same circuits*?

If your brain attaches a meaning to a past event that causes you to be fearful, and you put enough focus on it, it becomes *real* for you. This means that the anticipation of a similar event in the future will elicit the same response - even before it happens. When this happens again, and similar emotions are generated, the event is stored in what is referred to in NLP as a 'gestalt' - a collection of memories stored around a particular topic.

... for there is nothing either good or bad, but thinking makes it so.

William Shakespeare from the play 'Hamlet'.

Furthermore, the same event that happens to two different people may not elicit the same response from them. To one person, starting in a new school can be like a stone on their path of life, easily stepped over; to another, it can be like a boulder that becomes a blocker in their life (**Fig. 2**).

Fig. 2: Some situations feel like a stone to one person and a boulder to another.

*Walking someone down a timeline employs a kinaesthetic approach, and myself and Eleni would like to advise extreme caution with this, because it can inadvertently take someone back into a traumatic event. For this reason, using a visual timeline, whereby the person floats above their timeline, rather than physically walking it, is safer and equally effective. This is referred to in the section on Timeline therapy®.

How the person experiences it and the feelings they carry about it, will make a difference in the future. Situations in which feelings from past events adversely affect our present are situations in which Timeline can help.

Ways To Use Timeline

Timeline can be used in a number of ways:

- To create a compelling vision of the future – future pacing**.
- To bring resources from our past experiences to a future goal.
- To lessen the impact of a disappointing event (like a meeting that didn't go well).
- To change an unhelpful construct attached to a past event resulting in adverse effects now.

On one occasion on a course I was working with one of the group who had this recurring negative thought that she wasn't good enough even though she held quite a senior position in the company she worked for – she didn't know where this limiting belief came from. When she went back down her timeline, she recognised the point in her life where this idea had formed and we did some work to change this negative construct that she had put on this event. At that point, apparently unburdened, she took off down her timeline and went to a point in the future of her timeline, with me practically running to catch up. Whereupon she stopped and smiled broadly; a little surprised I asked her where she was now, "I have just bought a holiday home in France!" she exclaimed with a broad grin.

So Timeline is a very powerful exercise. It is advisable to carry out some elements of the process (e.g. Re-Imprinting, as developed by Robert Dilts), with someone who is trained in NLP, at least initially. Better still, book yourself onto a course and learn how to do it effectively and safely. In the meantime, I have set out a useful exercise at the end of the chapter for you to try by yourself, or (even better) for someone else to take you through. You can do this one kinaesthetically or visually.

**Future Pacing is term used in NLP where a person is associating into a point in the future to experience a desired situation. This has the effect of making that future goal more real and more compelling. This is often used to check out the effectiveness of a number of NLP processes not just Timeline.

Timeline Therapy®

This is a specific approach to Timeline developed by Tad James and Wyatt Woodsmall and is set out in some detail in their book: *Timeline Therapy and the Basis of Personality*. Tad James believes that the anxiety someone experiences is a warning message from the unconscious mind to focus on what they really want.Their approach involves finding the root cause of an issue, and releasing negative emotions accumulated from the past such as anger, sadness, guilt, hurt and fear, as well as removing limiting decisions that someone may have made about themselves.

(Note that Eleni is a Timeline Therapy® Trainer and this additional certification is available on her NLP Practitioner & Master Practitioner courses.)

Everyday Thinking And Doing: Consider This ...

Future pacing

Think about a future event in which you would like to bring your resources to bear (e.g. a presentation, an interview, an important conversation or a project). Note: This exercise can be done by walking it (kinesthetically), but it is often safer to do it by 'floating' i.e visualizing it in your head. This avoids revisiting any traumatic events.

Step 1: Carry out the exercise earlier in the chapter to establish whether you are 'in time' or 'though time'.

Step 2: Bring up your own timeline as described in the exercise. If you are 'in time', you will already be on it, standing in or floating above your present. If you are 'through time' you are likely to be standing or floating *beside* it, so move onto it. Now 'get to know' your timeline. Walk or float back down your timeline to some significant (and *pleasant*) events, and then walk or float forward to future (pleasant) events, like Christmas or birthdays. Then return to the present.

Step 3: From your present, look forward to the future event and see yourself there, handling it in exactly the way you want to. Notice what is different about you: how you are dressed, how you are holding yourself, how you are relating to others.

Step 4: Now walk or float back down your timeline, stopping at other events in your life when you have been resourceful and at your best. You don't need to search for specific events, let them

come to you as you go down the line. Acknowledge each along the way and 'collect' the gifts or resources each event gives you.

Step 5: When you are ready, walk or float back to the present, carrying all the resources you have gathered along the way and any others that present themselves as you go.

Step 6: When you are back at the present, roll these resources into the future on your timeline – like golden apples (perhaps leaving a golden trail as they go). These resources will be waiting for you when you need them, and specifically at the future event you had in mind.

Step 7: Walk or float forward in your timeline to that future event, noticing the resources you have laid out for yourself along the way. Then step into that future event in which you are handling yourself, and the situation, just the way you want. Notice how it feels to have got to this point, as well as the effect of the resources you have at your disposal. Notice what you are seeing, hearing and feeling when you are there. Notice how other people are reacting to you now.

Step 8: Look back from this future point to the present where you started and ask yourself: 'What do I know now that I didn't fully realise back then?'.

Step 9: Walk or float back to the present, noticing the decisions you made and your learnings along the way, and bring them with you.

Step 10: When you get back to the present, notice what you have learnt. How does that future event look to you now?

Part 5

Choose Your Words

Noam Chomsky, Linguist and Cognitive Scientist proposes that we cannot make changes to our thoughts and how we experience the world, until we change our language.

Taking this as our starting point we look at how the language we use reveals the blocks we put up in our way, how the power of language can build resources in ourselves and others, and even inspire!

Meta Model …

… noticing and challenging patterns of language that reinforce limiting beliefs

By Florence

Silence is the language of god, all else is poor translation.

Rumi, 13th Century Persian Sunni Muslim poet.

Everyday Conversations

Let me take you through my morning in town. I dropped into the hairdressers to make an appointment and the woman in front of me was complaining about the road-works in the street outside. "The council are always digging up the street for no reason!" The receptionist replied, "Yes ... they don't know what they're doing. It's time they sorted themselves out. There's no communication you know with the utility companies. They dug that same bit up a few months ago!".

I made my appointment and went for a coffee. The person who served me was complaining about a customer who had just left (there had been raised voices as I walked in). "That sort makes me so mad! They think I'm here just to be insulted. When I get a better job I'm out of here!". I sat down with my coffee and overheard a couple behind me discussing their son's problems with his teacher at school. "She's always criticising our Mark. She clearly doesn't think he's good enough for her class. I told her he would get a better education elsewhere. The trouble is they say we can't move schools mid-term!" The father then replied, "I have a mind to get this straightened out. I'm not having this nonsense – being made to feel like that when we go to discuss a problem. I'm going around to that school this afternoon!".

As you read this you will recognise these conversations – they're commonplace in towns throughout the country, if not the world. You could say it's just how people speak. In these conversations, there was little factual detail, yet the people whose conversations I overheard understood each other – or at least they seemed to. If they did start to infill their conversations with facts, they would have taken much longer. The woman in the hairdressers could have specified which council department was responsible for the situation, and how many times that section of road had been dug up in the last five years. To tackle the 'no reason' problem, she would need to have had a conversation with someone working for council or on the job. All of that would have taken time and it might be questionable what it would have achieved. The two people were doing what we call 'making conversation', harmless gossip in effect rapport building, which is probably what most of us do a lot of the time.

The conversation of the couple discussing their son's problems was more significant than 'making conversation', and arguably this was a conversation in which more specific information would have been important for what would happen next. The father was planning to go to the school to get things 'straightened out', despite having very little factual information (at least in the portion of the conversation that I heard).

All of these conversations contained patterns of thinking and speech called Meta Model 'violations'. In my explanation of the Meta Model, I am indebted to Jim, a delegate on several of my courses and now a friend. He complained bitterly to me one day that he just 'wasn't getting' the Meta Model. So I went home and thought how I could do better in my explanation the next day and I came up with the metaphor of a road to success and happiness with road blocks along the way. (**Fig. 1**).

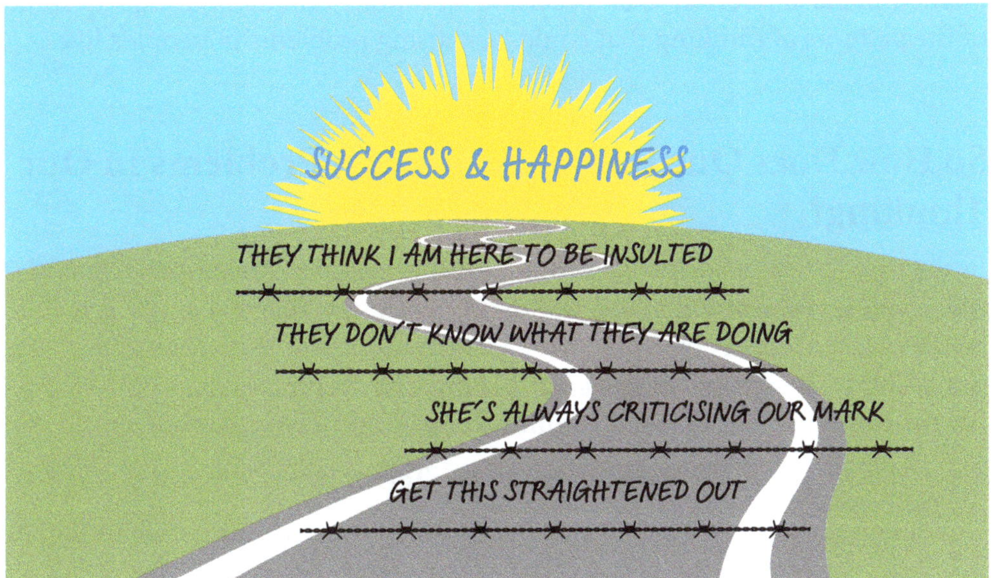

Fig. 1: Meta Model 'violations' – blocks on the road to happiness and success.

The road to success and happiness is in effect blocked by the flawed thinking that is evidenced in Meta Model statements and violations. Jim got it and exclaimed: "Why didn't you say it like that yesterday?!". Thanks Jim – that's the value of feedback!

In this chapter, I will look at these patterns, where they might cause problems, and how we can help ourselves and others by noticing them and asking questions to uncover any flawed thinking or 'lost' information that may be behind them.

The Origins of Meta Model

The Meta Model was the first formal model created by the original co-founders of NLP, Richard Bandler and John Grinder. It was published in 1975 in Volume 1 of *The Structure of Magic*. As Eleni pointed out (Ch.13), the prefix 'meta' appears a lot in NLP and means 'above' or 'beyond', so Meta Model (according to Dilts) relates to a "*model of our other mental models*". In other words, it refers to language that shows our 'map of the world'.

The Meta Model language patterns emerged from modelling the questioning style of Fritz Perls and Virginia Satir (both psychotherapists). They were skilful at recovering the lost information behind what their clients were saying. Noticing what someone says gives clues as to how they are thinking, and therefore how those thoughts may be getting in their way. So the Meta Model's origins were in a therapeutic environment. Bandler and Grinder, however, saw a wider application and they came up with a series of questions (sometimes also referred to as 'precision' questions), that aim to free up some of the patterns of thinking that could be causing problems in people's lives.

So How Does Our Language Indicate Problems In Our Thinking?

In their book *Encyclopedia of Systemic Neuro Linguistic Programming and NLP New Coding*, Robert Dilts and Judith DeLozier say that the basic principle behind Meta Model is that we make our own models of the world in our own heads and with our own language. It is simply our representation of the world not the world itself. This point is summed up in the pre-supposition:

The Map is Not the Territory

Our language has a 'surface structure' and a 'deep structure', as shown in **Fig. 2.**

- *Surface structure* is what we hear when we are in conversation with someone. It is our conscious mind expressing a thought that is only a 'shorthand' version of the original thought in the deeper structure.

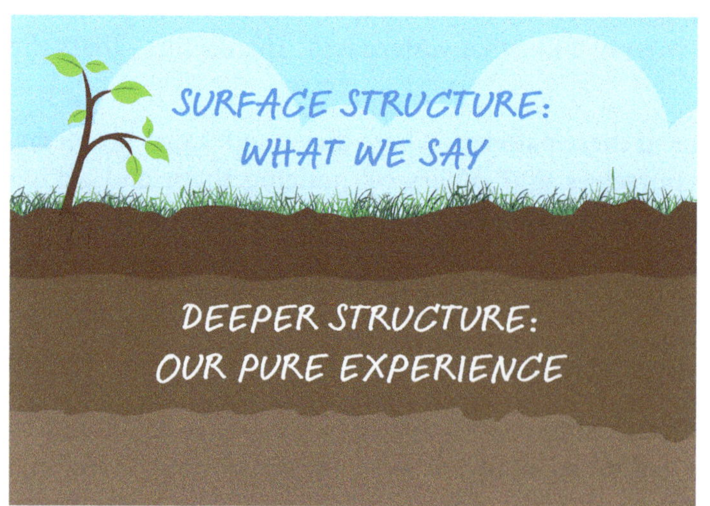

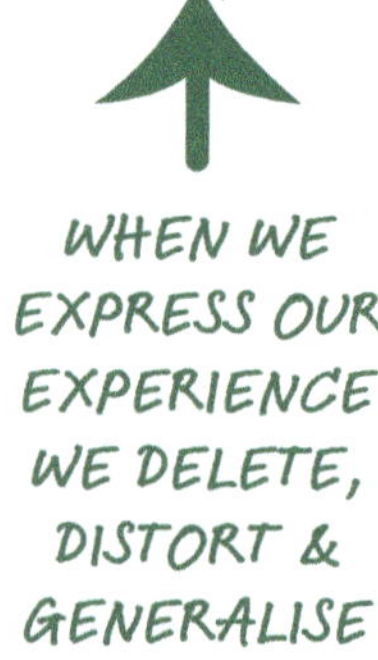

Fig. 2: Language has a 'Surface' structure and a 'Deeper' structure.

- *Deep structure* is the domain of our pure experience (what we see hear, feel, taste and smell) and it is held unconsciously. When this type of thought is expressed in language, it has been unconsciously deleted, distorted or generalised in the process.

Deletion, distortion and generalisation were described in Ch 3. They are the processes by which we create our own personalised map of the world as referred to in the quotation from Dilts and DeLozier. They help our learning processes and to manage the huge amount of incoming information. These same processes, however, have another side to them in the way they operate which have less beneficial effects:

- Deletion: we omit or over-simplify information.
- Distortion: we change information coming in to 'fit' with what we know or believe already.
- Generalisation: we take one example or one experience and make a general rule from it (which can lead to false assumptions).

As a result of these processes, an 'impoverished'* map of the world is evidenced by what someone is saying.

An example of this might be someone saying: "She doesn't like me". Hearing this, we might be tempted to sympathise or offer advice, in effect taking what is said at face value and interpreting it through our own map of the world. However, we can ask questions with the intention of helping the person to expand and perhaps modify the limitations they're holding in their map. As a result, they may question the validity of the statement they made, and may start to see things differently, so their choices in that situation are increased. Even if we simply ask "How do you know that?" the person is prompted to think how they came to that particular conclusion and may find scant evidence to back up their statement. It may have been driven by negative beliefs about themselves or the other person and such questions may prompt them to reappraise what they have said, and modify their view. As the filtering has been done unconsciously, the person will not necessarily be aware of the process (the deletions, distortions and generalisations) that led to their statement.

Bandler and Grinder used Noam Chomsky's** model of Transformational Grammar as a guide. Transformational grammar asserts that when we raise something from our deep structure to our surface structure (i.e. when we express a thought), we transform the meaning of the words. So the words we

*Impoverished is the process by which a person comes to have limited or no choice in a situation.

**Avram Noam Chomsky: linguist, philosopher, cognitive scientist, historian, political activist, and social critic.

use to describe our thought changes our perception of that thought. This is, in fact, the basis of all 'talking therapies' – transforming the language we use changes the meaning for us, and so our relationship to what we are describing.

It is worth noting that this works the other way too, in a potentially negative way; what we say (surface structure) feeds back to our deep structure, so if we say something (negative or positive) for long enough it also becomes part of our map.

Meta Model Patterns And Questions To Recover 'Lost' Information

Our everyday speech is littered with Meta Model patterns, sometimes called Meta Model violations. They are so commonplace that it's easy for them to slip by our notice and be left unchallenged. Here is a summary of the patterns that might ring alarm bells and questions you might ask someone else (or indeed yourself) to 'recover' information that has been 'lost' as your brain has filtered your thoughts.

"She thinks she's being clever"

This is an example of a 'mind read'. The speaker presumes to know what someone else is thinking and may even be convinced they are right, and their actions will reflect this belief. A possible question to get them thinking differently is: "How do you know that?".

"It's stupid to approach it that way!"

This is an example of someone expressing their opinion as a fact (aka a 'lost performative'). This way of speaking might get someone else's back up, and/or the person saying it may be reinforcing their own beliefs. Questions that may get them thinking differently are: "In whose opinion is it stupid?" or "By what standard do you judge that?".

"Meetings bore me!"

This is an example of 'cause and effect', whereby the speaker is putting themselves at 'effect' and therefore taking no responsibility for the situation, or for getting themselves out of it. One possible question to generate different thinking and help someone realise their own part in this is: "How do meetings cause you to be bored?".

"She hasn't invited me to the meeting so she doesn't think I've got anything to contribute"

This is a 'complex equivalence'. In statements like this, the person puts some facts together and reaches a conclusion that may be just a step too far. It may be true of course, but it is an assumption that they are making without checking it out. A possible question to get them thinking differently is: "How does not inviting you mean she thinks you have nothing to contribute?".

"I either apply for this promotion or I leave"

This statement is a 'pre-supposition' (of the unresourceful kind!). It pre-supposes something unhelpful; in this case, that there are only two choices. Question that might open up more choices are: "Who says there are only two options?" or "Could there be more than two options?"

"I never say the right thing"

This is an example of a 'universal quantifier' and it is usually an exaggeration. Other examples are the words: all, every, no one, everyone. Using this language, particularly in a business environment, can make what might be basically a good point seem ill-thought out, and therefore it may be easily dismissed. Two possible questions to get them thinking differently is: "Never?" or "Has there ever been a time when you have?".

"We shouldn't negotiate on this" or "I can't do that"

These are examples of 'modal operators of necessity and possibility' or, in simpler terms, limiting rules and assumptions that we impose on ourselves or on others. They can keep us on a narrow thinking track, or stop us from even attempting to do something differently. Possible questions to generate some new thinking are: "What would happen if we/you did?" or "What stops you?"

"My education was poor"

This use of the word education is called a 'nominalization'. Nominalizations are often a verb that has been turned into a noun – something that you physically cannot see and has a range of possible meanings. I often refer to these as 'fat' words (nouns that cannot be put in a wheelbarrow, unlike a table, for instance, and that cannot be seen, heard or touched). The danger is that the listener may make their own assumptions about what is meant – and then agree! Other examples are words like: success, communication, process, relationship. A way to recover what the person actually means is by turning the word back into a verb, or simply asking more questions about it: "How were you educated?" or "What do you mean by education?".

"I told him to man up!"

This is an 'unspecified verb' in that the speaker has not specified how the person is meant to do the thing they said. I was given this example during a conversation with an HR Director. It is unclear whether she noticed my eyes widening at her comment! I recovered her meaning by asking: "How specifically did you want him to do that?".

"I am concerned"

This statement is left hanging for the listener to potentially put their own meaning to it. It is known as a 'simple deletion'. For clarity you can ask: "About what?".

"Some people are never happy"

In this case, it isn't clear to whom the speaker is referring, and it may also be an exaggeration (called an 'unspecified referential index'). To check this out and avoid the ambiguity, you can ask: "Who do you mean by some people?".

"I want them to do more"

This is a statement I heard during another client conversation – a 'comparative deletion'. My challenge was to find out what the client's team were doing now, and what 'more' would look like. Not easy questions to consider, yet without his answers, we would not know whether we had succeeded or not. So I started to recover his meaning by asking: "Compared to what?" and "What do you mean by more?".

The correct titles of these patterns may be in an unfamiliar language, but what is important is starting to notice these patterns in everyday speech. When you do this, it opens up a way to help ourselves or other people to rethink some limiting patterns of thinking or assumptions. When we use language like this and it goes unchallenged, we not only express our limiting patterns of thinking – we are likely to be reinforcing them. We put these barriers to success and happiness in our own way.

The examples given above also have potentially negative effects for the person saying them, or others around them. We may hear patterns like these in far more harmless contexts in which it may be more damaging to a relationship to challenge them (not to mention, pointless). If someone says, "She is lovely", it would churlish to come back with "Who says?".

Even if someone is saying something with a negative implication for them, then helping them explore, and maintaining good rapport with them, requires a respectful, adult voice tone, to avoid interrogation. Our intention to help is the guiding principle here. Asking too many questions about a statement someone has just made could easily move from prompting a rethink to causing an argument. As ever, a good place to start is with noticing … and challenging our own thinking!

How Can I Use Meta Model Questions Effectively In My Everyday Life?

In one word: respectfully. There is a big difference between being able to drive a car and doing so within the law, and giving care, courtesy and consideration to other road users! So it is with Meta Model questions: without giving consideration to the other person, there is a danger of being intrusive or interrogating. If our intention is to help someone see the limitations in their thinking and getting them to think differently, then we need to create an environment that allows them to safely reconsider. In other words, we need to be in rapport with them to start with.

And then the question is, where to start? Someone may make a statement that is packed full of Meta Model violations. Look at this example:

> "My colleagues don't think I can do my job. They think I'm not aware of what they're saying about me, and they don't know how hurt it makes me feel. It's really unfair. I never get invited to their little private meetings. And I shouldn't have to ask, should I? They infuriate me!"

How many violations can you spot? Even this small statement is packed full of them. So where would you start? Part of the answer relates to the context in which you are having this conversation, as well as your relationship with the person, which is missing in this example. The answer, believe it or not, lies in my garage! Let me explain. The garage at our house looks like a train wreck, and when we are minded to tidy it up we are overwhelmed – we simply don't know where to start. There probably is a 'right' place to start, but what seems to work equally well is to start *anywhere*. Grinder describes playing with the jazz musician Herb Alpert and being concerned about getting his part wrong. Herb's advice to him, which John passes on to his students, is that "the only way to get it wrong is to stop playing". So (when in rapport and with respect), start anywhere that seems right to you. Whichever of the 'violations' you start with, you'll be starting the process of getting the other person to expand, rethink and open up more choices. My friend Bibian says it's like bathing a baby; even if you don't get everything, the baby will be cleaner when you finish than when you started!

Going back to that example in the previous page riddled with violations, you could challenge their 'mind read':

> "How do you know what they think?"

Or their 'modal operator of necessity':

> "What would happen if you did ask to join their meeting?"

The things to bear in mind throughout are your intention to help them and that asking too many questions may feel like an attack. So start anywhere that seems right to you and keep your questions to a minimum. Allowing the other person time to think and speak (and have your attention) will do more good than challenging every single thing they said.

Is It Right To Challenge Every Meta Model Pattern I Hear?

In short, I think not. As described above, it is important to be in rapport with the person to have your question accepted and to allow them to consider it. Furthermore, you will hear these patterns used at times (and on subjects) where it would be pointless – even aggressive – to challenge them. Take my story at the start of this chapter. Even if I had known the two ladies in the hairdressers, it would have been pointless to ask:

> "Are they *always* digging up the street out there? Has a week gone by when they haven't?"

Or:

> "What do you mean specifically when you say 'sort themselves out'?"

With regards to the parents of the schoolboy, it seems unlikely that they would have reacted kindly to any well-meaning intervention from me – a stranger overhearing their conversation – no matter how important it might have been for them to get clarification!

At other times, these language patterns may be used in a way that is unlikely to be a problem for the speaker. Here's a couple of examples:

> "The Lake District is a fabulous holiday destination!" (lost performative)

Or:

> "The sun puts me in a good mood!" (cause–effect)

It would be churlish and pointless to challenge these statements, better to just notice, smile and keep the rapport … at least, in my opinion!

And finally, there is the value of being allowed to vent – to let it all out, rather than bottle up frustrations. In these circumstances we will see little value in being questioned by someone else – much less hearing what their solutions are to the problems that have got us into this state. There may come a time in such conversations when questions and some reasoned thinking will help… until that time comes it may be wiser to keep your Meta Model questions to yourself !

Everyday Thinking And Doing: Consider This …

The starting point with the Meta Model is to develop your acuity for noticing patterns, ideally in 'safe' environment (especially if you are new to Meta Model). Here are some ideas.

Meta Model bingo

1. Have a copy of the patterns to hand while you watch a television programme or movie and tick off each one of the patterns you notice. Check for a 'full house' at the end. If you don't have a full house, it could be because some patterns weren't used. More likely than this, however, it may be that you're not picking some up as easily as others.
2. Watch another television programme or movie and just look for the one (or more) patterns that you didn't notice in the first part of the exercise.
3. You may need to be alone for this: watch yet another programme or movie, but this time call out the relevant precision question, (as indicated earlier for that Meta Model pattern), when you spot a violation.
4. During a meeting at work (in which you aren't directly involved in the conversation) take time to notice different patterns. (This time it is probably inadvisable to keep the score!)

Practise with a friend

If you have a willing friend, particularly one with an interest in NLP, this would be ideal.

1. Explain that you want to really listen to them and would like to practise noticing what they're saying and asking questions.
2. Ask them to talk about a real dilemma or issue they are experiencing currently.
3. When you have finished, discuss the effect your questions had on them and on the issue they discussed.
4. What did you do well? And what would you do differently next time?

Milton Model …

… the patterns of hypnotic language

By Florence

Where Will I Find Hypnotic Language in Everyday Life?

So the short answer is: in more places that you might realise at first:

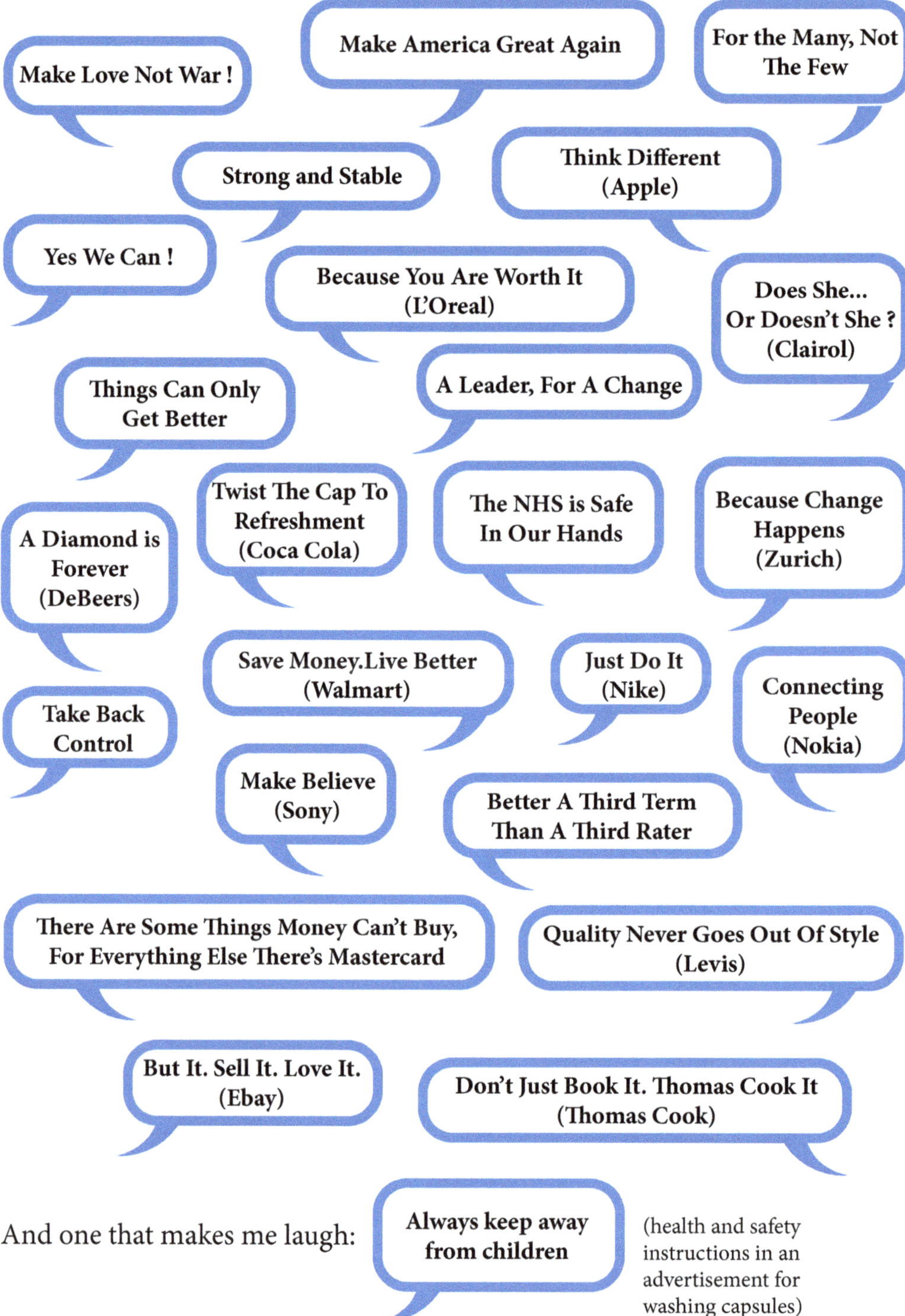

And one that makes me laugh:

(health and safety instructions in an advertisement for washing capsules)

Fig.1: Examples of hypnotic language in advertising and political slogans.

The statements in **Fig.1** are all everyday examples of the use of hypnotic language patterns, many of which you may recognise. It is used most noticeably in political slogans and in advertising, where a message needs to be communicated quickly and in a brief and memorable form. (The last one really makes me laugh: it is, of course, part of the health and safety instructions for laundry capsules.)

Crucially, advertising or political slogans like this must not say anything that the reader's conscious mind is likely to object to … so it needs to be 'artfully vague'! The use of this language in some political slogans can be questionable, but in NLP as with clinical hypnotherapy this language is used in a way, and with the express intention, to bring positive benefits to the receiver. Moreover, as NLP-ers working with any of the NLP boards we are bound by the code of ethics in how we use these and indeed all of our NLP skills. When you are ready to learn more, read this passage:

> *In this chapter, I want to talk to about Milton Model language and the value of being able to use it effectively. Sometimes it is referred to as artfully vague language and in some ways it is the mirror of the Meta Model.*
>
> *So as you read this passage, you may be wondering (and it's good to wonder) what the Milton Model is all about and how soon you will be able to use it elegantly and ethically in your everyday experience. Milton Model is about using artfully vague language that the conscious mind will accept and that takes a message to the unconscious without resistance. Some people believe that this is a form of communication that allows people to learn things easily, and that has to be a good thing, don't you think?*
>
> *The joy of this is when you start to notice the language patterns, you will find that you can use these more and more and to greater and greater effect. As I did a few years ago when Eleni and I were walking on beach on the beautiful Greek island of Amorgos. We were discussing our communication of hypnotic language on courses, as often people say to us, "I can't see yet how I can apply this in my everyday life!".*
>
> *Eleni said she normally replies with something like, "That's a great approach, because as you are challenging the use of this language, that will allow you to learn more easily". I agreed and said that I often added "You will start to become aware of the many applications for this language that emerge in your mind … applications that will be valuable to you as you move forward to more and more success in your life".*
>
> *My preference is often to tell a story to reinforce the learnings and day after day point out that we continue to make connections as we relax and go about our lives. And how good is it that the learning process continues effortlessly and unconsciously by just listening to a story? A story is in*

effect hypnotic language too, isn't it great we can access the unconscious just by use of a well-considered story?

I am guessing that you, like me, would want to feel confident using this language when you realise the benefits it can bring to you and others. When you do, you will be like an aircraft taxiing along a runway, gaining momentum ... until you take off ... and use all your learnings and gifts at will.

Consider for a moment how you felt as you read that passage. I wonder what you have noticed already? And how quickly you will start to notice the language patterns as you read on through this chapter.

What Is A Hypnotic State And What Is Hypnotic Language?

What we now refer to as hypnosis has been used in the context of healing since pre-historic times. The modern era of hypnotherapy, however, really begins with Franz Anton Mesmer the Viennese physician, from whom the word "mesmerism" is derived. His work influenced James Braid, a Scottish doctor, thought by some to be the first genuine hypnotherapist. In 1841 he coined the term 'hypnotism' which refers to the effect on the patient (or subject). His term placed significance on the *state* of the subject as being the key factor, rather than the skills or power of the 'hypnotist'.

The hypnotic state is also called 'trance' or 'downtime', whereby our focus is on our 'inside', and it is a very normal state for human beings to be in. (Uptime is when our awareness is on the world around us.) In fact, we are in a trance state frequently during our normal day: when we are driving long distances, or reading, watching television or listening to music, or daydreaming, or even when we feel confused. It is a state of relaxed awareness in which our focus in inward rather than on the outside world. As the examples above indicate, it is a state that we enter involuntarily in the course of our day – and deliberately when we are the subject of a trance induction.

The conscious mind can be critical and analytical, and when we are in a trance state it allows bypassing of the conscious mind, and gives direct access to the unconscious, making us receptive to new information. As long as the information is something that resonates with our unconscious mind and, as stated earlier, is not something our conscious will object to. The beauty of much poetry, for instance, is that it encourages the reader or listener to go 'inside' to consider its meaning for them, rather than being told directly what to think. Consider these lines in **Fig.2** from *Under Ben Bulben* by W.B. Yeats (the celebrated Irish poet and nationalist and sometime contemporary of my mother's). He requested them to appear on his headstone, and their meaning has sparked debate over the years…maybe as he intended!

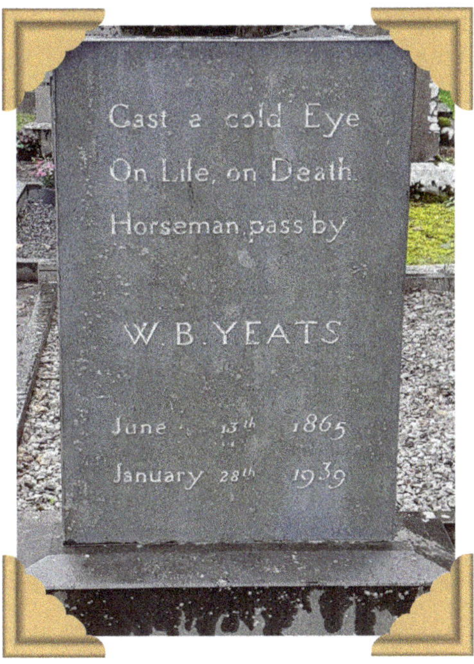

Fig. 2: The gravestone of W.B. Yeats at Drumcliffe, County Sligo in Ireland.

What Was Different About Milton Erickson's Approach to Hypnotic Language?

Milton Erickson was a clinical hypnotherapist who was modelled by Richard Bandler and John Grinder in 1974, and who gives his name to Milton Model Language. It is believed that Erickson did not 'know' what he was doing; rather, he trusted his unconscious to guide his clients into trance and went with what worked. He was therefore largely self-taught and believed that his clients' unconscious minds were capable, in the right circumstances, of coming up with their own creative solutions.

Traditionally hypnotic language was direct and authoritarian, in effect it told the subject what to do ("You are going into a trance"). The trouble here is that the subject's conscious mind can object to this. Although Erickson was known to use the direct authoritarian language at times, he developed and became known for his indirect, permissive approach. This is what Bandler and Grinder labelled as artful vagueness.

In contrast to the direct authoritarian approach, the indirect permissive approach involves saying something like: "You can go into a trance now or in a little while". Typically, words like *can*, *perhaps*, *allow*, *maybe* and *might* are used to make suggestions and they give the subject the illusion of choice. By being non-specific, the permissive approach allows the subject to infer their own meaning and interpret what is said in a way that is most relevant to them and their situation. An example of this is the phrase "You are learning many things". There is nothing to object to here because the speaker is not saying what those things are. This choice of words is likely to send the mind searching for and noticing what it is learning.

Key to Erickson's approach was:

- The rapport he built with his clients.
- His acuity and his observation of non-verbal signals from his clients, which he could utilise to pace and deepen the trance.
- His beliefs about his clients (a number of which have become NLP presuppositions):
  - We all have all the resources we need.
  - Behind every action is an unconscious positive intention.
  - People make the best choices available to them at the time.
  - There are no resistant clients, only inflexible communicators (he believed resistance was evidence of a lack of rapport).

He developed the use of metaphor and stories for therapeutic purposes (more on this in Ch. 20 on Metaphor) and coined the term 'brief therapy', a process whereby significant results could be achieved in just a few short sessions. He believed there was a wide scale of levels of trance and that 'conversational hypnosis' (when the subject was only in a light trance) could be just as effective as a deep trance. In this circumstance, a subject may be unaware of the trance or of the suggestion*.

By accessing the unconscious in this way, clients can be induced to shift their perceptions of a problem or difficult situation. When their perceptions shift, so does their reality or map of the world, and the limiting beliefs that were part of it are changed, freeing up their thinking and their choices.

So hypnotic language can be used very subtly, to the point where it can go unnoticed. Hence my point at the start of the chapter about hypnotic language being used, perhaps less reputably, in political slogans and advertising.

What Are The Milton Model Patterns?

Most of these are divided into distortions, generalisations and deletions (you will recognise the names of many of these patterns from the Meta Model), plus

*Suggestion is the process of causing uncritical acceptance of an idea in the client.

some additional patterns Erickson used. There is, however, a key difference with the Meta Model; in the Milton Model, the patterns are used mindfully, and deliberately made to be ambiguous. This has the express aim, as stated before, to access the unconscious directly, avoiding any resistance by the conscious mind and for the express benefit of the receiver. The purpose of this approach is to subtly influence another person's thinking. To illustrate the use of these patterns, I have included the slogans from the start of the chapter in their appropriate pattern.

Distortions

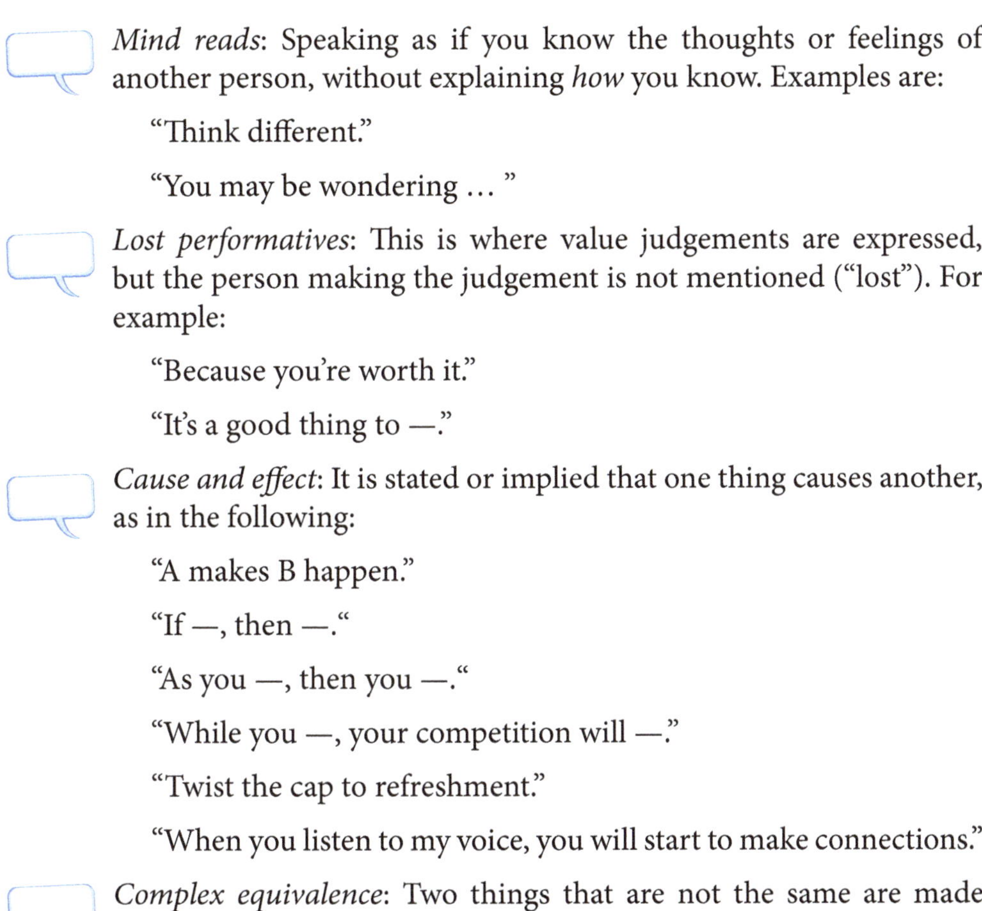

Mind reads: Speaking as if you know the thoughts or feelings of another person, without explaining *how* you know. Examples are:

"Think different."

"You may be wondering … "

Lost performatives: This is where value judgements are expressed, but the person making the judgement is not mentioned ("lost"). For example:

"Because you're worth it."

"It's a good thing to —."

Cause and effect: It is stated or implied that one thing causes another, as in the following:

"A makes B happen."

"If —, then —."

"As you —, then you —."

"While you —, your competition will —."

"Twist the cap to refreshment."

"When you listen to my voice, you will start to make connections."

Complex equivalence: Two things that are not the same are made equivalent, or one is taken as implying the other, or if one thing is true than the other must be too. Here are some examples:

"Save money — live better."

"Strong and stable."

"Learning is progress."

Pre-suppositions. All language pre-supposes something and in the Milton Model the pre-supposition is positive or beneficial in some way. For example:

"Yes we can." (Note the presupposition: the answer is yes whatever the question is, and that 'we' can do it together.)

"Take back control." (Note the presupposition: control has been lost and it can be recovered.)

Generalisations

Universal quantifiers. These are words such as *all*, *every*, *always*, *never*, *everyone* that over-generalize. Some examples are:

"Quality never goes out of style."

"All the things you are learning."

"It is always good to ---."

Modal operators. These are words that imply possibility or necessity. Examples include:

"Don't just book it — Thomas Cook it."

"A person has to think what's best for them sometime."

"We're going to have to do something different sooner or later."

Deletions

Nominalisations. These are processes (usually – but not always verbs) that have been 'frozen' and turned into nouns (my 'fat' words). They are abstract concepts that we refer to as if they were things, but we cannot 'see' them. For example:

"The NHS is *safe* in our hands."

"Because *change* happens."

"*Communication* between people is crucial to *success.*"

Unspecified verbs. These verbs do not specify 'how' an action will actually take place.

"Make America great again."

"Just do it."

"Continue to relax and you will know how to sort this out."

"You can run a tight ship when you take over the department."

Unspecified referential index. A noun or pronoun that doesn't refer to a particular subject (i.e. it has no 'referential index').

"For the many, not the few." (But who are the many? And who are the few?)

"One can, you know, make real changes." (But who is *one*?)

Simple deletions. Part of the information is missing, so the listener has to fill in the gaps.

"Diamonds are forever." (It doesn't say what this means – tempting to think this refers to a relationship if you are buying an engagement ring!)

"Make believe."

"As you ponder." (It doesn't say about what.)

Comparative deletions. A comparison is made without specifying what something is being compared to.

"Things can only get better."

"And it is going to mean more to you."

Additional patterns

In addition those above, Milton Erickson also developed the following:

Pacing current experience. This is where the speaker takes something that is quite obviously happening in the moment and often follows it with a cause and effect, a complex equivalence or a simple suggestion. In this way, the client's verifiable experience is linked to a suggestion (which is not verifiable).

"You are reading this example (*fact*), *and* becoming aware of the number of options there are with hypnotic language {*maybe/ maybe not*}, *and* so you are already forming ideas of how to use it (*the suggestion*)"

Ambiguity. This pattern is particularly noticeable in the political and advertising slogans at the start of the chapter.

"A leader, for a change."

"Connecting people."

"Always keep away from children."

"Make love not war !"

"Eats shoots and leaves."

Embedded commands and suggestions. These are suggestions embedded in a longer sentence that might stand alone as a phrase (or command) in itself. When spoken, they are often marked out by a subtle change of voice tone, or a pause, or a physical signal such as a hand gesture or glance while making the suggestion.

"Buy it, *sell it*, love it."

"I don't know how much *you are enjoying this holiday* yet."

"It will be good when you are able to *use hypnotic language patterns with skill* to help yourself and others."

Extended quote. These are long passages in which the client loses track of who said what to whom, so they apply whatever is said to themselves. Within the quote there can be a number of embedded commands, complex equivalences or other hypnotic language patterns. For example:

"When I was in a training course recently, one delegate said, 'I am so relaxed here, I am able to make so many links with working life", and then another person said, 'It's good, isn't it? I know I can use my learning straight away. She laughed and said, 'I just know the more I read, the more I learn, and the more I can use this knowledge to help myself and others and really feel I can fulfil my potential.'"

This pattern can be used even more simply in conversation when you want to give someone some information indirectly (they are not being given direct advice).

"My friend Eleni told me that one of her clients said to her —."

Tag questions. These are questions that are tagged onto the end of a sentence (often with a direct suggestion) that invites a 'yes' answer whether the client can respond out loud or not.

"Does she, or doesn't she?"

"It's good to learn hypnotic language easily, isn't it?"

Double binds. These statements offer the illusion of choice and often offer possibilities that are usually outside conscious choice or control.

"There are some things money can't buy – for everything else there's Mastercard."

"Better a third term than a third-rater!"

"You don't need to relax consciously. Your unconscious can do it for you."

Metaphor. This is explored fully in Ch.20.

Where Can I Use The Milton Model In Everyday Life and Work?

The exercises at the end of this chapter will give you some ideas and the opportunity to practise using this language. Here are some suggestions where you might use it.

- For business presentations.
- When pitching ideas to clients.
- In written communications in which you want to encourage, inspire or persuade your readers.
- Marketing materials.
- Website copy.
- Slogans
- Speaking or writing to yourself to encourage or inspire.

Everyday Thinking And Doing: Consider this …

As I write this, I don't know how much you are noticing these language patterns in the world around you … or even in this sentence! If you haven't already attended an NLP course you may do so in the future, in the meantime, let's make a start to recognising these patterns now:

- What do you notice about the title of this book *Everyday NLP*?
- If you would like to be able to easily recognise more of the patterns, and understand their value to you (and that would be useful, wouldn't it?) then go back and look at the passage in italics at the start of this chapter. Go through and annotate the passage as you notice the patterns used in every sentence.
- How about being able to put the patterns together for yourself and to increase your confidence in using them? Write yourself a letter, and in that letter reassure yourself how easily, effectively and elegantly you will be able to use Milton Model patterns to help yourself and others. When you have finished, read the letter out loud to yourself – better still get someone else to read it to you – and just enjoy the confidence it is demonstrating it has in you.

Metaphor …

… conveying messages in powerful ways

By Florence

Tell me the facts and I'll learn. Tell me the truth and I'll believe. But tell me a story and it will live in heart forever.

Native American Proverb.

When Do We Experience Metaphor In Everyday Life?

When I was a young child, like children the world over, my parents told me stories and read me fairy stories. When I learnt to read, I read stories for myself, sometimes enjoying some of them so much I read them over and over. These stories were really just more subtle versions of the morality tales of previous centuries, creating entrancing pictures in young minds and, along with them, key messages such as being kind, being honest and not judging people by appearances.

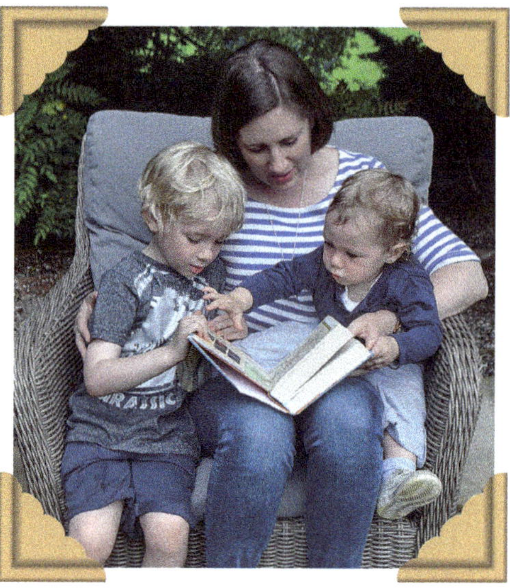

Fig. 1: We enjoy stories from the youngest age!

In my native Ireland, in the pre-television era, storytelling was a common form of entertainment. The *seanchaithe* (traditional storytellers) regaled their audiences with stories into the early hours of the morning. They might be oral histories or morality tales; a common theme for those wishing to discourage gambling was to tell the story of a gambler who was stopped on the way home by the devil sitting at a card table and invited to join him for a game!

This storytelling carries on in Ireland today. Recently, I was privileged to be included in the family birthday celebrations for my childhood friend Margo who was having a 'special' birthday. Our families have shared much together over the years and the evening was an invitation to sing and share our personal stories – each one building up the picture of her life, her experiences and what she meant to us.

This tradition of storytelling for conveying a message has passed in to the film industry. For example, the film *Avatar* has themes about how we treat the environment, and perhaps reflects on the behaviour of previous (and current) generations' treatment of native populations.

Storytelling (and this includes poetry of course) is evident in business presentations, in coaching, in meetings, in advertising, in selling, in sport, and in family histories. In effect, it is all around us.

What is Metaphor And Why Is It Important?

First of all, out of deference to my old English teacher Mr Seymour (again), here are the definitions of metaphor, simile and analogy.

- *Metaphor*: expressing or describing one thing in terms of another; equating two items (e.g. "Life is a bed of roses").
- *Simile*: to say something is 'like' or 'as' something else; comparing two items (e.g. "Reading this book is like bathing in chocolate").
- *Analogy*: less a figure of speech and more of pointing out the shared characteristics of two things (e.g. "She was like a swan, serene above the surface, paddling like hell below").

In NLP, all of these are all referred to as 'metaphor', as are stories. Metaphor is also a pattern of Milton Model language (Ch.19) because it draws the listener or reader into a light trance and takes a message indirectly to the unconscious (hence the value of stories in conveying a message to children and adults alike). In fact, the word metaphor comes originally from the Greek *metaphero* – to carry over, or to transfer.

There is an ancient Sioux saying:

The longest journey a man will ever take is from his head to his heart.

When someone hears or reads a story, they will derive their own meaning from it, consciously and unconsciously. Often stories are selected to convey a specific message to an audience, which – if given directly – their conscious mind might resist. This is why you will hear trainers tell stories and anecdotes to their delegates on courses; similarly, 'presenters' of all types to their audiences. They are delivering a message they want their listeners to take away – possibly without realising it at first.

You may remember the story that appeared earlier (Ch.11) about the Chameleon and the Leopard. And you may even be left wondering what the message of that story was. Effective stories do that. They send our brain off in search of a meaning for ourselves.

In the chapter on Meta Model (Ch.18), we refer to language having a surface structure and a deeper structure, and how when we express our deeper thoughts, they are subject to deletion, distortion and generalisation. Often the result of this process (and the difficulty of fully expressing our deeper thoughts) is that we use metaphor to try to carry the meaning of what we want to say. Moreover, as Carl Jung proposed, the unconscious mind uses symbols and metaphors to convey ideas or concepts that it cannot define in words, (you may remember Eleni elaborates on the importance of symbols in Ch.2).

Judy Rees co-author of the book *Clean Language: Revealing Metaphors and Opening Minds* calls metaphor "the native language" of the unconscious and points out that metaphors are present in almost everything that we say. In fact the use of metaphor is so commonplace that we probably don't always realise when we're using it. For example, you may hear someone say phrases like these:

"He's holding me back."

"I've had a hard day."

"She's a slippery customer."

"He's doing my head in!"

"I want the department to run smoothly."

None of these is meant literally – unless, in the case of the first one, someone is actually physically restraining the person who says it! Yet at first glance, they may slip by unnoticed – like this sentence in fact! Herein lies the trap and the opportunity of metaphor.

Some of the metaphors we use are not only evidence of negative beliefs or 'stuckness' in our thinking: as pointed out in Ch.18 our verbalising and repetition of them is likely to be reinforcing such beliefs or states. New Zealand psychologist David Grove recognised this and developed an approach that honoured the metaphor of one his clients for a difficult situation they found themselves in. By asking questions that developed and deepened the metaphor, he was able to work respectfully in their map of the world, eventually enabling them to develop their own way forward using their metaphor as a vehicle. An example of this is when someone described themselves as being caught in a trap. By asking questions about this 'trap', how the person was being held in it, and what they wanted instead, Grove's questions enabled his client to work out an escape plan.

His work was modelled by NLP modellers Penny Tompkins and James Lawley, who went on to develop a coaching approach that they called Symbolic

Modelling, using 'clean'* questions to work respectfully with the client's metaphor – without imposing any of their own thoughts about the client's situation. For more on this, see Eleni's chapter Listening, Silence and Asking Questions (Ch. 21).

Thus metaphor can give us a glimpse into someone else's map of the world, and provide indicators of how their thinking may be blocking their path to success and happiness. The same person can also unblock their own thinking by developing more resourceful metaphors, or taking on those offered by someone else, to illuminate a path forward.

Ordinary words convey only what we know already;
it is from metaphor that we can best
get hold of something fresh ...
but the metaphors must not be too far-fetched,
or they will be difficult to grasp,
nor obvious or they will have no effect.
The words, too, ought to set the scene before our eyes.

Aristotle, ancient Greek philosopher and scientist.

Are All Metaphors Equally Effective?

There are different levels of metaphor as outlined here – shallow, deep and embedded.

Shallow metaphors

These relate to a simple comparison, like a simile as referred to earlier in this chapter. They can be a little obvious and therefore (as Aristotle observed) they have very limited power for creating change (if that is the aim). Otherwise, as in the excerpt from a poem below, they can illustrate a point beautifully. In these 'isomorphic' metaphors, as they are termed, the relationship between the two things being compared is easily recognised:

Two girls in silk kimonos, both beautiful, one a gazelle.

W.B. Yeats from his poem
'In Memory of Eva Gore-Booth
and Con Markievicz'.

---

*Clean questions are those that are crafted with as little pre-supposition in them as possible (e.g. "What kind of –?" or "What would you like to have happen?"

Deep metaphors

These are often conveyed in a story that has several layers of meaning. They usually create pictures in the mind that the reader or listener is more likely to remember and reflect on both consciously and unconsciously. Because many meanings can be drawn from them, they are referred to as 'homomorphic' metaphors.

Embedded metaphors

These take the form of 'nested loops', so often beloved of comedians as they appear to veer from one story to another without finishing them, only to return to them later. They have the effect of confusing the conscious mind and 'leaving a door open' in the unconscious, which is waiting for the stories to be completed. They are very effective vehicles for carrying resourceful suggestions to the unconscious.

Sarah Frossell, my first NLP trainer, is a masterful story teller. She wove stories together and told them to us at the end of each day of the course. Her stories included 'clips' of an ongoing story about Blind Mouse. Even now twenty years on I think about that story, trying to remember what happened and how it ended. The last time I met Sarah, I asked her how it ended, and she just smiled. I guess she didn't want me to end my quest for a meaning. (I hope she smiles again as she reads this!)

Metaphorical stories have been used for centuries in a therapeutic manner. Today there are many books of stories available for use by trainers, presenters, teachers, parents and educators. I even have a section on my website called 'Telling Tales' (www.florencemadden.co.uk). These stories have been created by various course delegates to convey uplifting and encouraging feedback to one another. An example of one of these stories is 'The Chameleon and the Leopard' in Ch.11.

As much as we can enjoy and use other people's stories, we can also create our own – for ourselves – or to inspire another person or group. Here's how.

How To Write Your Own Story

If you want to use storytelling for the benefit of a group or individual and want to convey a specific message to them, these guidelines should help you.

Step 1: Decide on the 'message' or moral you want to pass on, such as believing in their own abilities, triumphing over adversity, or avoiding assumptions.

Step 2: Aim to be subtle. If you are writing for a specific individual or group they do not want to be able to identify themselves too obviously

in the story. So if the story is for a female, consider using a male character and perhaps have the main character an animal or object.

Step 3: Think of a parallel situation or metaphor for the message or moral you want to convey. For instance, self-belief might be conveyed using a magic mirror; triumphing might involve a race; avoiding assumption might comprise a variation on the 'beauty and the beast' theme.

Step 4: Create your story using all the representational systems (visual, auditory, kinaesthetic, olfactory and gustatory as appropriate) to bring colour, richness and interest to the story.

Step 5: Consider using other Milton Model patterns (Ch.19) if they fit. You could use *embedded commands* to reinforce key messages, or *extended quotes* to embed your commands further, as well as *tag questions* to draw the listener in even more.

Step 6: Avoid being too obvious. You want the listener to work things out for themselves, so leave the 'moral' untold at the end. A little bit of suspense and wondering leaves the unconscious mulling over the story. The aim is to get someone thinking differently about their situation, rather than tell them how to solve it.

Creating 'Nested Loops' To Embed Your Message Further

Nested loops, as referred to earlier in this chapter, are a way for inducing trance deeper still in those listening to your story, and they are a great way to embed key messages. They are also a device used by Milton Erickson, although he did not use this phrase to describe them. They create a state of curiosity in the mind of the listener and hold their attention as they inwardly question whether the story is complete. This has the effect of holding the curiosity and attention of the listener or reader until the stories are completed. The approach uses something called the Zeigarnik effect, after the psychologist of that name who noticed that people remember uncompleted or interrupted tasks better than uninterrupted ones. The basic structure of nested loops is as illustrated in **Fig.2,** overleaf:

A 'nested loop' can include two to five stories. Aim to tell up to three-quarters of each story before you reach the 'break point' (i.e the point where you break the story). Then start the next one without any explanation or acknowledgement that you have broken the previous story. And when you return to each story, make no explanation or reference to what you have done or are doing.

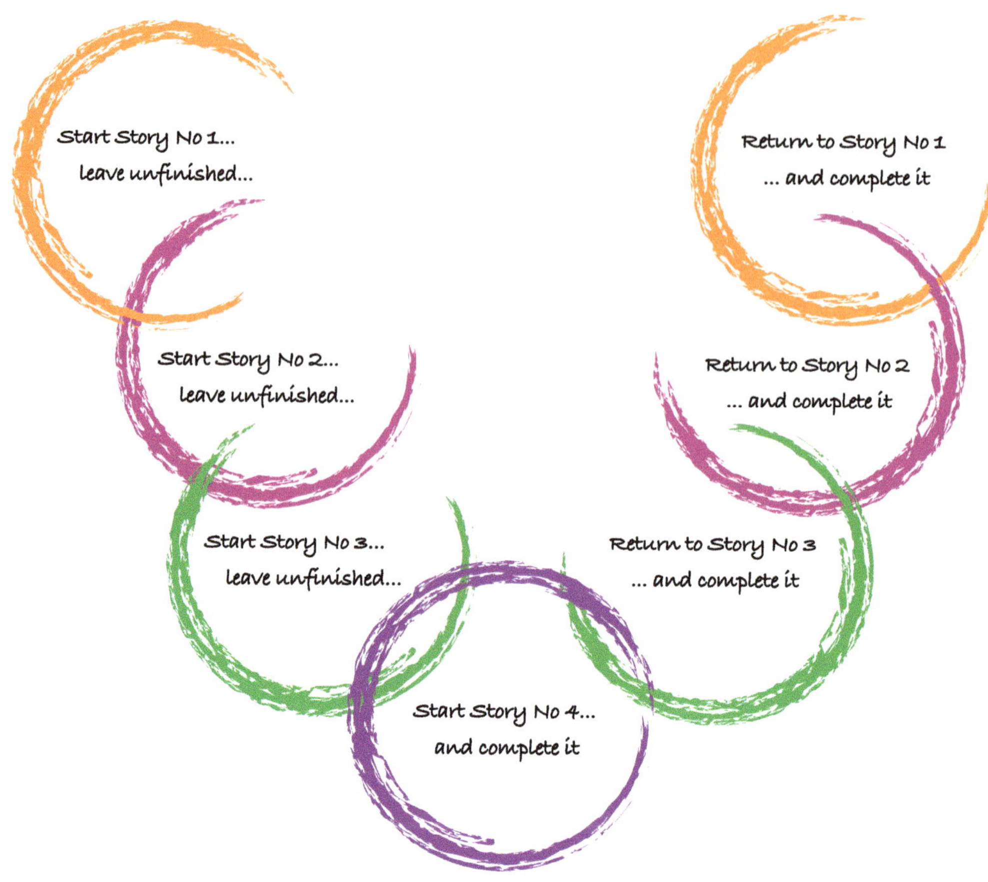

Fig. 2: Nested Loops.

When combining your stories, consider the message or moral you want to convey in each, and work out the best place to break each story so that one flows into the other. Confusing perhaps, but it should not be clumsy.

For an example of nested loops go back to Ch.12 and look again at my stories about my visit to the school and the manufacturing plant, which in effect enveloped the key messages I wanted to convey about rapport!

Physical Metaphors

As well as stories, we can also be inspired by other types metaphors too, as Eleni refers to in Ch.2 about the importance of symbols to the unconscious mind. Physical metaphors have the added benefit of giving us 'muscle memory' as well as a cognitive one. Possibly the best known of these is Tony Robbins' 'fire walk' whereby participants walk over hot coals. This physical metaphor is a powerful demonstration that they can triumph over adversity in their lives. Other physical metaphors include breaking wood or an arrow – they are powerful symbols for breaking through limiting beliefs.

Many coaches also use walking in the outdoors for their coaching sessions. This makes the link between moving forward and discovery – both literally and metaphorically. Similarly, many NLP processes involve the client moving their physical position, which is a strong reinforcement to their learning. Examples of this are Perceptual Positions (Ch.15) or walking the Timeline (Ch.17). And in Parts Integration (Ch.16), the client is quite literally weighing up their options in their hands.

And A Final Story …

I started this chapter by relating the fact that my parents, like so many others, told me stories as a child and that stories are used with people of all ages to convey important messages that the conscious mind may resist if told directly.

Well, I think my parents knew all that too. When I first left Northern Ireland and went to live in Scotland to take up my first management trainee role, I was very unhappy. I complained endlessly about where I was living and the work I was doing and how much I missed my homeland. Perhaps it was the rather immature note I was striking that inspired my mother, but one day a letter arrived from her. It wasn't her usual type of letter. She had written a story. It began 'Once upon a time …' and told the story of a little princess who was born to a family in which everyone loved and fussed over her, and she always got her way. Then as the little princess grew up, her education and ambitions took her away from her kingdom and she was very sad. Although the king and queen and the rest of the family still loved their little princess, they realised that to truly let her grow they mustn't rescue her, but simply show how much they believed in her.

I need not go on. I am guessing you've got the gist of it by now. Indeed, Aristotle wouldn't have thought the story particularly subtle. Yet it had the desired effect on me. From that point, I made a decision to get on with things and make the best of my new life! My mother never referred to that letter again.

The poet Seamus Heaney (who was also the brother of my husband's dinner lady !), summed up the power of poetry and (by implication, I think) metaphorical stories, by saying he didn't think that it/they could change the world, but could change how people felt about what was happening in it.

Everyday Thinking And Doing: Consider This …

Give some thought to situations in your life and work where you might convey your message more powerfully by telling a story. There are many possibilities: business presentations, training courses, client meetings, school assemblies, interviews and marketing materials among others.

- Pick an upcoming event in which you could use a story to convey your message persuasively and use the story writing guidelines to create the story. Or you could create several stories and experiment with the nested loops technique. Read them out loud to friends and colleagues and get their feedback.
- Think of an uplifting or encouraging message you would like to give to yourself, or a friend or your children, and write a story that conveys this message. If the story is for you, consider getting a friend or a family member to read it back to you for full effect.

If you would like to share any of your stories with a wider audience, I would be delighted if you sent them to me for inclusion in the Telling Tales section of my website www.florencemadden.co.uk.

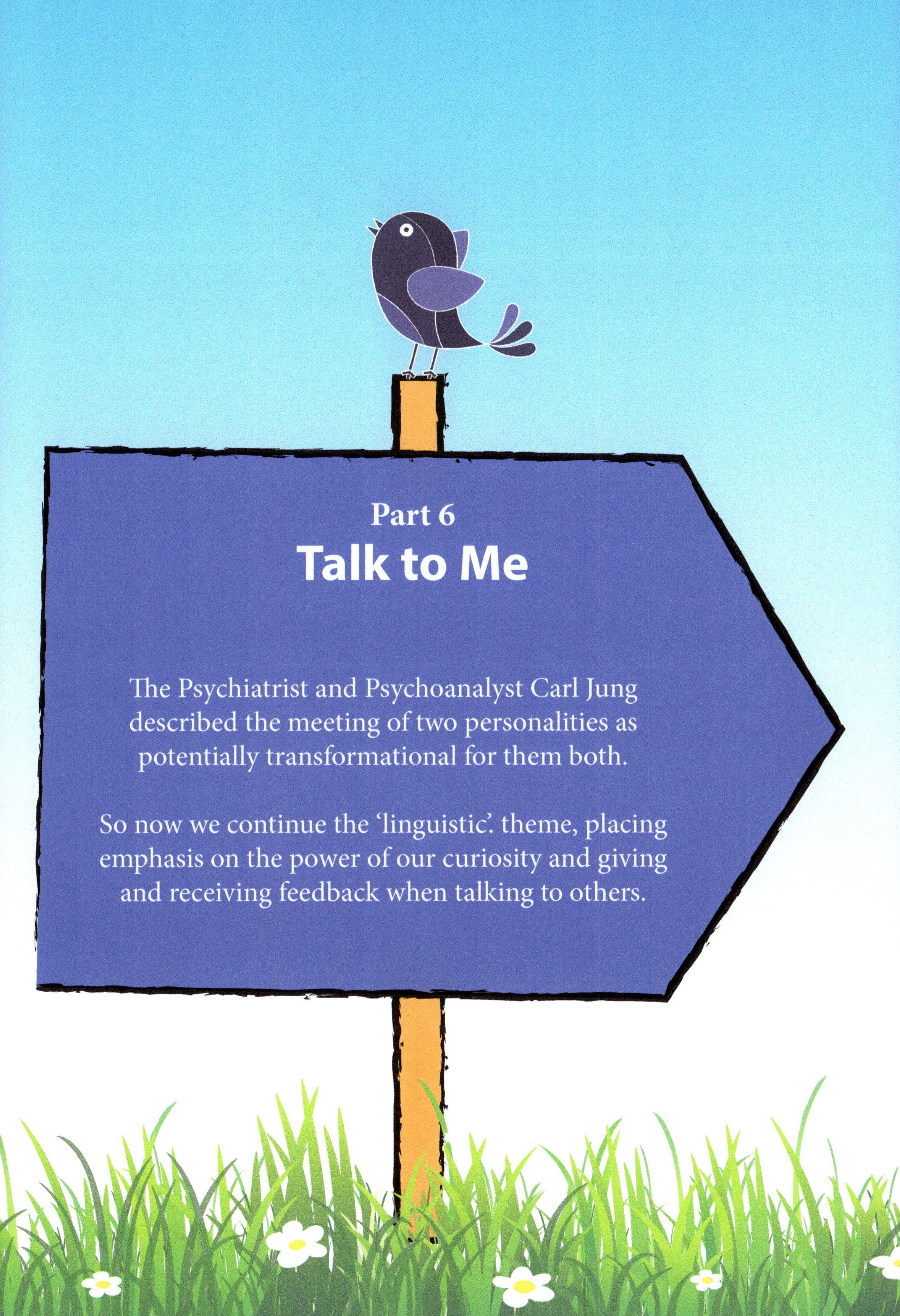

Part 6
Talk to Me

The Psychiatrist and Psychoanalyst Carl Jung described the meeting of two personalities as potentially transformational for them both.

So now we continue the 'linguistic'. theme, placing emphasis on the power of our curiosity and giving and receiving feedback when talking to others.

Chapter 21

Listening, Silence & Asking questions …

… creating the space and time for others

By Eleni

It is amazing how many hints and guides and intuitions for living come to the sensitive person who has ears to hear what his body is saying.

Rollo May, existential psychologist & author.

I used to open my mouth and say whatever was on my mind. There were filters like what is appropriate, polite and useful to share, but I lacked awareness of the tremendous opportunities to 'move' myself and others with language. Models like Meta, Milton and the Metaphors are good examples of how much more language is than just a communication tool. It is a filter within the unconscious which gives us immense power to choose the direction of our conversations and therefore of our reality.

In this chapter, I would like to focus on three fundamental elements that elevate the quality of our communication. They feature in Coaching and NLP courses alike. Nothing in NLP or in our everyday life makes sense without them – and as Rollo May indicates they can teach us so much more.

I am talking about:

1) Active Listening,
2) Golden Silence, and
3) Ecological Curiosity.

1. Active Listening

Most people do not listen with the intent to understand; they listen with the intent to reply.

Stephen R. Covey, educator, author & businessman.

Yes, Stephen. I was one of those people – I am sure in many ways I still am. My solution-oriented, 'Mrs Fix it' approach prompted me to quickly, cleverly and efficiently jump in to offer my point of view and a plethora of ways for the other person to move forward. I did listen. I was interested. Nevertheless, my belief was that the faster my response, the smarter I was. My belief was why waste anybody's time, when I could help instantly.

Despite having practiced listening – mostly to my inner voice – in spiritual practices since I was a teenager, it was only during my first coaching course, that I became far more aware of the benefits of active listening during everyday chats with friends, colleagues and family.

The extra time I was instructed to give my coaching clients taught me invaluable lessons. Where they felt stuck, just by me being there and holding the space for them to unravel their jumble of thoughts was enough for them to experience breakthroughs. Ideas that would otherwise remain 'locked' in their head, came flooding out, one after the other. There was nothing to interrupt them. They might stop talking, but they did not stop processing information. They just needed the luxury of having an interested ear to bounce these ideas around with. They wanted attention.

Active Listening, coined by Carl Rogers and Richard Farson (both psychologists) in their book of the same name, is not passively sitting drifting in and out of thoughts about our own to-do-list while the other person talks. Instead, we need to be present and sincerely interested in what is being shared. An attitude deprived of the urge to respond with opinions, advice or solutions.

During my coaching course, we used the book *Co-Active Coaching Skills* by authors Karen Kimsey-House, Henry Kimsey-House and Phillip Sandahl which reveals that there are three different levels of listening. The book is meant for coaches and I think that it is a must-read for anyone who regularly engages in conversations.

Here are the three listening levels:

Level 1: our focus is internal. We are focused on our own world. We listen to find a connection between what the person is saying and what this means for us or how it relates to us. We hear someone talking about their new house, we think about our own new house or the fact that we do not have a house etc.

Beliefs running at this level are: 'This is interesting to me' 'I can help them with that' and 'I will suggest a or b, maybe that will help them'.

Level 2: our focus is 100% on the other person. We concentrate on their words and context. We keep our own ideas and opinions out of the conversation. All our attention is on what the other person shares with us. There is a genuine interest in the other person's world.

Beliefs running at this level are: 'Each one of us has an interesting point of view on things' 'My time is well managed when I use it to listen to other people's stories' and 'I have respect for other people's journeys'.

Level 3: our focus is on energy and emotion. Listening becomes more global in the sense that even more subtle cues are picked up and our sensory acuity is heightened. We observe details in a totally different level and 'read' more accurately the non-verbal communication i.e. what is 'not' said. Our calibration skills develop and become more accurate. We sense the emotional states of those around us easier.

Beliefs running are: 'I am interested in people's emotions' 'I always find it important to learn more about my feelings and how I make other people feel'. and 'By my presence and energy levels, I can create more space for the one opposite of me to transform and move forward.'

We maximize the benefits of the Perceptual Positions technique (Ch.15) – the one where by moving from one chair to the other, we get different perspectives – when we also take into account the level of active listening of each person. As the person goes through each position in the exercise, he/she becomes even more aware of the listening level each 'chair' operates from.

Similarly, the **Parts Integration** exercise (Ch.16) – a chat between two or more parts of ourselves – enjoys greater results when we become more conscious of the listening level of each part.

In general, the more attentively we listen in these two essential NLP practices, the more we develop Active Listening levels 2 & 3. As a result, we build a life-long strategy of understanding and negotiating more efficiently.

2. Golden Silence

We all crave silence sometimes. Silence in our head and silence in our environment. Silence from that constant chatter within and silence when we listen and when we talk. Often, we talk far more than is beneficial for our progress. A pause can make a world of difference. It creates magic.

When we focus on our internal dialogue, insights and solutions start streaming from us and we feel far more energized and confident. Our need to dominate conversations starts to fade.

To anyone you're engaged in conversation with, silence communicates:

- 'You are important and what you say is important',
- 'I respect you',
- 'You have the freedom to express yourself, I am listening, I am interested in what you have to say'.

The above are all phenomenal self-esteem boosters for the speaker and the listener. These messages build the confidence of the speaker and this in turn strengthens the relationship between the speaker and the listener. Imagine, what it feels like to be able to do that for the people around you.

I still have the following quote vivid in my mind when I entered Ernest Hemingway's house, the famous novelist, during my visit in Cuba:

A human being needs two years to learn to speak,
and fifty to learn to be silent.

As a coach, knowing when to be silent enables the client to elaborate more on a subject, develop new ideas, feel heard and respected and come up with his/her own solutions. The coach also gains a better understanding of what the client is about and there's potential for lots of observation and self-observation for both coach and client.

The key for the coach is to ask himself/herself when he/she is about to speak:

1. Am I about to give direct or indirect advice? For what purpose?
2. Am I about to ask a directive question? Whose agenda am I following?
3. Has the client really finished processing thoughts and releasing emotions?
4. Am I about to ask/talk from a place of good intention, ecological curiosity and open-mindedness?

The art of coaching is to know when to be silent and when to break that silence.

It is now commonly acknowledged that practicing silence is not just for coaches as meditation is not only for spiritual people. These skills are essential for every professional, business owner, spouse, parent, friend and family member.

Nowadays, we probably have more noise around us and within us than ever before. Living in cities, bombarded by the social media, the gigantic technological advancements, we have enough stimuli and 'busy-ness' 24-7. But these things are not necessarily the root cause of the issue.

It is worth checking with ourselves and the constant chatter in our own mind. When we manage to silence our mind, we calm our mind and we listen better to our inner voice, we succeed in finding our peace and quiet in all levels.

Peace, peace of mind, mindfulness, the power of quiet are imperative for our survival, quality of living and world peace.

Silence is the sleep that nourishes wisdom.

Francis Bacon, philosopher.

3. Ecological Curiosity – Questioning

The Meta Model (Ch.18) opened the way to dozens of other language related models. However, what is significant is that this first model was a questioning model. Let me explain.

I went through my childhood with a values system where you did what you were told. Why? 'Because I told you so.' Was the typical parental response. Nowadays, I would like to believe that every parent encourages questions. The teenage years can be hard on those parents who have cultivated a culture where questions are not appreciated. A teenager's role is to double check if and when the status quo works. And when they find any 'window' for growth, they better ask questions for the sake of all of us.

Similarly in organizations of all sorts, in governments and law enforcement, you want to have a "Questioning Habit." A healthy strategy to assess and evaluate processes and procedures. Why do we do this? Why do we not do something else instead? Is there a better, faster, cheaper way? Is there more than anything a more ecological and fair way?

I recently watched an interview of Supreme Court Judge Sonia Sotomayor in the United States of America who said something that touched me deeply: she made a distinction between 'justice' and 'fairness' and that they do not necessarily mean the same thing or lead to the same actions and how this was one of her biggest challenges in her role. Our justice systems are there to reinforce the law, not always being fair to the ones involved. One more reason to create the space for more honest dialogue around our laws, the foundations that again glue us all together. Away from rigidness, we touch the heart and that makes the world a better place.

Types of questions

The below are just a few categories of different types of questions. The more we practice and seek to empower ourselves and others, the more we come across new ways to question and vice versa.

Open/Closed questions:

Technically, open questions give freedom to the other person to answer any way they want. Closed questions are ones that are answered with yes/no, right/wrong etc.

An example of an open question is: *How have you been?* It clearly gives the other person the freedom to talk about what he/she wants.

An example of a closed question is: *Are you going to the party?* The answer is yes or no.

Both have value. Open questions open up the conversation, and as result, the person asked the question is invited to talk more and expand on his/her views – and that means we get to know them better.

Closed questions serve to close conversations, to confirm decisions after evaluating possibilities, enabling the person to move forward with one of the options.

To be able to know the difference and master when to use which one is as much of a life changing experience as it is a life-long practice.

Probing questions *(Meta Model questions):* What? Who? Where? Specifically?

This is how NLP started and you've already read about this in Ch. 18 by Florence. In short, probing questions which provide us with details. They contribute to precision and clarity in any description of events.

Active questions/How questions: These questions help a client process and focus on actions and results, they are useful questions that are focused on active, future-oriented change and on implementing solutions that help drive client solutions and success. For example…

'What is the first step to …?'

'How will you achieve this?'

Clean language questions: *How? In what way? And that...what is it like?*

Clean language – devised by David Grove in the 1980s – is about asking questions without any presupposition. They allow the other person to choose where to go and expand further in their thinking, they shower the other person with respect and steer clear of contaminating or directing your own thinking on to the other person.

'How are you?' is pretty clean. Asking *"Are you tired?"* instantly creates an image of ourselves…as tired! That's how the brain works! We've inadvertently influenced the other person.

Our words cannot NOT influence and create images, sounds and feelings for others and so we are all influencers in that sense. The type of influencer we are is largely determined by how clean we keep our questions.

Backtrack frame/Clarifying questions: Replay the client's words to be sure you have understood or let them reappraise what they have said.

Person A says: 'I called and no one answered so then I went to the movies.'

Person B replies: 'You called to see if they wanted to come with you to the movies or were you planning to go to the movies alone anyway?'

What if questions: This hypothetical approach gets the client to erase history and personal barriers and reconsider a situation, a relationship or an issue in a new light. A reboot type of process.

What would you do if you had a magic wand?

***Rhetorical questions*:** These are questions asked for emphasis and to provoke our thinking rather than expecting a reply.

'Would you believe it?'

'Why me?'

'Could I possibly love you more?'

Leading/Presupposing questions:

'What time will you go to the supermarket?' This clearly implies you are going to the supermarket. These questions are better used when we are more experienced in how to use language and, as they can turn into a massive mind-reading exercise and can create misunderstanding.

Judge a man by his questions rather than his answers.

Voltaire, French writer, historian and philosopher.

Be A Question Designer

A habit I've developed during the last 15 years is to regularly add to my questions list. When I hear a great question, I note it down. When I get results, I reflect on the questions that led to them. In my journal, I have a special section I use to re-evaluate my questions. When out of nowhere someone asks you "that one-million dollar question", it opens the door to opportunities you never thought existed!

Just like fashion designers, every season, decade and era inspire a different set of questions.

The questions to ask when designing a question are:

- What information do I want to elicit?
- Do I want to
    - retrieve data,
    - elicit emotional states,
    - create a plan for a goal,
    - challenge,
    - connect,
    - find out what is important?

The type of questions we ask will depend on our intention.

So, as a summary, a few things to always have at the back of your mind when it comes to questions, are:

- Keep it simple, keep it clean – do not presuppose
- Keep it positive – construct images and sounds that benefit everyone
- Keep it open

The Answer Is In The Question

Question everything. Learn something.
Answer nothing.

Euripedes, Athenian playwright.

As much as we all ask ourselves tens of thousands of questions every day consciously and unconsciously, they tend always to be the same sort of questions and they've been created by our very own mindset. When we pay more attention to other people's questions, let alone listen to the far more powerful questions of a trained coach, our world expands.

Even if there is no immediate verbal answer, it does not mean that there are no inner workings taking place. This is also what makes questions in books and seminars so powerful – everyone in the audience can answer internally for themselves or carry the question within for a while and find an answer in their own time. And our unconscious is a goldmine when it comes to finding answers because it operates at so many different levels simultaneously.

People tend to mainly seek answers, but in reality, the solution nearly always lies in the question.

Powerful questioning aims to establish a strong sense of empowerment and 'invites' others to reflect and open-up to new possibilities, such as:

- to think about the problem/situation from a different perspective,
- to give them the freedom to search for answers at a deeper level,
- to make their own decisions and find out what they really want,
- to help them realise what's important to them and what gives them the most satisfaction.

A Guru In Bali

Back in 2008, I attended a silence retreat in Bali, organized by Art of Living, a volunteer-based, humanitarian and educational organization, founded by Sri Sri Ravi Shankar or Guruji (his sweet nickname).

Along with 3000 other equally excited people and in the presence of Guruji, we practiced some elaborate yoga poses, got into some serious soul searching and we were silent for 3 full days. No phones, no room service, no books, no television, no gestures, no eye contact. Just focusing internally.

Finally, we broke our silence, and the retreat was about to finish. To our surprise, it was announced that Guruji wanted to thank us for our week together and he would meet us in his hotel suite for a few minutes…grouped by country of origin.

Remember, we were 3000! Sometimes, coming from a smaller country has huge advantages! Being the only Greek, the organisation put me together in a group of 6 coming from other 'smaller countries' who I had already met during the previous days. So, while Guruji would briefly have a moment with hundreds of people from India, Australia and America, just the 6 of us would get to spend 5 minutes with him.

When our turn came, waiting outside his hotel suite, we were all thinking about that ONE important question we could ask him about our life. All except one guy, who was busy with his new gadget – a flashy smart phone. This was back in 2008. "Really? There's a holy man in there, you should be meditating, not playing with your phone!" We teased him and giggled!

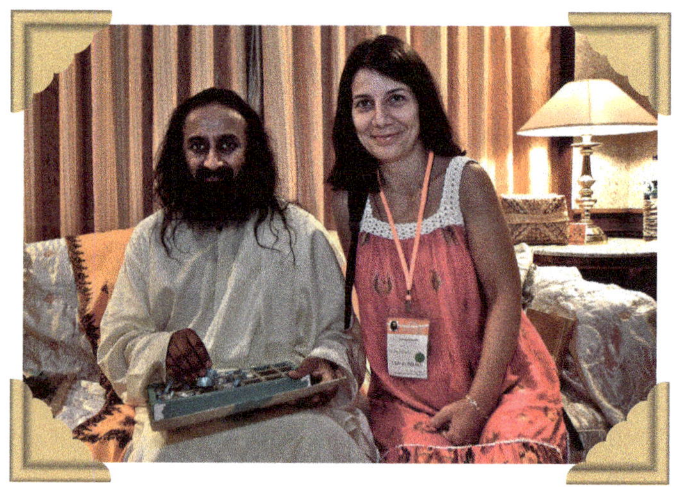

Fig. 1: With Guruji in Bali in 2007.

Then, the door opened. The security guard nodded we could go in. Guruji, sitting on a red sofa with a box of chocolates in his hands and a broad smile on his face, welcomed us. As we started making our way towards him, gadget man put his phone in his pocket…but not quickly enough…Guruji saw it. In a funny shuffling of his white robes, he took out the exact same phone and said to our friend: "Oh, please, come sit next to me and teach me how this thing works. I've just been given one."

The two men spent our 5 minutes decoding the phone's settings while we ate chocolates. As the security guards gave us the sign to leave so the next group could come in, I heard Guruji say: "Ah, and that one question you wanted to ask me…you know, well YOU know the answer."

Everyday Thinking and Doing: Consider This...

- From the people you live with and spend time with, who do you consider good listeners and what makes them good listeners?
- How often do you practice silence? What is your relationship with silence?
- As a child, what was your preference: to comply and do as you were told or question things and even rebel at times?
- What are some of the favourite questions you like asking?
- And here is a powerful question for you that holds a key to your heart: What do you love doing?'

Chapter 22

Powerful Feedback …

… receiving and giving feedback to make a difference

By Eleni

If you are irritated by every rub, how will your mirror be polished?

Rumi, a 13th-century Persian Sunni Muslim poet.

One of the first assignments I had for my NLP Coaching Certification was to ask for feedback about myself from people I was related to in my various roles in life. Fifteen years later and I can still feel both the thrill and the worry about what they would say about me. I thought in black and white terms, the fixed mindset way, that my good friends would praise me, while others would touch more on my shortcomings.

Thanking everyone for their time in sending their feedback was part of the process and I could not help asking myself, what would happen if someone said something untrue about me? How could I possibly not respond to that? This was part of the exercise too. But believing in the process, I sent my questions and waited, holding my breath.

The Feedback I Received From Jo

Some people responded right away, some took their time, some responded with just one line. And some did not answer at all. The biggest surprise came in the form of an email from my friend Jo – not the most pleasant surprise, but a game-changer. At times, he said, I came across as 'dishonest'. Those words cut right through to my heart. And yet when he explained what he meant, it made sense.

He talked about pseudo-modesty. "Eleni, when you get a promotion, you always crack a joke. You say things like 'Who knows? They might fire me in a month'. You know that won't happen, but you act as if you're apologising for your success and you downgrade it. You do this with lots of things you succeed at."

He had a point. Instantly, I connected my behaviour with my upbringing. My parents, grandparents, our whole community were all about 'modesty'. Since I was young, I had been encouraged not to share details of my A+ grades at school. "Eleni, not everyone has got good grades today. Next time, you might not get a good grade yourself. Be mindful of other people's feelings."

The same with my new shoes, our new sofa – anything. No need to 'show off'. On the one hand, this was a powerful and noble message, that helped me be empathetic and raise my emotional intelligence. On the other hand, I had picked up the habit of making fun of myself when I achieved things, not because I did not love myself but because I felt I had to keep the parts that I was most proud of to myself. It was an eye-opening moment, coming through the honest and gentle feedback from Jo.

The whole journey of receiving feedback shone a new light on my blind spots and helped me feel more appreciated at the same time. Feedback was a skill to be learnt. From providing and receiving reckless, occasional, random and low- quality feedback, I started shifting to a well-thought out process with steps and principles.

Not initially a core module of NLP as such, Florence and I worked a lot on feedback with Sue Knight during our NLP Trainer Training course. Sensory acuity, rapport, emotional intelligence, language, the meta model, goal-setting, and so on: all that NLP is, comes together in feedback and the importance of incorporating it in our daily routines. Receiving feedback, giving feedback and feeding it all back to ourselves – it's life in a nutshell. After all, we have the NLP presupposition "There is no failure, only feedback". This is an empowering belief that helps develop a growth mindset.

Receiving & Giving Feedback: *the basics*

Before receiving or giving feedback, please check:

- your emotional state
- the emotional state of the other person, and
- the best time and place to do it.

Then when giving feedback:

- keep it brief and to one or two points at one time
- rehearse it and find the appropriate language

Receiving Feedback

Before we offer anyone our view, it is useful to learn how to be at the receiving end of someone else's thoughts first. And that involves open-mindedness, resilience and high self-esteem. Often, I run into an unconscious notion that feedback means criticism. But that is a myth.

Feedback can be both positive and negative. We receive both kinds daily. What counts is understanding our own reactions to both types. How do we go about that? What is our personal take on people's comments about our behaviour? How can it help us see clearer? It can hit a nerve when someone asks us to improve or to change; similarly, we might unconsciously reject praise or feel uneasy about being given a compliment.

When you receive feedback, check any beliefs around perfectionism, failure and disappointment that could get in your way; then replace them with beliefs that promote listening to a different outlook on things, learning and flexibility that nurture feelings of 'deservingness' and 'accomplishment'. When we can do this, we will be happy when someone recognises our efforts, and we will listen attentively when they want to help us improve in certain situations. We will start to stand tall, to enjoy progress and to laugh healthily at our mistakes. We will get new learnings, get inspired and go on to inspire others.

Once we are convinced about the benefits of feedback, we should generate a habit of not only welcoming it, but also *initiating* it regularly. We want a constant flow of new insights, which in turn makes us more insightful and helps us move forward. By establishing feedback as a routine, we learn to manage our emotions much more efficiently.

Ask for feedback from people at work, friends and family. Ask for feedback from the people whose opinions you think you know as well as those whose opinions you fear the most! Remember to thank anyone who offers the observations, for their gift, time and energy. Different outlooks on situations enrich our experience. And being appreciative and considering what others tell us creates bridges and can be a tremendous factor for building rapport.

Interpreting Feedback

One day, during a course, a delegate shared that she was quite negatively surprised that most of her friends had mentioned how short for time she always seemed to be. Yes, she was busy with wonderful plans, but she also had time to relax a lot, she told us. After a few more questions, she admitted that she talked a lot about all things she had to do while she was out sharing a meal with her friends. She realised where they had got the impression that she was always short of time.

After yet more questioning, she started to wonder if their message was more about how they felt when she was with them? Could it be that by her mentioning her 'full day', they did not feel she was fully present while being with them, and therefore they were not valued by her?

Pay Attention To 'Unfair' Feedback, too.

Can people be unfair and hurtful in their comments to us? Yes! And if they are, why should we even consider their opinions in the absence of any good intentions? Because even when none of it makes sense at that moment, by 'parking' their comments it might make sense later. If you receive the same 'unfair' feedback from the same (or a different) source, it will speak volumes. At the end of the day, when our self-esteem's bucket is full, even the malicious motives of someone or jealousy are irrelevant; there are lessons to be learnt for us everywhere. Furthermore, it is getting clearer and clearer that anyone who attacks us could just not find a more ecological way to express themselves at that moment. Have envy and jealousy never happened to us?!

We may resist or ignore feedback because we have misinterpreted it, or because we have intense negative emotions from our past experiences. If we are deeply hurt by feedback, it might have more to do with previous emotional wounds, our insatiable need for approval, or an inability to let go at some level. These issues have more to do with us and our own 'reality' than the person who gives us feedback.

I would not advise anyone to sit and take nonsense and verbal abuse by anyone. This is not what this is about. It is simply about taking a moment to reflect how we 'attracted' any piece of negative feedback we receive. It is when we choose to learn from it, find the silver lining, even see a hidden compliment in it that our relationships benefit the most.

Giving Feedback

How give Positive Feedback

There is another myth that *constructive* feedback relates to 'points for correction'. I would like to challenge this idea because, from everything I've read, experienced and witnessed, there is nothing more constructive than positive feedback.

It is not negative feedback that drives people away. Mostly, it's the positive feedback they never receive – the unexpressed words of encouragement and support, the 'what works' bit, the appreciation. How often do we criticize others and how often do we acknowledge their accomplishments?

It is difficult to take feedback on how to improve, when the person delivering it does not acknowledge our strengths also. Did the 'feedbacker' take time to praise them? Was it enough? Was it done repeatedly? Regularly? Consistently? Convincingly? Enthusiastically? A person's career can reach great heights when they're around leaders who see their unique talents. A person's life can change in a heartbeat if others express their belief in them. Positive feedback embraces celebration, confidence, empathy and forgiveness. It goes hand in hand with the NLP presupposition "Everyone does their best with the resources they have available".

Positive Feedback Traps

Remember the prime directive of the unconscious (Ch. 2) that goes: "the unconscious does not process negatives"? By focusing on wrongdoings or what needs improving, our brain gets programmed by images we do not want. When we concentrate on 'a colleague being late' and ask them *not* to be late again, we in fact advise them to be late … again! Alternatively, when we pick up on the times they were on time, and acknowledge them, we unconsciously and technically help create internal representations of 'being on time'.

Let me just describe some common attempts at positive feedback that fail miserably:

- Comparing someone with their previous self, highlighting the previous mistakes: "Well done! I remember what you were like last year and how no-one could depend on you."
- Comparing someone with ourselves: "Well done! Much better than me. I'm so bad at this."
- Comparing someone with someone else who is not present (a third person): "Well done! Not like Marvin who we fired last year because no one could depend on him."

All three examples take the spotlight away from what the person does well and shifts it to what someone else does or does not. Praising by comparison and celebrating someone by bringing someone else down never achieves the desired results, and it never will. Every parent will agree to the failed practice of comparing siblings. None of the children gets a boost in their confidence. Instead of a bridge, this kind of feedback promotes friction.

How give Feedback for Improvement

If there *is* room for improvement, it's important to raise it.

Before you do, check:

- Whether you have previously offered the same person considerable and regular positive feedback.
- Your own motivation behind giving the feedback (what is it you want to achieve by offering this?).
- Whether it is the person's pattern or a one-off error.
- When delivering the feedback, make sure you are in *rapport*!

After all of the above are taken into consideration, go ahead!

The 'Giving Feedback' Tips

Regardless of whether we are providing positive or negative feedback, here are a few tips to bear in mind:

Be Clear and Take a Moment to Explain

When you say "You are amazing" in a work context, explain why you think this, and how the person's amazingness contributes to the team's great energy or company goal. Give arguments and reasons to support your positive feedback. Then your feedback becomes more memorable and easier to accept, and the person feels more cared for and valued because of your extra effort. In the same way, just saying "You're impolite" will leave another person wondering, or feeling frustrated or angry – because there is nothing specific for them to work on.

Keep It About Your Impression – It's All You Have

When you feedback your opinions, share how their actions made *you* feel and affected *you*, whether that's in a positive or negative way. Stay away from assumptions like "I can tell you're a good employee". Say instead "When you take the time to discuss my plans, it means a lot to me".

Emotional Intensity Rules

Positive feedback needs to be delivered with emotion! The unconscious (our crew) thrives on emotion, regardless of which emotion. When we develop beliefs that move us emotionally, such as when we see beauty in action and thought, our crew instantly direct its attention there – and that brings us more of it! So, the rule of thumb is: positive feedback has got to be delivered with more emotion than negative feedback.

Do the Maths, aka Be Balanced

Powerful feedback is conscious, regular and more than anything balanced feedback. This means we do not *only* offer or accept positive feedback, because that would lead us to what is called positive toxicity – a tendency to see things not as they really are, but to have an eye and an ear only for the positive side of things. This is one-sided and creates another set of problems.

Just do the maths and use the result to improve the feedback you give.

Each day, how many times do you make time to celebrate your and other people's successes? How long do you take to prepare for both positive and points for improvement feedback? Which of these types of feedback moves you the most? Find ways to measure your progress and be clear about the facts and figures where your energy goes.

A fact to consider: Putting more emphasis on what is missing, suppresses feel-good hormones. Our limiting beliefs thrive in this environment. Positive feedback triggers dopamine production and other feel-good hormones to be released from the brain – meaning people feel happier and are therefore more productive. The choice is ours!

Evaluate the Feedback You Give Regularly – Ask for Feedback About Your Feedback Skills

Run a check on your feedback quality: how is your feedback perceived? Is it coming across the way you intended? And if yes, has it helped? How do people at the receiving end feel about it? Has their self-confidence or performance increased? Think about it yourself and find out from other people how they experience it. Equally important, has your relationship with them grown? Have authenticity, trust, and openness prevailed?

'Perception is Projection' check!

Before or after you offer feedback, make sure you reflect on what you are going to share. Could what you share also apply to you too? It just so happens that more unconsciously than consciously, when we are unhappy with our own performance in something, we notice the mistakes of others more easily. Carl Jung's quote comes in handy here:

Everything that irritates us about others can lead us to an understanding of ourselves.

By thinking in a 'perception is projection' fashion, we reap the benefits ourselves of every single piece of feedback we offer to others.

Feedback Breakfast

On a Sunday morning each month, since our children were three and four years old, we have held feedback-breakfast sessions. We have always made sure the kids got their favourite food on the table and had breakfast with the big Family Book to note it all down!

Victor, our youngest, would always kick off the session with his triumphs over the past month (since the last feedback-breakfast session). I still remember how, during his very first session, he went on for twenty minutes recalling each cookie he had been offered on one single day. In comparison, Isabelle would be proud of every single friend she had made – at the supermarket, in the mall, at school, and so on. Right from the start we knew what moved them both.

Then it was our turn as parents to share what we thought we had done well, and to note it down in the Family Book. Once everyone had completed their list of successes, we would go back to Victor to hear where he thought he could improve and we all followed after him.

Then, after again everyone had spoken, three of us each time would take turns to say what we considered as the fourth family member's triumphs and points for improvement.

Ten years have passed since we introduced this habit and it still unites us. It makes us talk, reflect, bond, exchange ideas, negotiate, re-align our goals and aspirations, and ask for and give support. It is delicious!

Fig.1: Nourish your mind with effective feedback sessions!

Feedback at Work

As a leadership coach, I have the joy of working with gifted leaders who juggle multiple high-value, high risk projects and rise to all sorts of challenges. The pioneers among them embrace feedback and go out of their way to arrange 360-degrees of it! The mere fact that they hire me as a coach, proves they value feedback.

Typically, it is a confidential and anonymous form of feedback from the people they work with.

What inspires me even more is when leaders create a culture of open communication, whereby their peers and managers and anyone reporting to them are welcome to offer them any type of feedback, at any time, and are convinced that it will be appreciated, without fear of their job being in jeopardy. This is an ultra-hip soft skill – the art of believing in and leveraging other people's wisdom, and as a result maximise your potential and theirs.

Self-Feedback

Just as it is important to keep an open mind to feedback, so it is equally important that we offer ourselves feedback. From us to us – with love!

Step back at the end of the day and assess your thoughts and actions. Self-talk is powerful. It helps us build on confidence, motivation and encouragement, which perhaps we did not get from our parents, teachers or bosses. We can learn to acknowledge our accomplishments, encourage ourselves, and let go of all the negative emotions that hold us captive.

Ask for feedback from yourself and give it to yourself. Now that is *empowerment*.

The Life Spheres Coaching Model

The below is a model I created to help coaches concentrate on the essential ingredients of their craft! The truth is, being reminded of these ingredients, not only benefits coaches but everyone in any conversation.

As you go through the flow of this Coaching Model, you will notice that there is no clear beginning or end. There are words together, side by side, all essential at any moment during any interaction. Their intention is to catch your eye and help you re-focus on them. The more you feed them to your conscious and unconscious, the more these skills get integrated in your day-to-day communication.

Every Monday, in our family, it's Educational Evening; just 20 minutes of an inspiring video. From films about geography and history to lessons of kindness and contribution; from documentaries about Mozart and Einstein to series about our planet. Anything. On one of these Mondays, we watched an interesting Ted Talk about 'Frientimacy: the three requirements of all healthy friendships' by the author Shasta Nelson. The three requirements were: positivity, consistency and vulnerability. We all recognized relationships where we have all three and other relationships where we can do better in these three areas.

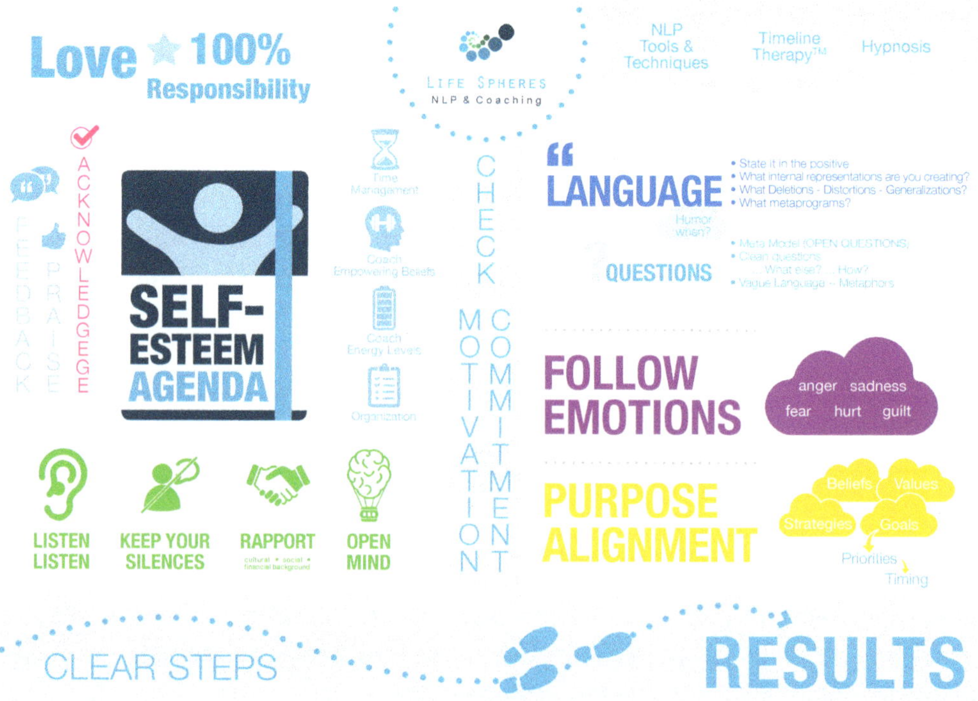

Fig. 2: The Life Spheres Coaching Model.

The Life Spheres Coaching Model (Fig.2) is hanging near our television set and as I reflected on these three requirements, my eyes roamed from one word to another connecting them with one or two or three of these requirements.

I saw the word **Love**, up left (positivity, consistency, vulnerability), then **Purpose** and **Alignment** (consistency), **Acknowledgment, Praise** and **Empowering Beliefs** (positivity), **Listen**, **Silences** and **Follow Emotions** (vulnerability).

Then, I focused on the **Self-Esteem agenda**, the key to deeper levels of connection with ourselves and others and the source for high energy levels and a life with purpose. Self-esteem, how deserving we feel deep inside.

Positivity, Consistency and Vulnerability, three powerful concepts to boost our self-esteem!

Florence's Feedback

May 2017 at the International NLP Conference organised by the Association of NLP in London and I had just finished my presentation on 'Sleight-of-mouth patterns' – 'what is that?' I hear you wonder, you will find out more in Ch.24. As everyone left the room, Florence stayed behind to offer me some feedback.

She took her time telling me what had worked in my presentation. She talked for ten minutes straight and managed to find elements in my talk that I did not even know existed, and how they had changed her way of thinking – for the better. Then she paused. She looked down and then up again and she carried on talking, about more insights and inspirations she got from it. I will remember that moment for the rest of my life. It was a vote of confidence, and it was delivered convincingly.

Fig. 3: Together with Florence at the NLP International Conference in London 2017.

Writing this book together involved giving continuous feedback on each other's chapters. We had to raise our game. We had to dig deeper into what I've shared with you in this chapter to get our points across, to keep our motivation and meet target dates! Living in different continents and in different time zones, we turned even more to our feedback practices to ensure we made successful decisions about everything in the book, while maintaining our harmonious friendship (and even taking it to a new level). The book in your hands is important to us; our friendship is more important still.

Everyday thinking and Doing: Consider This …

Think about the last time you received feedback and how you felt about it.

- Whose feedback do you appreciate?
- How often do you ask for feedback?
- Think of someone you do not really like and write twenty things that they do well. See what happens in your body and mind.

Part 7

Reset The Picture

The Anthropologist and Social Scientist Gregory Bateson pointed out that when we refer to the world is it as it is, or as we see it?

We can learn to change our own maps of how we see the world, and those of others, by reframing, asking questions, changing state and shifting perceptions.

Chapter 23

Frames and Reframing …

… shifting our thinking by changing how we look at things

By Florence

There are some people who see a great deal and some who see very little in the same things.

T. H. Huxley, English biologist and comparative anatomist.

How We See It Isn't Necessarily How It Is!

Frames are all about context and how we choose to look at things. I often remark about how much I learn from the delegates on my courses. Recently one person in particular taught me a great deal about 'reframing' things outside the training room.

At the end of my courses, I always make it clear to the delegates that I'm happy to stay in contact with them, and that my service to them as individuals carries on after the course. And I really mean this, as their learning is very important to me. Recently I got an email from someone who had been on a course with me a year previously. She sounded very upset. I felt very strongly that I wanted to help her in any way I could, but my own workload meant I had very little time for myself. I questioned whether I should get involved, and worried I was taking on too much. As it would be a few days before we could speak again, she specifically asked if I could suggest anything she might read. So I sent her a draft of my book *The Intention Impact Conundrum*, which was still being typeset at the time. Then we arranged to have a chat. By the time we talked again, she had read most of the book. She was clearly energetic and upbeat and reported delightfully how the book had helped her reframe how she saw things at work. Far from being someone that may need a lot of my time and help, it took very little from me; just by 'being there' for her, she had helped herself. By making contact with me she paid me a huge compliment – she did not place a burden on me at all. On top of that, our conversation shifted my own state and she left me laughing out loud that day.

And that is the essence of 'reframing'. Sometimes we see things from a one-dimensional, negative perspective and in that moment we can't see that it is only one angle on what is happening. The event or sequence of events that we see may be a fact, but how we interpret them (and the assumptions we make) can have a huge impact on our state, and our well-being and relationships.

Where Do We Experience Frames And Reframing In Everyday Life?

When we set out the scope of a project at home or work, we talk about desired outcomes and individuals' roles in achieving them – we are in effect setting a 'frame' so that those involved know what to expect.

We also see 'reframing' just about every time we hear politicians on the television or radio. Very often we hear this referred to as 'spin', whereby facts are reinterpreted to give a desired message. This is even sometimes done with wit and good humour, such as Ronald Reagan in 1984. During his presidential campaign he 'reframed' the concern from a journalist that he was too old to be President in this way: "I want you to know that also I will not make age an issue of this campaign. I am not going to exploit for political purposes my opponent's youth and inexperience".

More often perhaps, the idea of putting a 'positive spin' on events has gained notoriety in the political forum. Nonetheless in our everyday life, reframing in our conversations with others (and ourselves) at home or at work, can be used for much more wholesome purposes. For example, we may encourage another person to 'look at a situation in another way' and present them with an alternative interpretation of events that they had not considered, perhaps changing how they feel about it.

So in NLP the 'frames' we choose give us context and guidance for our actions or our thinking.

What Is Important About Our Choice Of Frame?

Think about the pictures or photographs in your home and the frames they are held in. Did you choose the frames yourself? What led you to choose those particular frames? Are there frames you would want to change? If so for what reason?

We frame a picture to draw attention to it, to protect it, or enhance some element of it. In NLP, the purpose of framing or reframing is much the same, it is about giving something context and meaning, and taking our attention in a particular (more resourceful) direction – and sometimes it is about offering a measure of protection also. The basic premise of this is that when we have an experience, it is not the event itself that is significant – it is how we interpret it (as discussed in Ch.17 Timeline).

It is not so much what happens to you as how you think about what happens.

Epictetus, Greek Stoic philosopher.

Examples of reframing

Consider these examples of reframing in everyday situations.

- A researcher's work is criticised by a very senior person in their field. The researcher believes this criticism diminishes their work and, as a result, they are down and depressed. If they choose to regard the senior person's feedback as showing interest in their work – that this person considers their work worthy of their attention – they may be flattered, even encouraged. With the passage of time, which often has the effect of 'reframing' situations, the researcher may look back later in their career with amusement on the episode.

- A football coach is concerned about a new team member who seems very forthright and opinionated during team meetings. Their behaviour is ruffling the feathers of the other players, who expect the new person to be taking more of a backseat. The coach then discusses this 'problem' team member with another coach, who is of the opinion that this behaviour is just what the club needs – someone to challenge and bring in fresh thinking. The coach then starts to see the potential in the new player rather than the problems they are creating.

What Can 'Meaning' And 'Context' Reframing Achieve?

Reframing is all about how you choose to view a behaviour or a situation – it is this that gives it meaning. When we choose to 'reframe' something, then our thinking about it, and hence our feelings about it, change also. There are two types of reframe that are commonly used:

'Meaning' reframe

The first example above is a 'meaning' reframe. In other words, it relates to the meaning the person attaches to something that happened. You may notice a link here to the precision questions, (questioning flawed thinking), referred to in the chapter on the Meta Model (Ch.18). These questions in many cases aim to prompt a reframe e.g. the statement "She doesn't like me" is a negative mind read. By asking the question "How do you know that?", we invite the speaker to reassess what they said. If they don't have any specific evidence to back up their original statement, they may reframe their thinking.

An example incorporating a complex equivalence is:

> "She hasn't invited me to the meeting. She doesn't want me there".
>
> This can be reframed by finding a different meaning for this behaviour to one that is causing the problem:
>
> "She may think that your time would be better spent getting on with the project, and that she can fill you in later."

Or:

"Could there be any other reason she may think attending the meeting is not the best use of your time?"

As you can see, a meaning reframe looks at the 'intention' behind the action, and when this is reassessed the feelings attached to the action are changed.

'Context' reframe

The second example above is a 'context' reframe. Behaviour in a certain context might be regarded as a problem, but when viewed in another context it could be beneficial. Some ways of changing a context may be to look at the frame size, the location, the time, or even the age of the person involved. To clarify this:

- *Frame size:* The new employee's behaviour in the example might be seen as disruptive in the context of a team meeting, but from a company perspective he or she may be someone who isn't prepared to go with the status quo and could prove to be an agent for change.
- *Location and time:* Flippant behaviour at a funeral may seem inappropriate but could be seen as motivational in an office environment.
- *Age:* A child who refuses to eat a certain food might be regarded as stubborn but viewed at another stage in their life this behaviour may relate to someone who knows their own mind and won't be pushed around.

The NLP Presuppositions (Ch. 9) are also an invitation to reframe an event, our own behaviour, or that of someone else, in a more resourceful way.

What Are The 'Standard' Frames In NLP And How Are They Used?

There a number of commonly used frames in NLP that can help to guide our own thinking and that of others we meet or work with:

'Discovery' frame

This is a useful frame for a training course or team meeting. The object is to encourage participants to learn by experimentation and allowing themselves to take 'risks'. The outcomes in this frame are learning and acceptance of the concept that there is often much greater learning when we make mistakes and take lessons from them.

'Open' frame

As with the discovery frame, this can also be used on training courses and in meetings. It creates an opportunity for participants to ask questions, to seek clarification and to share insights on any topic, as long as it is relevant to the gathering.

'Outcome' frame

This frame is about evaluating events in the light of an outcome you set out to achieve. It might be a way of framing your own thinking, or for use with a group to keep the focus. It is also useful for keeping on track when unexpected discussions or events occur.

'As-if' frame

This is useful for exploring possibilities, such as: if such and such were to happen, how could we handle it? Another use is to motivate yourself, or a group, to strive for a desired outcome by imagining you had already achieved it. For example, what you will see, hear and feel when you achieve it. Using this frame as a starting point makes it easier to plan a route to achievement and find a way around any obstacles.

'Agreement' frame

This frame is about finding some agreement or common ground and 'winning yourself a hearing' by showing respect for the views of others. It relates to phrases like

- "I agree and —" rather than "I agree but/however —".

  The words but and however tend to diminish the agreement that comes before.

- "I respect —." Or "I appreciate —."

This means you may not agree but still want to demonstrate your acknowledgement of someone else's view or intention.

'Back-track' frame

This frame can be used in two ways. To check out understanding by playing back what has been said to the speaker using their words and tonality; or to 'back track' to the last point of agreement (e.g. before a meeting gets stuck or fractious).

'Contrast' frame

This is a way of selling an idea or approach by contrasting one idea with some alternatives, which typically shows the preferred option in a better light. For example: "We can invest in this new system which will prepare us for the next stage in our development, or we can just leave things as they are till the current system breaks down and deal with the fall-out then".

'Relevance' frame

Sometimes a member of a group in a meeting can go off topic. By asking "How is that relevant?" the meeting can be brought back on track, or provide the person with an opportunity to explain why their comments are relevant. I have been very glad to use this frame in the past when I didn't think what someone was saying was relevant. When I asked the question, it seems their input was indeed relevant and the question helped them clarify their point.

'Ecology' frame

Ecology was referred to in earlier chapter. It considers the wider impact of a decision or course of action on the larger systems of which it, or we, are a part, such as a team, an organisation, customer base, family, even the planet. It relates to whether the decision or proposed action respects the integrity of yourself and others. Ideas that seem viable when first suggested can have much wider ramifications and unintended consequences.

'Appreciative' frame

In common with an 'Appreciative Enquiry'*, this frame draws attention to what is working well as well as possible forgotten resources that could be built upon to achieve an outcome. This is not a 'traditional' NLP frame, yet it can be very useful for assessing a situation, as opposed to going down the "What is the problem?" route. The key benefits of the appreciative frame are that it raises morale and builds on current strengths. An example could be when seeking to improve internal customer service, is to look at the successful processes in external customer service.

* Appreciative Inquiry is an approach to organisational change which focusses on doing more of what is working well.

Everyday Thinking And Doing: Consider This …

- Think about interactions you have had with colleagues or associates in which you have been left angry or unhappy. Then consider:
  - How do you know what their intention was in that situation?
  - Could there be another intention behind their behaviour that you haven't considered, which may change your feelings about the situation?
  - Could their behaviour be useful or desirable in another context?
- Consider a difficult meeting that you have attended recently. Could the use of one (or more) of the standard frames set out above have led to a more satisfactory or smoother outcome?
- Think about a forthcoming meeting. Given the agenda and what you know of the participants, which of the frames might you choose to adopt that would be helpful?

Sleight of Mouth Patterns …

… prompting new perspectives using questions

By Eleni

The limits of my language mean the limits of my world.

Ludwig Wittgenstein, philosopher.

Here's a parent–child conversation that you might recognise:

Child: "Everybody's talking behind my back at school."

Parent: "How do you know everybody's talking behind your back?"

Child: "Erwin told me."

Parent: "How does Erwin know everybody's talking behind your back?"

Child: "I don't know."

Parent: "The fact that Erwin told you that doesn't mean it is true. It just means Erwin thinks that, which doesn't say much about anything else."
Child: Looks at parent.

Parent: "I remember when I was your age, Laura said something similar to me, but then I found out she wanted to be my friend and didn't know any other way to get my attention.

Child: Looks at parent with more interest.

Parent: "Who specifically do you think talks behind your back? Do you think even Suzanne does, who was here yesterday, who you played with all day?"
Child: "Of course not! Suzanne would never do that!"

Parent: "You see? That's not everybody. So, what's more important? You spending the rest of your evening trying to figure out something that doesn't make sense, or going outside to play with Betty who just called and asked what time you will be coming out?"

Child (smiley, calmer): "Thanks, mom, I'll go out and find her" landing a kiss on the parent's cheek.

Next day:

Parent: "What happened with Erwin?" (unsure whether it was a good idea to bring it up again)

Child: "Who?"

Sleight of Hand – Sleight of Mouth

We have the power of choice over our response to any statement. We've already touched on some linguistic tools for doing that, including the 'reframes' in the last chapter. It's time to expand our choices and reframes even more about expressed limitations that come our way. Robert Dilts noticed how Richard Bandler would always 'win' an argument by responding in some specific ways. Dilts decided then to create a list of possible responses, with the purpose of challenging any limitations in the thinking and believing of another person, during an argument. His list became what we call the fourteen Sleight-Of-Mouth (S.O.M.) patterns.

Sleight of hand is a mix of techniques used mostly in close-up magic, whereby magicians can manipulate objects, like cards and coins, without the audience noticing. Advanced sleight of hand requires months or years of practice.

Magicians direct our attention and re-frame our memories, and they temporarily alter our reality.

Similarly, S.O.M. patterns can magically loosen up our fixed ideas and open the way to new beliefs and possibilities. They prompt us to re-visit beliefs, and challenge those that hold us back. We get outside our own 'box' – to a bigger 'box' – until eventually we get to a whole new building or planet! They are tools that help us work on a more flexible mindset every single day.

We cannot solve our problems with the same thinking we used when we created them.

Albert Einstein, theoretical physicist.

No, as Mr Einstein shared with us almost a century ago, we cannot. And we cannot change our thinking if we keep using the same language and holding the same beliefs. The S.O.M. patterns serve to shake up any 'limiting ideas' that keep us stuck and powerless; they open up new points of view and eventually replace limiting thoughts with empowering ones.

The four aims of the S.O.M. patterns are to:

- change the meaning
- change the cause
- change or challenge the comparison
- change neurological levels.

The Basic Structures of S.O.M. Patterns

First of all, let us take a look at a couple of the most common structures of **beliefs**. You are already acquainted with the Meta Model distortions of 'Cause & Effect' and 'Complex Equivalence'.

These are a starting point for applying the S.O.M. patterns, here they are again:

1. If 'A' … then 'B' (or 'A' because 'B')

2. 'A' = 'B' (or 'A' means 'B').

Here are some examples of these types of beliefs.

1. *If* I had more patience, *then* I would be able to keep my job.
2. *Because* I come from a poor family, I will never have the same opportunities as rich people have.
3. The fact that she doesn't call me *means* she doesn't like me.

We had the honour and the pleasure that Robert Dilts has read our book and of course this particular chapter. He offered his invaluable feedback and he also shared some powerful reminders about the S.O.M. patterns, that truly help us 'be the difference that makes the difference':

- The goal of the effective use of Sleight of Mouth patterns is to awaken and widen people's maps of the world. We want to ensure that we deliver them through a curious and supportive mindset.
- Written examples of Sleight of Mouth are tricky because tone and relationship are so important for how the words are received. Something intended to be helpfully provocative can sound confrontational or even nasty.
- Eventhough a S.O.M. pattern can come in the form of question, an answer, or just a statement, framing something as a question always makes it easier to receive and reflect upon.

Before I give you some S.O.M. patterns examples, let me briefly go through each one, and explain what they are all about.

In Fig. 1 overleaf I have split them into groups of three and four, each group picked out in a different colour, simply to make the learning process easier. The groupings are simply so your brain can retrieve them and use them more easily.

1 **Metaframe:** We often start these with "I imagine you are saying that because …".

2 **Reality strategy:** The key question here has to do with how we know something is like this. For example: "How do you know …?".

3 **Model of the world:** This offers a different point of view – i.e. someone else believes something different.

4 **Apply to self**: We take the key words of each part of the belief, and we make up a sentence with them, not necessarily related to the initial belief but using the same words (or derivatives of them).

Sleight of Mouth Patterns

Persuasion skills – Belief reframes

Reality Strategy
How do you know this is true/untrue?

Model of the World
Point out how other people have different beliefs

Intent
Mind-read the intent of the belief (Secondary gain)

Counter Example
Offer or ask the exception of the belief

Meta Frame
Expose the real, deeper reason of the stated belief

Change Frame Size
How would the belief look different if viewed in different context?

Apply to Self
Create a new statement from the words stated in the belief

Cause & Effect — Belief

Cause → Effect (Evidence) — Meaning

A = B
Complex Equivalence

Redefine
A does not mean **B**, it means **C** and this is **D**

Chunk Up
Exaggerate to illustrate the silliness of the belief

Chunk Down
How specifically does A = B

Metaphor
What story with parallel can you offer?

Hierarchy of criteria
What is more important than that?

Consequence
What could happen as a result?

Another outcome
What is the real Issue?

Fig. 1: Sleight of Mouth

5 **Intent:** Here we seek to understand or guess the motive behind a statement – what it is that they want to gain with this belief? We've already talked about 'secondary gain' – this S.O.M. pattern aims to find the secondary benefits of a limiting belief. Otherwise if there weren't any, we would not still keep it.

6 **Consequence:** The questions here are usually in the form of "What will happen (or not happen) if …?" This forces the other person to see the consequences of maintaining their belief.

7 **Chunk down:** The key word here is 'specifically', as in "What is it you think specifically about …?" We want to ask for specifics.

8 **Chunk up:** Here, we are free to make a wild assumption and exaggerate it to the point that the other person's statement becomes ridiculous.

9 **Metaphor/analogy:** As you might expect, this offers an analogy, or a story or some example that provides a different opinion from the one they stated.

10 **Change frame:** Exactly as the name of this SOM suggests – change the frame, by making it smaller or bigger.

11 **Hierarchy of criteria:** A typical question here would be "What is more important – A or B?" Take what they seem to find important and put it opposite another important value of theirs. This can require a bit of guess work!

12 **Counter-example:** Just like the Model of the World above, offer them another example. This usually starts with something like: "Really? Has there been (or not) a time that (it was not as it you stated)?"

13 **Another outcome:** The phrase here is "The issue is not *this* – the issue is *that*".

14 **Redefine:** Simply put: "A does not mean B. A means C and that means D".

Eventhough the possibilities for creating S.O.M. patterns are unlimited, I hope I manage to keep things as simple as possible, so you start incorporating them in your everyday conversations right away – practice and start experiencing the benefits.

So here are some simple examples using the three limiting beliefs already given and Robert suggested some S.O.M. examples of his own which I underlined for clarity for you to marvel – treasures coming straight from the master!

Limiting Belief 1: "If I had more patience, then I would have been able to keep my job."

1. **Metaframe:** "I imagine you have that belief because you are impatient to become more patient."
2. **Reality strategy:** "How do you know that?"
3. **Model of the world:** "What people do you know who got acknowledgment from their bosses for their patience?"
4. **Apply to self:** "Impatience opens doors to opportunities."
5. **Intent:** "What do you want to achieve by being impatient?"
6. **Consequence:** "What will happen if you keep thinking about the job you've lost?"
7. **Chunk down:** "How specifically did your impatience cause you to lose your job?"
8. **Chunk up:** "So if you were patient, would you just be in that job forever?"
9. **Metaphor/analogy:** Someone once said 'To be impatient is to be hooked on the future'
10. **Change frame:** "In the bigger picture of employment, successful people likely have a combination of patience and impatience about the right things."
11. **Hierarchy of criteria:** "What's more important? Thinking about what went wrong or creating new opportunities in your career?"
12. **Counter-example:** "Has anyone else been impatient and still kept their job?"
13. **Another outcome:** "Is the real issue whether you can keep a job or not, or is it what you learn from what happened?"
14. **Redefine:** "Is it about the job, or is it about your self-confidence and the degree to which you can now strengthen your self-belief?"

Limiting Belief 2: "The fact that she does not call me *means* she does not like me."

1. **Metaframe:** "Do you believe that the only reason that you would not call someone is that you don't like them?"
2. **Reality strategy:** "How do you know that when someone doesn't call, they don't like you?"

3 **Model of the world:** "My brother doesn't call me during the week because he knows we're busy and doesn't want to disturb us."

4 **Apply to self:** "You're so like me – we like connecting!"

5 **Intent:** "What do you want to achieve by waiting by the phone?"

6 **Consequence:** "What will happen if you keep thinking about her not liking you?"

7 **Chunk down:** "Can you say specifically in what way she doesn't like you?"

8 **Chunk up:** "My cousin hasn't called me for ten years – does that mean he doesn't like me?"

9 **Metaphor/analogy:** "Last year I was into this man and we used to bump into each other wherever I went. He seemed interested in me, but even though he could have got my number from mutual friends, he didn't. A year later, we started working for the same company and after we became friends, one Thursday, I found a note he'd left me with some flowers asking me out."

10 **Change frame:** "As you look back over all of the calls you have received in your life, have they all been from people who like you?"

11 **Hierarchy of criteria:** "What's more important, her calling you or you calling her to find out if she needs anything?"

12 **Counter-example:** "Has there been anyone who did call you and didn't like you?"

13 **Another outcome:** "The issue isn't whether she likes you, but whether you like yourself."

14 **Redefine:** "It's not about who's calling who, it's about being willing to re-evaluate your expectations and that means giving freedom to people to do as they want."

Limiting Belief 3: "I come from a poor family, therefore I'll never have the same opportunities that rich people do."

1 **Metaframe:** "Have you ever considered that what allows people to discover and create opportunities is more likely a function of how rich their mental model of the world is than the amount of money they have?"

2 **Reality strategy:** "How would you know if you had the same opportunities as rich people?"

3 **Model of the world:** "My grandfather comes from a poor family and he believed in using his own initiative and hard work to create opportunities."

4 **Apply to self:** "There's a poverty of spirit when we give up."

5 **Intent:** "What do you want to achieve by saying you're poor and don't have the same opportunities as rich people?"

6 **Consequence:** "What will happen if you keep thinking about the possibilities you didn't have?"

7 **Chunk down:** "What opportunities do rich people have specifically?"

8 **Chunk up:** "So, if you're rich, you just clap your hands and things magically happen?"

9 **Metaphor/analogy:** "Birds aren't rich, but they can fly!"

10 **Change frame:** "If you looked carefully at history, I wonder whether you might find that there were just as many rich people trapped by their wealth and poor people driven by their circumstances to see or create opportunities that the wealthy were incapable of perceiving?"

11 **Hierarchy of criteria:** "What's more important? Thinking about rich people or creating chances to move forward?"

12 **Counter example:** "Has there been anyone who wasn't rich and had the chance to lead a successful life?"

13 **Another outcome:** "The real issue isn't whether you're poor or not. The real issue is whether you're smart enough to find ways to progress in life."

14 **Redefine:** "It isn't the poor who lack opportunity. It's the poor rich people sitting crying about their bad luck and stuck in a negative mindset."

Self-SOM-ing!

Of course, what makes S.O.M. patterns even more interesting is their use *internally*. Remember all those crew members who are negotiating inside us all the time? When we pass on the SOMs patterns to our unconscious as a way of thinking and talking, we have more choices in the way we communicate with people around us. But also, more than anything, we expand and improve ways of communicating between our own parts. It all just happens 'under the hood', with the amazing result that solutions suddenly emerge out of nowhere. Our destiny changes course miraculously!

In his book, *Beliefs: Pathways to Health and Wellbeing*, co-authored with Tim Hallbom and Suzi Smith, Robert Dilts uses some of the S.O.M. patterns in the domain of health and wholeness. With the power of metaphors, counter-examples and more S.O.M. patterns, the authors share a whole range of conversations with astonishing twists and turns.

Ethics and Ecology

Sleight of hand makes magicians powerful. It is a tool. Sleight-of-mouth patterns are also a tool in our own hands, and are used every day by journalists, politicians, public speakers, managers and parents, both consciously and unconsciously. It's in our own hands to learn how to use them, to maximize our conversational experiences as well as our winning minds.

A car can save a life, or it can take a life. Social media, when used appropriately, benefits us all; when not, it can have detrimental effects. They are just tools. The same goes for S.O.M. patterns, what we do with it sits with each of us.

The more we use them, the more we also learn to identify (consciously and unconsciously) the most effective ones to use as for responding in any discussion.

Happy to share?

Before the kick-off of the corporate courses Life Spheres delivers to organizations, each participant has a brief 5-10 minute talk with myself to make sure I answer his/her questions and that the training is something they welcome and happy to go to. As I share with them that the Life Spheres courses are quite experiential and hands on, once in a while, a participant will share back during these 1-to-1 sessions, that they are a bit shy or introverted and not sure to what extent they can share anything at all with their colleagues.

My response varies of course but the common factor is a reframe SOM pattern. Most times, it sounds something like this and if you read between the lines, you might already recognise some of the patterns.:

"For me, sharing is not an obligation, it is making sure from my part that should anyone want to share, they get the time and space to do so. Everyone is invited to share what they want to share, when they want to share it. It is not about having to share, it is about you having the opportunity to express your opinions and experiences and feel listened to."

Award-Winning Night!

It's a Thursday evening and I receive a call from a client who was nominated for an award at one of the most prestigious nights of the year for his industry. He is distraught. For the previous two years he was also nominated, but on both occasions someone else won. He's not sure he can go through it again. He says, "If I don't get it for the third year in a row, I'll be the biggest loser in the industry".

Me: "I can imagine you'd rather stay home and not have to face anyone if you don't win it."

Client: "No, it's not that. I want to go and face everyone no matter what happens."

Me: "Okay, so what will happen if you continue thinking you won't win?"

Client: "I won't win and I'll feel horrible whether I stay home or not."

Me: "Has there ever been anyone who didn't win for a couple of years and then finally got it?"

Client: "Are you kidding? Most of them didn't win it the first time. Michael won it after five years!"

Me: "So are all these people losers according to you?"

Client: "You know the answer to that."

Me: "It seems to me that the issue is not whether you win or lose, go or not go. The real issue is you haven't yet felt proud about your nomination and given yourself a big pat on the shoulder for what you've already achieved."

Client: "Okay, I'm running late now. Thank you and wish me luck!"

Next day:

Client: "I won."

Me: "You're only saying that because you can't wait to take me out and celebrate!"

Client (laughing): "Tonight?"

What Neuroscience Has To Say?

Neuroscience and magic get closer and closer by the day. In their book *Sleight of Mind*, Stephen Macknik, Susana Martinez-Conde and Sandra Blakeslee offer a glimpse into the neuroscience of magic and the secret principles that can unlock questions about how our minds work.

As V.S. Ramachandran MD PhD (author of *Phantoms in the Brain*) says: "This is a highly original book. Science and magic have much in common. They both take seemingly inexplicable events and provide elegantly simple answers that enthral the observer. The authors have done an admirable job in exploring this idea and suggest ways in which the two disciplines can cross fertilize each other."

Singing S.O.M. Patterns in London, May 2017

I was about to present on the SOM patterns – a subject considered by many to be technical and complicated. As you know, there are fourteen patterns and I had just an hour and a half to cram them all in. Then I got an idea. What about using singing and dancing, two of my ultra-favourite states, to move body and mind to present them?

Believe it or not, I spent two months looking for songs that had the same lyrics as the SOMs patterns, hoping I could make them more memorable inside my head, in my communication, and for my audience. I even went so far as to use the S.O.M. patterns to challenge any limiting beliefs around me singing these songs for my presentation at the conference. I guess I enjoyed the risk and, if nothing else, we all moved on the beat of the S.O.M. patterns.

I put pictures of the singers on stickers and glued them to both sides of a CD, to use as coasters for our cups. No, the CDs did not have the songs on them. They were simply meant to get people's attention when they were having coffee with a friend. They would look at the coaster and choose one to practice during their conversation, like "How will I know?" by Whitney Houston (reality strategy) or "Your intention is good" by Elvis Costello for (intent).

I guess, I find song lyrics, sounds and music the ultimate reframes in our lives, metaphors to move people's minds and touch their hearts.

Everyday Thinking and Doing: Consider This …

SOM patterns are part of our everyday life. Take these three suggestions and transform your reality daily – easily and while having fun!

- Start by identifying limiting beliefs you hear from other people or your inner voice. Then pick up two of the SOM patterns and create relevant questions or statements for this belief.
- Which S.O.M. pattern did you notice you already use in your conversations?
- Who do you consider to be a great 'reframer' in your environment? How do they do it?

Anchoring …

… access resourceful states easily

By Florence

Let no one ever come to you without leaving better and happier. Be the living expression of God's kindness: kindness in your face, kindness in your eyes, kindness in your smile.

Mother Teresa, Catholic Saint.

What Is An Anchor?

A few years ago I joined Eleni on the beautiful Greek island of Amorgos where she runs NLP courses every summer. It's not on the 'hot' tourist trail, so the peace, chilled-out atmosphere and natural beauty is a magnet for those 'in the know'. One day, in the gorgeous Aegiali bay, a yacht appeared and dropped anchor (**Fig.1**). The rumour soon got around that the occupants were Tom Hanks and his family. We didn't get to see him, unfortunately, hard though we stared down from the cliffs, but he stayed at anchor there for nearly a week. Clearly, he knew that when you find a place you want to be, the best thing is to drop anchor and enjoy the experience!

Fig. 1: A grainy image from Aegiali Bay of the yacht in question!

Anchors in NLP do not refer to boats, but they do serve the same purpose: they hold us in a particular state (good or bad!). Anchors are also naturally occurring; think about your reactions when you drive on a motorway and see flashing blue lights coming up behind you, notice how quickly the feelings you associate with them come to you. Or think about when you return home after being away for a while and see the faces of your loved ones; or certain smells that bring back feelings, like the perfume or aftershave of someone you love, the smell of sun cream, or the smell of hospitals. What about a favourite piece of music that comes randomly on the radio and stops you in your tracks? All of these are anchors – and of course as Mother Teresa taught, we are anchors for other people too! Some anchor pleasant states and others less so. Nonetheless, they demonstrate a power that is worth harnessing – which is why anchoring has become perhaps the most widely used NLP technique.

Anchors are usually quite personal to us, in that a specific 'stimulus' does not necessarily create the same feelings in another person. For example, when I come home, I bury my nose in my cat's fur or in my dog's coat. They smell good to me. But more than that, their smell is powerfully linked to the love and comfort they bring.

And it is strong feelings that create anchors of any kind. The limbic system structures in the brain are involved in many of our emotions and motivations, such as fear and anger, also feelings of pleasure as those experienced from eating and sex. It also determines which memories and stored and where, based on how large an emotional response an event invokes. At the start of each of my courses I invite the delegates to set the Ground Rules and most times one of their rules is to have fun learning; I usually respond to this by pointing out that we tend to remember things we enjoy! I do not elaborate on what I mean – their naughty laughter suggests we are thinking on the same lines! I like to think this goes some way to anchoring the learning on my courses.

An example of the power of 'naughtiness' as an anchor is when Eleni and I trained together as NLP trainers (with Sue Knight in France). We each had to a run a session for the group and mine was on anchoring. As the group were experienced in NLP I thought I would do something that is less often referred to, known as Sliding Anchors. While I was explaining to the group how to do it, I innocently explained that they needed six inches of skin that could be easily accessed for drawing your finger down it. I had in mind a finger or stretch of forearm of course, (certainly no other part of someone's anatomy!); but it was too late, the group had dissolved into fits of laughter. When they regained their composure. Someone said, "Wow that's some way to set an anchor!". Now I giggle every time I deliver an anchoring session. (Eleni was still laughing when she persuaded me to include this story.)

So, an anchor simply makes a connection between a stimulus of some sort and an emotional state. And what can be created inadvertently or naturally can also be done deliberately, as you will learn.

The Origins Of NLP Anchoring

In their book *Frogs to Princes*, John Grinder and Richard Bandler set out how to deliberately set anchors, specifically for anchoring powerful positive states. They were inspired by the way that Milton Erickson induced resourceful states in his clients when they were in a trance state (by using his language). Bandler realised that often people will feel good for a specific reason, and in his view the aim of having an anchor was to feel good at any time for no particular reason.

Anchors are built by association and repetition. The importance of repetition for the unconscious mind in the learning process was discussed fully in the chapter on The Unconscious Mind (Ch.2). You're probably familiar with the story of Pavlov's dogs, who were taught to associate the ringing of a bell with the act of being fed. After some time, just the sound of the bell made them salivate – they did not need to see or smell their food.

A key element for setting an effective anchor is to start with an intense experience and build the anchor by repetition, then several anchors can be 'stacked' one on top of the other.

How To Set And Stack An Anchor

A simple and convenient way to set an access an anchor is, (as I attempted to explain in on the course France!) is on your hands or ears. Here is the process:

Step 1: Choose your 'state'. The starting point is to choose the 'state' you want to anchor (e.g. a state of confidence, calmness, excitement or relaxation).

Step 2: Pick intense experiences. Then think about specific times in the past when you have felt the chosen state strongly. It is good to set your anchor by thinking of at least three intense experiences of the state.

Step 3: Set your anchor point. Decide where you are going to set your anchor point. It needs to be easily accessible, but not in an area that you would touch inadvertently (e.g. the palm of your hand; this would be easily touched and the desired state would be quickly deteriorated by other less desirable states. Popular choices are the ear lobes or finger knuckles).

Step 4: Set your anchor at the right time. The optimum time to set your anchor is when the feeling is growing in intensity – *before* it peaks and starts to dissipate, as shown in **Fig. 2.**

Step 5: Press on your chosen anchor point. Think back on your first chosen experience in which you felt the desired state. Associate into it, and as the feeling starts to intensify press down on the anchor point with one of your fingers. Make sure you take your finger off

before the state dissipates. Repeat this process as you recall the other experiences of this state, thereby stacking each new experience on top of the other.

Step 6: Revert to your normal state. Shake your hands or walk around for a few seconds.

Step 7: Test your anchor. Do this by pressing on your chosen anchor point and noticing whether (or how strongly) the chosen state returns.

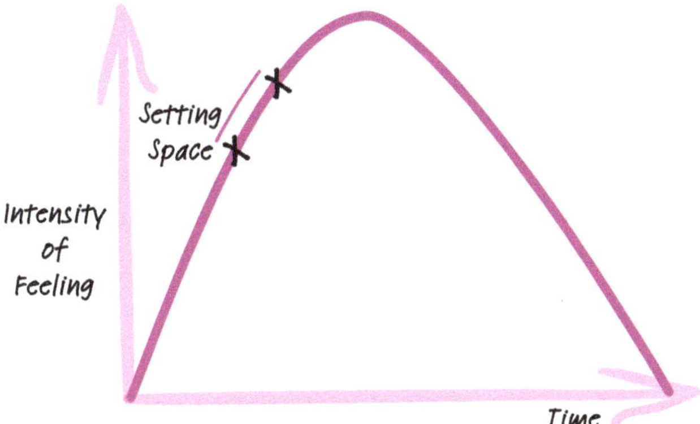

Fig. 2: The optimum time to set an anchor.

If the anchored state is not sufficiently strong you can repeat the process by recalling further experiences of the desired state. Thereafter, you can continue to stack more anchors on the anchor point whenever you experience the desired state.

Creating Anchors Using Physical Movement And Visioning

Circles of Excellence

On one occasion I received a worried phone call from a friend who was preparing to do a business presentation. During her last presentation she had suffered a panic attack and this time round she wanted to stay calm and confident. She knew about the Circles of Excellence technique and asked me to take her through it over the phone. This is the process we followed.

Step 1: First, we established how she wanted to feel during her presentation (to stay in a calm, confident state).

Step 2: I asked her to think of three situations in which she felt that state, from any aspect of her life.

Step 3: I then asked her to set out a 'Circle of Excellence' on the floor in front of her. This meant envisioning an area about the size of a hula

hoop, flat on the floor, and telling me about its colour and appearance. I asked her to make it the exact shade and brightness that she wanted it to be. Some people envision a circle with a shaft of light shining on it, or one that is showered with sparkles. As the facilitator, you go with what your client chooses.

Step 4: I invited her to think of her first situation and associate into it and, as the feeling intensified, to step into her circle. When she was inside the circle, I asked her to 'ramp up' the feeling and then step out of the circle, just before the feeling peaked, thus leaving the feeling in the circle.

Step 5: We repeated the same process for her other two situations.

Step 6: She tested her circle by stepping back in to it. When she felt that the feeling was strong enough, I asked her to 'pack up' her circle and take it to another area of the room. This represented where she would be doing her presentation.

Step 7: She then unpacked her circle and stepped into it, this time associating into her presentation. She was delighted to find that the feeling of calmness and confidence was still there! And her feelings about doing the presentation had shifted. She 'packed up' her circle with the intention of taking it with her on presentation day.

We carried out this process over the phone because we were unable to meet and because she already had some familiarity with it. The process is robust and relatively easy for anyone who is unfamiliar with NLP. My friend was delighted to report her presentation went well, and she has continued to use her personal Circle of Excellence ever since, stacking more good states on to the original anchor and making it very powerful indeed.

Another way to achieve a desired state

Sometimes clients find it hard to think of three situations in which they had a strong experience of their desired state. In these circumstances a useful alternative is to get them to think of someone who demonstrates the state the desire, and associate into that person. They can then take the other person's state into their circle….in effect modelling them !

Chaining Anchors: creating an anchor when the current and desired states are far apart

If the 'Desired' and 'Current' states are very far apart, the gap may be too great and some interim steps are needed to get the person to their desired state e.g. a person may be currently terrified of public speaking and they want to get to enjoyment of the experience. This process is called Chaining Anchors, which you can do using spaces on the floor:

Step 1: Start by helping the client identify their 'desired' and 'current' states as in the example above it could be moving from terror to enjoyment of public speaking.

Step 2: Next, help the client to identify the intermediate steps to get to their desired state (usually 3-4). In this example these could be: annoyance at the 'terror' reaction (note this is an 'away from' state, Ch. 13 Metaprograms), then into more 'towards' states of calmness and anticipation of success. Mark out spaces on the floor for each of these in a sequence you can step through as in **Fig.3**:

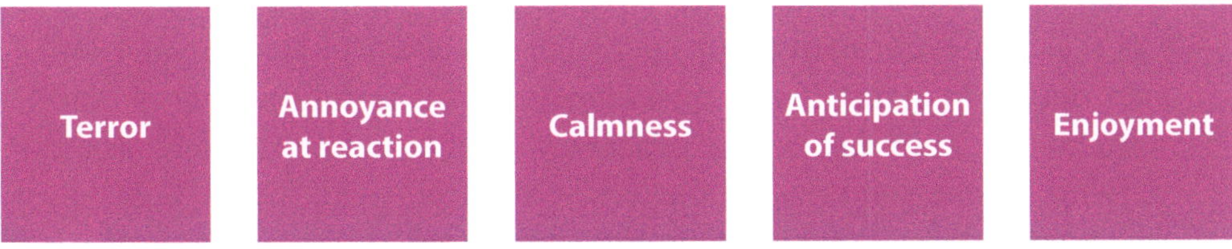

Fig. 3: Chaining anchors on the floor.

Step 3: Now using the process for setting an anchor, get the client to step into each space in turn and elicit and anchor that state to the space. You can reinforce this by getting your client to simultaneously anchor the states onto each knuckle). Be careful to 'break state' in between each one. Now for the chaining.....

Step 4: Get the client to step into the first space (current state) and fire the anchor, as soon as it peaks, release the anchor by moving into the next space firing off a new anchor. When this peaks, release that anchor by moving into the next space and firing off that anchor. Do this all the way to the desired state. In this final anchor encourage the client to make this state as intense as possible by ramping up the colour, light, sounds and feelings to be just right. (See Ch.26 Submodalities.)

Step 5: Test by firing off the anchor for the first (current) state, if the process has worked the client will rapidly go the desired state. If not repeat steps 3 and 4 until the changes are embedded.

Step 6: Future pace: get the client to imagine a time in the future where they would previously have had the undesired reaction and get them to notice how they are thinking about this differently now.

This process can be done as described by one person taking another through it or you can do it for yourself. If for any reason you don't choose to use spaces on the floor to mark out the different states, you can set each of the states on adjacent knuckles and follow the process in exactly the same way.

Everyday Thinking And Doing: Consider This …

- Take some time to notice positive anchors you already have in your personal or work life. For example, you may have particular clothes that make you feel good during a meeting or an interview, or a piece of music that relaxes you. Noticing these natural and spontaneously occurring anchors can be very useful and they are often the most powerful.
- The next time you find yourself in a situation where you are feeling in a particularly resourceful state, anchor it! And use every opportunity to stack up other positive states on it as they occur.
- Is there an event coming up in which you want to ensure you're in an optimum state? If so, consider what that optimum state is, and anchor it using any of the processes outlined. Alternatively, ask a friend to take you through the Circle of Excellence process. This will allow you to really focus on your desired state.

Submodalities and The SWISH Pattern …

… using the finer details of our representational systems to effect change

By Eleni

Arrange whatever pieces come your way.

Virginia Woolf, English Writer.

Change A Dark Day To Light

A decade ago, and my mother and I are chatting away in her kitchen. She doesn't look her normal sparkly self. I feel the urge to ask her: "Mom, could you close your eyes and think of a happy event in your life?". My mother closes her eyes and within seconds the tears are rolling down her cheeks. She is shaking. I ask her to open her eyes and tell me what happened. With the saddest look on her face, she tells me that she could not find any happy events anywhere in her mind. It was all black.

My heart skips a beat and I ask her to close her eyes again and take a pin with her (mentally in her mind) and if it is still dark, to start poking it with the pin until she finds a ray of light. Sure enough, a couple of minutes later, she starts crying again, but different tears; she has managed to see my birth.

You see, with my father's passing just a couple of years before that moment in the kitchen, and grief was still overshadowing everything else. Not that grief ever miraculously disappears. I once heard someone say, "We don't let go of grief, we move forward with it". But it only took one small sharp pin to create a hole to unveil the rest of my mother's reality and she was at least able to smile again.

Emotions Move Us!

When we talk about family, education and work, more and more often you may hear the term 'Emotional Intelligence', or EQ. Most scientists nowadays will tell you that it is even more important than our Intelligence Quotient – what we know as IQ. Smart is one thing, emotionally mature is a whole different game. Being aware of and managing emotions makes a difference!

Let's not forget that the little emotions are
the great captains of our lives
and we obey them without realising.

Vincent van Gogh, painter.

Memories and experiences turn into beliefs and values, and they carry emotions. We talk about happy memories and sad memories; we actually speak of memories where the meaning we gave to them elicits a specific emotion.

The degree of ease or tension in our bodies comes from our self-talk. Our spiritual, emotional and mental state influences our physical one. As important as fitness, sports and nutrition may be for our health, it is by regularly taking care of our emotional world and bringing balance to it that protects our 'ship'.

What Are Submodalities?

In Chapter 11, Florence took you on a tour through the representational systems – visual, auditory, kinaesthetic, olfactory and gustatory – so you know that we use our senses to see, hear and feel the world outside us, and with their help we also represent the world inside us and recall our memories. These representational systems are also called modalities.

A picture can be in black and white or full colour. A sound can be loud or quiet. A taste can be sweet or bitter. A smell can be strong or mild. A feeling can be felt in different parts of the body and have variable intensity. These aspects of modalities were introduced into NLP by Richard Bandler, and are called submodalities. They are the building blocks of our experience, we store and represent experiences in different ways depending on the emotions they evoke. So by changing the submodalities associated with how we internally represent a memory or a belief, this gives us the ability to influence and change any emotions associated with them.

This is exactly what Florence did on that plane in Ch.1, when she was thinking of an unpleasant conversation. She changed the submodalities of her internal representations, by letting go of an undesired emotion and as a result feel better. She changed the colour and the size of the image in her mind, then dissociated herself from it by sending the image to a distant cloud, far away from the plane. In this way, she re-arranged her 'visual' submodalities.

You can do the same with any representation. Notice each time you shift a submodality – does the emotion get more or less intense? This is the main principle behind shifting submodalities, which is that you are actually able to adjust them. Testing submodalities one by one shows you how your brain stores memories, beliefs and values, and allows you to get to know yourself better and take control of your emotions.

Types Of Submodalities In Each Representational System

Some of the different types of visual, auditory and kinaesthetic submodalities are shown in **Fig. 1,** overleaf.

Visual Submodalities	Auditory Submodalities	Kinaesthetic Submodalities (sensations & feelings)
Location (use both hands to show where in relation to your body you see the image inside your mind)	Location (where/what is the source of the sound?)	Location (whereabouts in your body do you feel sensations/ feelings?)
Size of picture (be specific)	Sounds or Voices?	Intensity (strong or weak?)
Associated or Dissociated?	Volume (loud or soft?)	Movement (continuous or in waves?)
Colour (black & white or colour?)	Pitch (high or low?)	Temperature (hot or cold?)
Brightness (bright or dim?)	Speed (fast or slow?)	Pressure (hard or soft?)
Motion (moving or still?)	Duration (continuous or intermittent?)	Texture (rough or smooth ?)
Speed (if moving – fast or slow?)	Harmonious or discordant	Speed (e.g. of heartbeat)
Framing (does it have a frame around it or not?)	Rhythm	Duration (continuous or intermittent?)

Fig. 1: List of Visual, Auditory and Kinaesthetic Submodalities.

Beliefs, Emotions And Re-arrangements!

I imagine that many of us, while experiencing the emotion of anger, have heard someone saying something like: "You have no reason to be angry. You have your family, and food, and a roof above your head. You should be grateful." Similar reactions might create a series of limiting beliefs such as:

- Anger, sadness, fear and pain are bad.
- Do not talk about negative feelings, they bring you – and others – down.
- Smile at all times.
- Forget what happened!

I'm sure you can recognise several generalisations, deletions and distortions here that could be challenged – this list is a good recipe for an *un*authentic life. We all carry limiting beliefs about turning a deaf ear to our inner voice, choosing sacrificial situations over win–win ones, not expressing ourselves, not taking any kind of risks. These statements are thinking habits that hand out *distress, intolerance, entitlement, the need for instant gratification, feeling incomplete and tendencies for perfectionism.*

Now you understand how our unconscious organises our beliefs and memories, by changing their submodalities, we can 'move' those beliefs and memories and look at them in a different way as if we move them from let's say one cabin to another on our ship. In this way, we create a different emotion around them. Here is an example of how we work with submodalities to shake the foundation of a limiting belief:

Steps for Letting Go Of A Limiting Belief

First, think of two beliefs:

- A limiting belief that you would like to change, a belief that is holding you back. Let us for example use 'I am not good in job interviews.' Let's call this Belief 1.
- A belief that we used to believe in the past but not anymore, preferably something neutral like 'I used to believe that milk is good for everyone and now I know that this statement is not true.' Here, we want a belief deprived of emotions (neutral) so there is minimum resistance or doubt about the fact that even though we used to believe it in the past, our unconscious is pretty clear that it is not true now. Let's call this Belief 2.
    - Close your eyes and think about Belief 1. You will probably within a few minutes have an internal representation inside your head. There is no real need to focus on the content of this representation, we will only work on finding out its submodalities.
    - So, now that you got the internal representation, elicit the submodalities of Belief 1 (the limiting belief): 'I am not good in job interviews'; this means going through the list of all the visual, auditory and kinaesthetic submodalities and identifying how you represent the belief; if you don't use each representation system (if there is no sound, for example), just ignore these submodalities altogether.
    - Open your eyes (break state).
    - Close your eyes again and think of Belief 2.
    - Just like with Belief 1, elicit the submodalities of Belief 2.
    - Open your eyes (break state).
    - Now, compare the submodalities of Belief 1 and Belief 2 and find the differences between them. This comparison is called **contrastive analysis.**
    - Close your eyes again and think again of Belief 1.
    - Start changing the submodalities which differ from those of Belief 2, to those of Belief 2. For example, if the image of the representation of Belief

1 was in fact a movie and that of Belief 2 is a picture, you turn Belief 1 to a picture. This is called **'mapping across'.** So, without actually changing the content of our 'movie', we just turn it to a picture. By facilitating this change, we teach our unconscious to also place the limiting belief in the cabin/category of statements a.) we used to believe in the past AND b.) we do not believe them any more now so the limiting belief starts losing its grip over us.

Now test the effect: how do you feel about that old limiting belief now?

Joe Dispenza is one of those science writers who fully grasps the role of emotions in transformation. In his book *You Are The Placebo*, he provides scientific evidence and case studies that show how our own thoughts, emotions and beliefs generate chains of physiological events in our body, and how we can influence the whole process. He also describes his personal wake-up call after having an accident that would probably leave him paralysed for life according to his doctors. Despite such a prognosis, he refused any operations and decided to just not let any negative thoughts enter his mind. One month later he walked back to work. He could easily have believed the belief that he would never walk again – and yet he managed to turn the situation around and get the result he wanted by focusing on 'his own empowering beliefs' that got him back on his feet.

Steps For Installing An Empowering Belief

You can similarly work with the submodalities of an empowering belief that you would like to believe in more or install afresh.

Think again of two beliefs:

- An empowering belief that you would like to strengthen, like ' I am good at job interviews'. Let's call this Belief 3.
- A belief that we are pretty certain about and is quite neutral at the same time, for example 'The sea is blue'. Let us call this Belief 4.
  - Close your eyes and think about Belief 3.
  - Elicit the submodalities of Belief 3.
  - Open your eyes (break state).
  - Close your eyes and think about Belief 4.
  - Elicit the submodalities of Belief 4.
  - Open your eyes (break state).
  - Compare the submodalities between Belief 3 and Belief 4 and note the differences **(contrastive analysis).**

- Close your eyes again and think again of Belief 3.
- Bring up Belief 3 again and start changing the submodalities that differ from those of Belief 4 to those of Belief 4 **(mapping across).**

How do you feel about this strengthened belief now?

By going through the steps above, you will notice differences between submodalities. Here are some of them:

- **Digital submodality:** It is either switched on or off. For example, "associated" or "dissociated" (it can only be the one or the other).
- **Analogue submodality:** It has a scale. For example "How dark is a picture?" or "How loud is a sound?" (there is grading).
- **Critical submodality:** The one that makes the biggest difference and that has the most intense feeling attached to it.
- **Driver submodality:** When this type of submodality changes, other submodalities also change. Location and associated/dissociated are often drivers. When we change the location inside our mind, or we move from associated state to dissociated state, often the other submodalities shift as well automatically.

N.B. Sometimes the Critical and Driver submodalities are the same.

My mother, Florence and science writer Joe Dispenza, as mentioned above, in a way all re-arranged their submodalities and changed their experience within their head and as a result they all felt better!

Science is pretty clear now about how every thought we have can reach the furthest and tiniest cell in our body and affect it. A strong body strengthens the mind, and vice versa. Moving our body provides us with more solutions and inspiration than using our brain alone (as in Ch. 15 Perceptual Positions where we physically moved from one chair to another).

With submodalities, we 'move' things around in our head and work on a different level of flexibility; as a result we 'move' emotionally. When we emotionally move to more resourceful states, our mind becomes more flexible and resilient and subsequently our body too, enjoys more flexibility and vibrance.

The Swish Pattern – Step by Step

The Swish pattern is one of the earliest NLP techniques and it helps us change how we think about something that annoys/irritates us. In effect it is something called a 'Pattern Interrupt' in that it breaks the relationship between the 'Cue' state and the undesired response that this triggers. E.g. being asked to do a presentation and then going into a panic about it.

It works by replacing one picture in our head with another one, so by mainly focusing on the visual submodalities. Here are the steps:

- Identify the **undesired state** (or unwanted response) in yourself, and precisely what the **Cue** state is that triggers it. How do you get in this state?
- Close your eyes.
- Do you have a picture inside your head representing this undesired state?
- Once you have a picture, describe it briefly. What would you see if you were to reproduce a scene of a situation where, for example, you get into a panic? Identify the elements that intensify your reaction.
- Associate into it. As strange as it may seem, associating into it and intensifying it briefly helps.
- Open your eyes (break state) and put this image to one side.
- Identify the **desired state** (a powerful positive state of your choice). How would you like to feel instead? This is the moment to tap into as many internal resources as you can, such as confidence, creativity, active listening, etc.
- Close your eyes.
- Do you have a picture? If you need to, intensify the key submodalities in the picture.
- Be dissociated, so you see your body in the picture.
- Open your eyes (break state).
- Close your eyes.
- Bring back the undesired picture to its full size and place the desired one, just small, in the bottom corner of the first image, just like this:
- Now comes the Swish! Either say "swish" out loud to yourself many times in a row, quickly; or even better, ask a practitioner or friend to say it. Every time you say

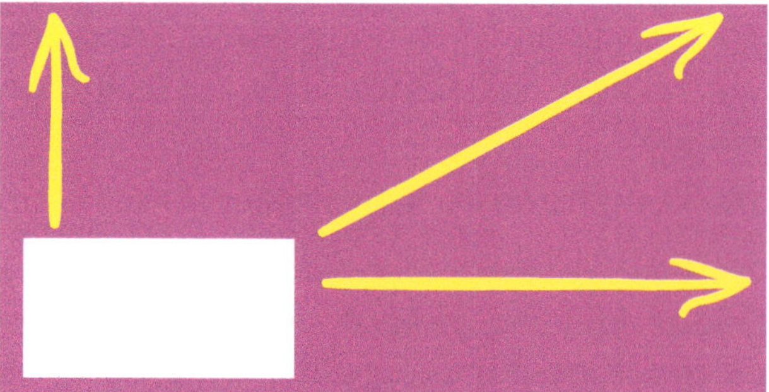

Fig. 2: Place the desired image in the bottom corner of the undesired one.

or hear the word "swish", do two things at the same time: (i) rapidly shrink the image of the undesired state and recede it to a distant point, while (ii) exploding the desired state into full view, big and bright. Speed is the important part of this technique: remember "Swish, Swish, Swish"!

- Repeat this step at least ten times.

Enjoy the results!

Important: Note that the swish pattern is only meant for minor annoyances and minor negative feelings – definitely not for trauma-related issues.

Take 100% responsibility when you use the pattern. For example, if you want to stop being upset with the traffic around you while you are driving along the street in your car (which will be the first picture you create in your mind), you create a second picture in which you see yourself to be in the same street but with a new more resourceful reaction – choosing a resourceful internal dialogue and being calmer. In this second picture, you can even see yourself turning the situation around and for example using the time waiting to listen to music or audio book.

Creating a picture that shows the roads empty, though, implies the world needs to change first for you to get to a more resourceful state and this is a less powerful mindset overall and the results not as striking.

Virtual Reality – Your Reality

In a movie theatre, we manage to find ourselves in different worlds and experience different sensations. With close-ups, landscapes and soundscapes, the storytelling becomes more compelling. By adjusting the visuals and audio, audiences may cry or cheer within seconds.

We live in the virtual-reality (VR) era, where experiencing a 3D movie or a roller-coaster with special visual and sound effects is part of everyday life. You could say books and fairy tales were the predecessors of virtual reality as through their words we are still able to find ourselves in faraway places. The explosion of VR and AI (artificial intelligence) simply take the simulation and optical illusions to a whole new level. Just think how Google maps allows you to literally stand in front of your house … on your computer screen!

I watched Chris Milk's TEDx talk recently, in which he talked about using VR software to create 360-degree movies to capture how what it is like in a refugee in a camp, or in other places that desperately need our help. He uses these movies for the United Nations, so political leaders and decision-makers can literally be in the position of those in need. His talk title was called 'How virtual reality can create the ultimate empathy machine'.

The question is, do we really need these mediums? Our brain feels reality and imagination in the same way. When we can successfully choose images and sounds in our mind and adjust their submodalities, we can do anything! Then there's nothing even virtual about it as it becomes our reality. This is also the power of visualisations. With submodalities, we play with our memory, we dream consciously, we plan and we capture the extraordinary brilliance of 'cooking' our dreams in our head – we change the meaning of a belief or experience and improve our reality.

Ready for submodalit-ing and swish-ing?

As effective as submodalities can be, the practice of changing them needs to be used appropriately.

I would never advise anyone to use submodalities alone to stop smoking. A deeper knowledge of how the unconscious works is necessary for their safety; smoking, drinking and other 'distractions' do often serve a purpose and have secondary gains. They may harm one part of the body, but they also take care of the excessive stress that our unconscious does not have the means to deal with otherwise. Unless we find out about ourselves and start exploring our deeper needs and beliefs, quitting a bad habit with such one technique risks to create another problem a few months later, as the unconscious will not yet have a more ecological alternative to release stress. Not feeling significant enough or good enough within is a common source of stress.

Before quitting bad habits, start installing new good habits. For example, a habit of celebrating your steps forward in life, no matter how big or small they. The crew of our ship defines priority according to emotional intensity. By regularly and wholeheartedly celebrating our small steps towards a goal as well as others', we instruct our crew to 'move' this 'direction of feeling' and replicate similar conditions. Regular broad smiles, belly laughs, powerful words, little dances and warm hugs communicate how important a 'good news' event is and takes precedence over other not-so interesting or pleasant events. We feel more significant and in sync internally.

Get Organized! Start Uncluttering and Tidying Up!

Speaking of re-arranging beliefs from one cabin to the other, I thought it would be beneficial to touch also on some re-arranging and uncluttering of our physical environment – the bottom lowest neurological level (Ch. 6). Florence had doubts about marrying submodalities and uncluttering tips in the same chapter. Finally, she agreed to me combining the two in the same chapter; even if they would never marry, they could 'sleep under the same roof in separate bedrooms'. Thanks, Florence!

You see, I find that there is a parallel relationship and a correlation between our emotional and physical states and mental and physical clutters. I would like you to go through the following suggestions and notice what happens in your life.

Time and time again, people tell me how after emptying a drawer that they seldom used helped them find a solution to a long lasting problem out of nowhere; how throwing away unnecessary possessions was followed by closing new deals in their business; how putting their wardrobes in order helped them manage their time better. The common factor is that their life moved forward and they felt a whole lot better, after tidying up and re-arranging 'things', just like in our head with submodalities!

Here I will briefly go through a few crucial life 'spheres' that you might regularly re-organise:

- **Home and office:** Physically go through every room, check the cupboards, bookcases and store rooms, and make a plan to clean them up and organise them!
- **Electronics:** Now this is a big one to sort out, with impressive results when it is sorted! Up until a decade ago, technology took up nowhere near the amount of space it takes up in our life now: thousands of emails in our Google accounts, hundreds of pictures on WhatsApp, and a constantly full inbox at work, with little guidance how to keep them 'clean'. It's all new to most of us and it's still clutter! This type of clutter is a good mirror of our organisation skills in our brain which again affects our emotions.
- **Finances:** Another massive one! How quickly can you find bills and contracts and credit card statements? How are they all organised so you know exactly what your income and expenses, or (equally important) what opportunities do you have to make more money? I'll say no more. I trust you to add this one-million-dollar habit to your monthly to-do list.
- **Relationships:** As spontaneous as we would like to be at getting together with our friends, the quality of our friendships also needs following up. Relying on social media or planned group gatherings does not send the message to our crew that we are 'serious' about our friends and family.

  Making an effort translates into our friends believing that we value them and think about them; this process takes time and organisation.

Everyday Thinking And Doing: Consider This ...

So you may be wondering what difference learning about submodalities can make to your life or how quickly you can make real change for yourself and others? To experience a little of this you may like to try out an exercise similar to the one Florence described in Ch. 1.

- Think of a conversation or meeting where you felt mildly dissatisfied with the outcome. On a scale of 0–10 (where 0 denotes it didn't matter to you at all and 10 denotes it was very important to you), choose a conversation that scores no more than 5.

    - Think about your chosen scenario. See it in your mind's eye as a still picture or a video. Notice your feelings as you see it and check it on your 0–10 scale.

    - If the image is in colour, turn it into black and white (or vice versa). Then, in your mind's eye, or with the help of your hands, squash the picture down and down, smaller and smaller to the size of a postage stamp, for example, then open your hands and watch it float away from you. Keep it moving through the air until it becomes only a dot, then too hard to see at all. Now pay attention to your feelings and rescale them from 0–10.

    You may find your feelings have not changed entirely, but the likelihood is that they have been *altered* by what you did.

- Submodalities are all about getting easily into emotional states we like! To have maximum benefit of this NLP technique, being aware of what we feel when and what/who makes us naturally feel good, helps us make better choices and reproduce more of these feelings. When we feel good, our self-esteem and confidence gets a boost and vice versa.

  So, take your journal and write down how you feel about your nearest and dearest. Choose three of the closest people to you.

    - Write down <u>who</u> is good for your self-confidence.

    - Write down whose self-confidence you are good for.

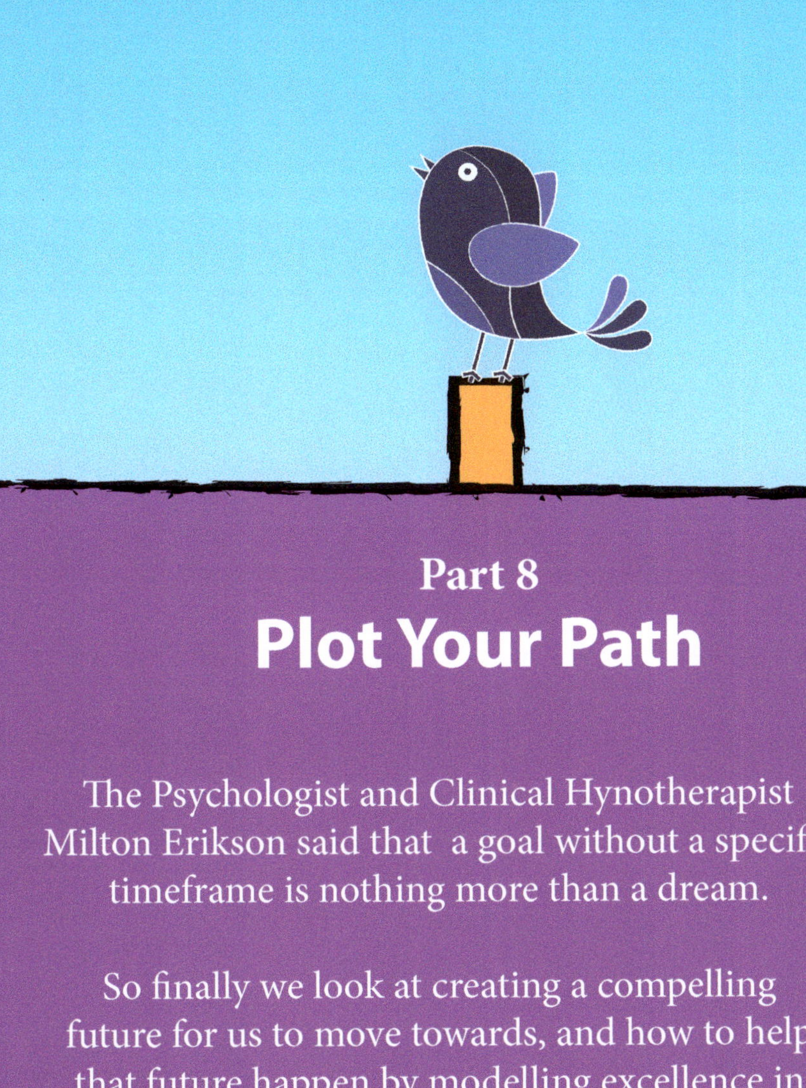

Part 8
Plot Your Path

The Psychologist and Clinical Hynotherapist Milton Erikson said that a goal without a specific timeframe is nothing more than a dream.

So finally we look at creating a compelling future for us to move towards, and how to help that future happen by modelling excellence in ourselves and in others.

Modelling Strategies …

… reproducing excellent results

By Florence

Fools talk of imitation and copying, all is imitation.

Thomas Gainsborough English portrait and landscape painter, draughtsman, and printmaker.

What Is Modelling?

When my neighbour's daughter was two years old, she was at a barbeque in our garden with some other friends who had a little boy called Charlie. He was only a year old. Someone else at the party was larking about on our ride-on lawnmower, and little Rosie stepped into action, putting her arm around little Charlie to lead him away from any danger. We smiled and commented about how she was just like her mother in her desire to take care of others. I saw Rosie earlier today, she is now twenty-seven years old. This time she was helping her mother with their newborn lambs. Both women were dressed alike for the job in hand and working together seamlessly. From childhood to adulthood, Rosie has been 'modelling' her mother – completely unconsciously.

Modelling is something we've all been doing from birth. Eleni referred earlier

Fig. 1: Modelling others to recreate their results or behaviour.

(Ch.2) to the imprinting and modelling periods of our life, when we learn our beliefs and values from significant others in our lives and consciously or unconsciously 'model' them. In our teenage years this modelling can become more conscious; we may have 'heroes' that we model, in terms of how we dress, style our hair, speak and behave. In casual speech, this is sometimes also referred to as 'channelling' someone.

In NLP this early learning process is often referred to as 'intuitive modelling', whereby we learn without language or by asking questions. This forms at least part of many approaches to modelling. By simply adopting the physiology and movement of another person we can learn a great deal about how they do what they do and even a little of how they are feeling – whether they are an expert presenter, skier or cook. (You may remember this phenomenon was referred to in earlier chapters – specifically Ch. 15 Perceptual Positions.)

There is perhaps a cautionary note to be sounded here about modelling: when as a teenager we model one of our 'heroes' we might want their look but not necessarily other parts of their life which may not be quite so desirable. So when we refer to modelling someone in NLP, we are only modelling their specific skill not the whole person. John Grinder makes this point about modelling Milton Erickson. He says he was initially cautious about modelling him until he could figure out how to model his skill without also 'taking on' his illnesses and disabilities.

In Ch.1 I referred to my realisation that NLP is about being the best version of myself. By modelling the skills of others and adding these to our own, we can do just that – we don't have to be someone else !

What Is A Strategy?

How we do what we do is a strategy. We have strategies for how we get up in the morning, for choosing what we eat, for exercising, for becoming attracted to others, for resolving conflicts (and for starting conflicts), overeating, and avoiding exercise – to name but a few! As Richard Bandler says:

Failure is nothing more than a chance to revise your strategy.

Anonymous.

We are usually unaware that we are using a strategy, because it has become habitual and the sequence of thoughts is not in our conscious mind. So it may strike us as odd that we have strategies for behaviour that doesn't serve us well – as we do for our effective behaviours. Because of this, we repeat our mistakes – fortunately when we realise it, we can make different choices too.

I was coaching a new manager who was struggling with her team, and one very strong character in particular. So I asked her, "If you had to teach me how to allow her to dominate in a department meeting, how you would do it?"

Her first reaction was to laugh at the very idea that there was a process (aka strategy) here. Then she started to speak. Her strategy started at a point before the meeting, by visualising how this person was likely to behave. This created a feeling of dread and a knot in her stomach. Then she went on to describe what she did in the meeting room. She carried on setting out her (previously unconscious) strategy for 'allowing' this member of the team to 'take over'. Then she looked at me and started to laugh: she realised in that moment that since she could identify each part of her strategy, she could make different choices and change it!

A strategy can therefore be defined as a sequence of internal and external experiences that create a particular outcome, and can be described in sensory terms – visual, auditory, kinaesthetic, olfactory, gustatory, auditory digital, etc.(Ch.11). These are the terms we use when we 'code' a person's strategy.

How Do We Know When To Revise A Strategy: The T.O.T.E. Model?

In 1960, George Miller, Eugene Galanter and Karl H, Pribram set out their T.O.T.E. Model and it was subsequently introduced into NLP by John Grinder, to describe how strategies run. In any aspect of our lives we might have a desired state and a current situation that do not match, as shown in (**Fig. 2**) This is when we can be prompted to revise the strategy.

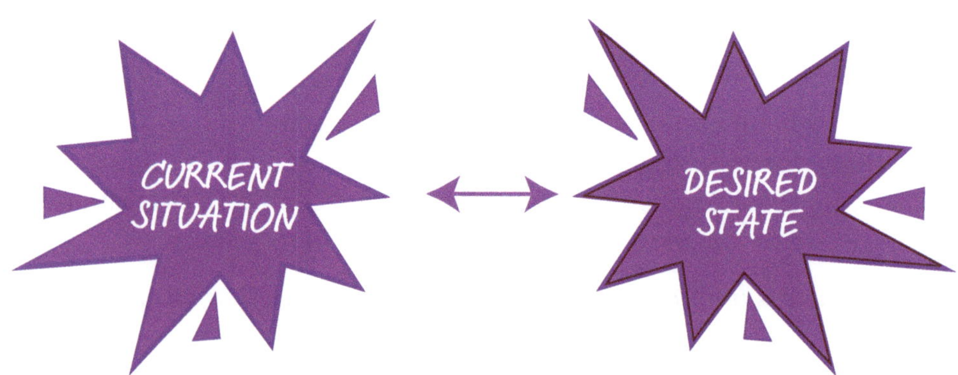

Fig. 2: Our strategy is how we attempt to move from our Current situation to our Desired state.

The first '**T**est' or trigger for running a strategy is noticing when a current situation does not match the desired state. This starts the strategy **O**perating to address the 'gap' between them. In a second '**T**est', the two states may match i.e. the desired state has been achieved, then the strategy **E**xits i.e has completed successfully. If they do not match, then you recycle through the strategy, as shown in **Fig. 3**, adjusting the strategy or the criteria for the desired state.

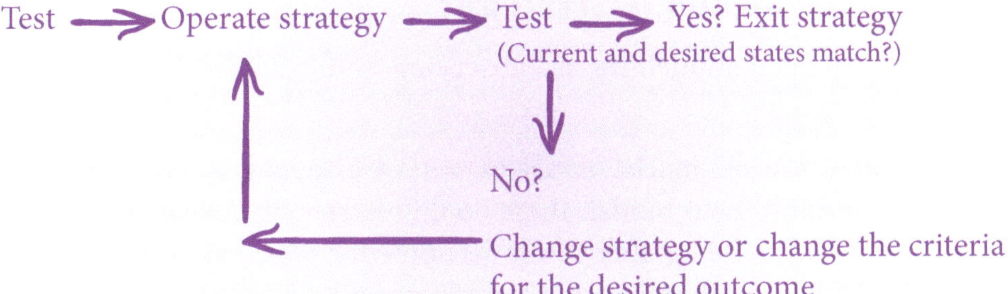

Fig. 3: The T.O.T.E. model.

To illustrate this in an everyday situation, imagine you're out shopping for a new coat (your desired state). You decide beforehand what you want the coat for, what you want to wear with it, the colour you prefer, and how much you would like to spend. This is your buying strategy, and it is the first test or trigger. You then go around the shops to search for the ideal coat. At the end of the day, you haven't found what you're looking for – this is the second test; you have not achieved your desired state. So you may decide to recycle your strategy, perhaps go online to shop, or to change the range of acceptable colours or your budget, in which case you could revisit the shops. If you find what you are looking for in the shops with your revised criteria or by going online, then the second 'test' is passed and you exit your strategy.

Study the past if you would define the future.

Confucius, Chinese Philosopher.

He has a point! And most of us can reflect on many occasions when we have done just that. This is why recognising that we are running a strategy (that doesn't work for us) is the first step, allowing us to adopt a more effective one. This can be done by modelling another person, or ourselves. Very often the behaviour or approach we desire in one situation may be one that we already use in another. We just don't always realise it.

An example of this is a lady I know who struggled to speak up in business meetings at work. Yet when her daughter had a problem in her school, she went to see the Principal and had no problem expressing her views. I pointed this anomaly out to her and asked her what was different when she went into the school. She replied that in the conversation with the Principal she felt she had the right and responsibility to speak up for her daughter..........I then asked her how she would be in work meetings, if in her mind, she saw her rights and responsibilities there also. She didn't need any new skills, she needed to see herself differently and shift her own thinking; and when she did her effectiveness in her role at work was transformed!

When you think about certain skills you'd like to develop in yourself, consider whether there other areas of your life in which you demonstrate the skills already.

How Can We Model A Strategy?

Robert Dilts' defined modelling as "observing and mapping" the effective behaviours of others.

We have choices. We can model ourselves, *and* we also have a rich resource of other people around us to model: these could be friends, colleagues or even people in the media. Being able to model someone who exhibits a skill we would find useful is another way to learn and grow.

When I did my original NLP training, I modelled Ann, another delegate who was also a trainer and had a particular skill in building rapport easily with new groups when they arrived. I asked Ann to (literally) walk me through what she did with the new groups. I noticed everything – where she went, how she looked, how she moved – as she described what she did. Sometimes I asked questions and she had to pause as she wasn't able to answer these easily.

It is common for the person being modelled (the exemplar), to be unaware of their own strategy. It is worth noting that the modelling process can be really useful for the exemplar too, because when they become conscious of their own strategy, they can use it more easily in other situations. As referred to earlier (Ch.19), Milton Erickson wasn't fully aware of how he achieved the results he did.

What I learned from modelling Ann that day became part of my strategy for building rapport and it has remained my strategy ever since. Thank you Ann, I hope this pleases you as you read it all these years on!

There are a number of ways to approach modelling and in the book *The Bumper Book of Modelling*, Fran Burgess identifies four distinct classes of modelling methods. I have summarised them briefly here. If you want more information, go to Fran's fabulous book. It is a goldmine.

Intuitive

This is the approach that is most akin to our early childhood experience of modelling. The modeller in this approach works instinctively, seeking to access the deep structure of their exemplar without questions or language. They start with being in physical rapport with the exemplar, whereby the modeller enters what John Grinder describes as the 'know nothing state'; they suspend or distract their conscious mind, and trust their unconscious mind to absorb and learn from the person they are modelling.

Expressive

This approach relies on movement, art and music as vehicles for expressing the inner structure of what someone is experiencing. It relates directly to the unconscious (Ch.2) and is particularly useful for self-modelling – expressing what is difficult to convey fully with language. I refer to the Generative Coaching work of Stephen Gilligan and Robert Dilts (Ch.14), and specifically to the idea of developing a somatic (of the body) gesture that symbolises and anchors your COACH state. This is an example of an Expressive approach to modelling, in this case self-modelling.

If I could tell you what it meant, there would be no point in dancing it.

Isadora Duncan, dancer and choreographer.

Metaphoric

It is commonplace for us to express ourselves in metaphors and symbols in everyday conversation. It is a way to access the deep-structure patterns of our experience. In working with someone else's metaphor, the modeller can ask questions to explore it further and generate new thinking. Symbolic Modelling (as developed by Penny Tompkins and James Lawley from the work of Dave Groves the New Zealand therapist) is one example of this type of strategy.

Cognitive

This is the approach most typically quoted in NLP books and taught in NLP training. Rather like the examples I set out earlier in this chapter, this is where the modeller starts by observing the exemplar, perhaps second-positioning them (this is where the modeller takes up the physiology of the exemplar). The modeller then begins to ask questions to build up a detailed sequence of how the exemplar does what they do, making each part of the sequence explicit. This approach is explained further in the next section. My earlier example of how I modelled Ann is a combination of cognitive and intuitive modelling.

The Cognitive Modelling Process

To model someone whose skills or strategies you would like to acquire, there is a simple process to follow. Here, I cover both 'implicit' (intuitive) modelling (you observe and 'become' the person you are modelling) and 'explicit' (cognitive) modelling (you consciously elicit each part in the sequence of performing the skill). This is how it goes:

Step 1: Choose your exemplar. This could be one (or more) people who have demonstrated excellence in the skill you would like to acquire.

Step 2: Observe your exemplar in action. if possible, observe them first without asking any questions. Take up their physiology and allow yourself to 'become' them as they do what they do (in other words, second-position them). Notice what you learn from this. This element is the aforementioned 'implicit' modelling, and is akin to the intuitive modelling approach.)

Step 3: Ask them questions to establish the sequence of what they do. Start by asking them to associate back into a time when they were doing 'the skill' and then ask how they know when to start doing what they do – and then what they do next, and so on – until the sequence is established. Useful questions are:

"What is the first thing that makes you —?"

"Then what happens?"

"What kind of —?"

"What happens just before you —?"

"What lets you know to —?"

"What's important about —?"

"What do you do if it doesn't go well/work?"

The sequence is expressed in sensory terms. Remember the woman who was struggling to manage her new team. Her unhelpful strategy started with a *visual picture* in her head of the likely behaviour of the problem team member, and this was swiftly followed by an internal *kinaesthetic feeling* i.e. knot in her stomach.

Step 5: Check out the sequence. Once you have established the sequence, 'play it back' to your exemplar to spot any gaps, and add in any missing pieces. Sometimes the exemplar's eye movements help fill in the gaps, although they are not consciously aware of them (Ch.11). It may also be helpful to offer suggestions when your exemplar is 'stuck' – but be prepared to be wrong! Either way, your suggestion, even if it is incorrect, might just help them realise more about what they are actually doing.

Step 6: Check out what is essential and what isn't. Not all parts of the sequence may be essential, so test out which parts are significant by checking what would happen if it is left out. Here's an example: someone who is particularly effective at running meetings may say that they aim to get to the meeting room before any participants arrive. You could ask them how it would affect their performance if they arrived to find that some participants were already there. If, on reflection, that would make no difference, then it is not an essential part of their strategy.

Step 7: Try it out. Having established the essential sequence, try it out and notice what difference it makes. Consider any adjustments you might need to make.

Step 8: Pass on your model. Your model of their strategy is now ready to be passed on to others.

If you are using more than one exemplar you might do steps 1–4 with a few people before pulling together the common or essential parts of the model.

Modelling Yourself as a Learning Tool

Modelling the success of others is a useful strategy obviously, and as in my earlier example of the woman who found it difficult to speak up in meetings, we can also model ourselves. The behaviour or results that we want in one part of our life could easily be a behaviour we demonstrate in other areas. When we recognise this, we can notice what we are doing differently and transfer our successful strategy to other areas of our lives. Perhaps surprisingly we can also learn from modelling our unsuccessful strategies too. My other example in this chapter was about someone who allowed her meetings to be hi-jacked by a member of her team. By recognising she had an unconscious strategy for this, and becoming consciously aware of it, she realised she simply had to invert her old strategy to get the outcome she wanted. So self-modelling brings awareness and clarity that enables us to make different choices.

As we have mentioned elsewhere in our book, Eleni and I first met on a course with Sue Knight in France in 2009. Sue deftly spots the behaviour or pattern that might be holding you back and she makes you feel more consciously how that pattern or behaviour is impacting on you. In effect she too is getting you to model yourself, really feel what you are doing, thereby opening a door for you to change.

Knowing how we get the results we don't want, is a fabulous way to figure out how to get the results we do want.

Everyday Thinking And Doing: Consider This …

1. Pick a skill that you would like to improve in yourself:
    - Consider who could be exemplars for you.
    - Arrange to observe them in action. Second position them, and allow yourself to 'become' them. Notice what you pick up from each person that you observe.
2. If you have the opportunity to do so, take your modelling of their skills one stage further. Follow the process above to build a more

detailed sequence. Notice what the exemplar was not aware of and what they learned about themselves from the modelling process.

Note: Be careful to pick only a small 'chunk' of what your exemplar does (e.g. focus on how an excellent presenter gets themselves ready to speak). Modelling is a detailed process – tasking on too great a 'chunk' may be very time consuming – possibly even unnecessary.

Well-formed Outcomes …

… making the outcomes you want desirable and achievable

By Eleni

You have your brush, you have your colours,
you paint the paradise, then in you go.

Nikos Kazantzakis, Greek writer and Noble Prize winner for literature.

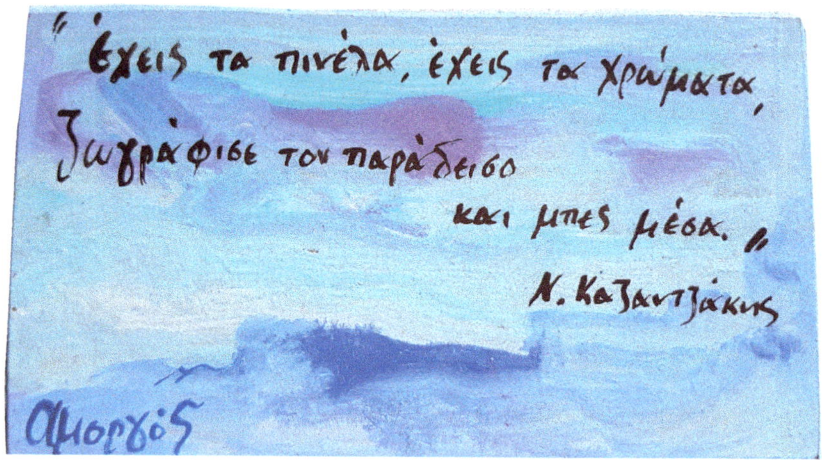

Fig. 1: The Kazantzakis Plaque.

One of my fondest memories with Florence was on Amorgos island in Greece when we discovered a shop with quotes written on plaques by Nikos Kazantzakis. He was a Greek Nobel prize winner in literature in 1947 whose books I grew up with and which played an important role in shaping me. On one of these plaques was written the above quote by the writer and I knew I had to give it to Florence. Little did I know we would become co-authors of this book five years later.

For me, this one sentence of his captures our unconscious beauty exquisitely: first and foremost, the responsibility that showers us with empowerment, secondly the unlimited potential of our imagination (as Carl Sagan points out!), and thirdly our need for internal freedom. To achieve all three takes courage and a decision to look within and decide what story we want to write for ourselves.

Imagination will often carry us to worlds that never were,
but without it we go nowhere.

Carl Sagan, astrophysicist and cosmologist.

Carrying the ideals and way of living of my parents and society around me, my main goal was to enter the University of Thessaloniki. Finding out what I truly wanted to do with my life was secondary to that and brainstorming or thinking out of the box was not essential. It seemed that getting into university was the general definition of success. I was committed one hundred percent, but I had zero percent enthusiasm for it. So, I did it, but it took me eight

Fig. 2: Florence & I on a boat off Amorgos.

years to actually complete my studies. I felt no happiness and my self-esteem suffered.

For our story to be paradisal, celestial and ambrosial, being the captain of our own ship and owning our goals is vital. Plenty of times we want things and yet we are not fully behind them. We want them because we were told to want them, or because we believe they will make someone else happy. Our own enthusiasm may not be there, though. In these cases, despite our own conscious convictions, our unconscious will place hurdles and resist.

This leads me on to a few questions for you.

- Have you defined what happiness/success/a fulfilled life is for you?
- What are your strategies on how to go about achieving the above?
- How do you get motivated? What makes your world go round?
- What do you love doing?
- What will the reality you dream of look like?

Answering the above questions and defining our ideas of 'paradise on earth' or 'success situations' – whatever name we want to give it, offers us the gift of responsibility to imagine it, to tap into the internal resources we need to create it, and to enter a safe and exciting place from where we can begin to achieve our dreams.

Once we have a clear mental image of our dream scenarios, we recognise our successes easier. We go after our goals more easily and we are more comfortable when they manifest before our eyes. We develop a habit of acknowledging talent and results in us and in others. We contribute to a society that builds success on love and wisdom.

In order to create, there has got to be an inner fire inside. That's when we can follow through with our goals: when they were our idea and because they are meaningful to us. Becoming an NLP trainer was my idea and it adds meaning to my life every day. It makes my heart sing and gives me inner peace.

Believe it to see it!

Once during a presentation, I was asked how come I focus more on beliefs and not goals.

Focusing first on goals, we might actually be hindering our own progress towards them. We may find out that the time we spend aiming in a certain direction, despite lessons learnt and our achievements on the way, was actually not the direction we wanted to take our life at all.

When we have a fixed mindset, it creates a fixed set of goals. In a fixed mindset we might be happy with a certain job, friendship or holiday destination, but it will not be able to see beyond those things. It is a continuous growth mindset, with constant work on our beliefs, that sets us free, enabling us to regularly re-evaluate our goals and re-write our story. There is always room to outgrow our own set of goals towards a vision we did not know was possible.

I often explain this way:

'I'll believe it when I see it' is part of a fixed mindset.

'I'll see it when I believe it' is part of the energy coming from a growth mindset.

Once a friend of mine laughingly admitted that he does not believe it, even when he sees it.

As for beliefs, nothing can beat the force of our own self-belief. The more we believe in our own power, the more we believe we deserve life the way we envision it, the more our path ahead opens wide. When we believe we deserve it, the universe serves it. Our goals develop into something we could not grasp before. They get redefined.

And more focusing …

Two points are massively important to understand and practice when it comes to goal setting:

1. Remember in Ch.2 the pink elephant with the big blue ears I was asked during my NLP Practitioner course *not* to think of, regardless of my best efforts I did see in my mind? That was about the Prime Directive of the Unconscious where we do not process negatives. Just like with my example

on 'I do not want stress' in the same chapter, when we focus on not wanting stress, it will be just that we will create an image and program our mind with.

The bottom line is when setting goals, say it the way you want it. Do not say *stress*: say, *relaxation* or *peace of mind*.

2. Do you also remember in Ch.3 Everyday Thinking and Doing when Florence asked you to apply the 'red' filter? The red colour was just an example, a metaphor if you will about where we draw our attention at any given moment. As a result, we will see more red objects.

   The same way, we are far more effective when we focus on every detail of what we want. This way, we give our mind a map of where to navigate, and the more details this map has, the easier and faster the ride.

   This is what the goal-setting SMART model is about (SMART is an acronym for Specific, Measurable, Achievable, Realistic and Time-bound). To make goals SMART, we have to identify precisely what we want to achieve.

   "I want money" becomes "I want a monthly salary of 2000 euros starting from July 2019". It is specific about how much money you want and when you want it. Then, we check how achievable and realistic this goal is and we work with our beliefs. To make it even smarter, we fill in more specifics, building a picture or a movie in our head: "How will I achieve it? Where will I achieve it? When will I have achieved it? Whose support do I need to help me achieve it? What tools and resources will I need?"

The Magic Recipe of Well-Formed Outcomes

In NLP we use the term 'well-formed outcomes'. This is about goals PLUS PLUS! To make our goals into well-formed outcomes, we go beyond just stating specifically what we want; we ask ourselves the big questions about internal freedom and deservedness. We question our motivations and the impact on others of what we want to achieve. We dive into our strategies to prepare and programme our mind to receive our desired outcomes.

Here are some key components of going from SMART-ing to well-formed outcom-ing.

- State your goal in the positive.
- Expand your language when stating it – add new words, expressions & structures to express it.
- State it in the present tense; use the word 'now'.
- Write it down.

- Use empowering beliefs (affirmations).
- Re-evaluate regularly.
- Acquire the necessary skills and resources.
- Identify possible limiting beliefs and limiting decisions that you could encounter on the way to achieving it.
- Be ecological, with trust and honesty, and be congruent with your behaviour; create win–win situations.
- Take ownership and massive action.
- Add in enthusiasm, passion and joy; act as if you *internally* see, hear and feel so that your attention directs itself towards external and internal resources necessary for achieving the goal.
- Celebrate with each step that brings you closer to your goal, no matter how small it is!

This very last item on the list brings me neatly to the next section.

Progress Versus Perfection – Small Does It!

I remember playing chess with my father for hours on end when I was young – probably the happiest memories I have of us together. There was silence, focus and strategy. Beating my father for the first time was a dream come true! He was startled too, with pride and confusion combined in his face when he realised his king had nowhere to go. I was just eight years old.

The years passed and I won and lost hundreds of chess matches in Greece, and as part of a team in Amsterdam. Sweet team triumphs and bitter losses brought me to tears. All that said, it was again because of my friend Simon's solid chess-playing advice that I had a breakthrough in my game.

Instead of aiming for the king right from the start, he aimed for just one pawn. That was it. One point. That would make sure he had the advantage and then he would go for another pawn. They were small wins but consistent wins, that ended up winning the game. This simple strategy changed my whole outlook on life, and my dreams. Just like in a game of chess, our goals are achieved bit by bit, little by little, every day.

Our unconscious craves for progress – not perfection. Our crew rejoices and gets our self-esteem boosted with small and regular steps towards our goals and by building unshakeable habits that give us small wins every day. Then we get a regular pat on the shoulder meaning "Well done!".

My good friend Simonetta (it's in the name, I tell you!) is a great example of this. She has always been adamant about making her bed up every morning like one in a five-star hotel. That is still her first goal each day and she achieves it with flying colours!

Never discourage anyone who continually makes progress, no matter how slow.

Plato, Greek philosopher.

Well-Formed Outcomes That Can Always Be Added To Your List!

We have a whole universe within us. Every part of us deserves to feel accomplished and making progress (Parts Integration Ch.16). The naughty, the playful, the part that loves cool surprises, the nice and the mean parts, the common and the uncommon parts. Their progress is our progress. If we miss out on one, we will feel the consequences.

Next to all other well-formed outcomes we usually decide to pursue: relating to family, work, finances, assets, holidays, communication and negotiation – how about including a few related to your emotional management & wellness?

How would you like to feel today? Set some goals!

FUNess!

Are your parts connected, and having fun? Work at it. Build your emotional world to feel more connected and fun. Honour those parts of you! Be specific in identifying how much fun you want to have every day, with whom, and in what situations. Align your activities with your goals to create more pleasure and enjoyment in your everyday life.

Do anything, but let it produce joy.

Walt Whitman, poet.

KINDness

Plan one conscious act of kindness every day. Everything begins with altruism, and it should not be limited to those close to us and those who wish us well, but should extend to strangers, and animals, and every living thing! When we purposefully plan to help, support, share and serve, we fill our body and mind with enormous amounts of energy and satisfaction.

When you're faced with a choice, choose to inspire, choose to empower, choose to stand for those who have lost the will to stand for themselves.

Orly Wahba, author of 'Kindness Boomerang'.

CLOSEness

Hugs are not meant solely to console us during difficult times. When we remember to laugh, and create pleasant emotional situations every day, then hug in joy, pass on positive feedback and appreciation to our crew, and other people, we again invest in positive change within. An optimal state. Hugs move our body – in a direction of inclusivity. How far, how deep, how wide do we want to expand to feel content and appreciate ourselves and our life?

We need four hugs a day for survival. We need eight hugs a day for maintenance. We need twelve hugs a day for growth.

Virginia Satir, family therapist.

Bellavista, Santiago de Chile

All paths lead to the same goal: to convey to others what we are.

Pablo Neruda, poet and Nobel Prize winner.

Six months ago, I found myself in Chile. Was it a goal to be there? Yes. It became one when one of my great corporate clients booked me to deliver an NLP Practitioner course in Santiago de Chile. On my free day during the course, I was planning to finish this chapter, the one you're reading now and the last one in the book, and I found myself in the neighbourhood of Bellavista. Enjoying the lovely view from a street-side café, just before I turned on my laptop, I realised how close I was to Pablo Neruda's house (another Noble Prize winner whose work changed so many lives). Ten minutes later, laptop back in its bag, I entered his ship-shaped house and immersed myself in all its glory and symbolism.

Neruda had three houses in total and they were all full of ship-like features. Next to his amazing poetry, the passion we shared about the sea spoke to me even more. His dining table was narrow, like on a ship, so the people gathered around it would stay close. The windows were round, and he had a wavy-shaped Captain's bar. His furniture and possessions were from all over the world, from Iran and Russia, France and India, China and Italy.

At that moment, I realised that despite having asked so many people to draw 'their ship' on my courses, I had yet to draw mine.

As soon as I got back home to Malaysia, I was ready to envision what my ship would look like – what 'Eleni' would look like. In the meantime, I called Florence and asked her to email me an image of her ship. A day later, a Noah's Ark landed in my Inbox, along with two words: Embracing all!

And so, as I was about to start to draw my ship, my twelve-year old son Victor came up and asked what I was doing. I told him why I was staring at an empty piece of paper, and he smiled and asked what ideas I already had. I told him that I was trying to decide between a yacht, a cruise ship and a surfboard. Without hesitation he said, "Mom, you have to decide on the symbolism! Is it romance, luxury or action you're after?"

Boom! I had my answer! It was a surfboard! *I* was a surfboard, in mainly three different states, either gazing at the horizon from the beach, or in action going places and creating or having lots of fun on the waves!

Now, it was my daughter's turn to come and help me out. Belle listened to my idea and looked at my first sketches and as always, in her supporting and sweet way, she asked me about my surf pictures in my head and the colours that were important to me. She translated both them quickly and produced drafts. Since that moment, I took my time and it was during a Business Communication Skills training in the Philippines when I finalized my three main emotional states surfboard.

Fig. 3: Florence's Ark picture & Eleni's surfboard picture.

The Mind Museum, Manila in the Philippines

And so, the book was not yet finished. Like a lighthouse throughout this whole writing process, Florence's words, from the 1965 movie '*Agony and the Ecstasy*' where Pope Julius II asked Michelangelo when he will finish painting the Sistine Chapel, echoed in my head. His answer: "When I am finished!"

Even though there may not be much of a resemblance between those two men and us, I found Florence's metaphor touching. She was creating space and time for both of us to get inspired and enjoy the process. (Between you and me, she was keeping up with our schedule with far more precision than I was!)

And so, I found myself in Manila, in the Philippines, six months after Chile. My hotel was in the Bonaficio district, next to The Mind Museum.

Oh, no…oh, yes!

Oh no, because I had decided to close the curtain on this last chapter which had been pending since Santiago and now, there was a museum about the mind, right there, calling my name! Oh yes, because I could not imagine a more appropriate place to visit before I finally finished Everyday NLP.

As I entered the museum, I felt a profound sense of awe. This was no ordinary place. The greatest minds of science were there – their words, their stories, their experiments. This is the quote that greeted me upon entry:

We are all connected.
To each other biologically. To the earth chemically.
To the rest of the universe atomically.

Neil deGrasse Tyson, astrophysicist.

A couple of hours later, having indulged in dancing waters, shadow boxes and holograms, Galileo's tour of the solar system, and displays on Foucault's Sublime pendulum and the Earth's rotation, I was alone in my hotel room again, inspired, and with hundreds of notes from the Mind Museum to follow up on. I finished my dinner in my room, then called the hotel staff to collect the giant trolley it was served on before going to sleep.

Twenty minutes passed and I was still waiting, so I played a game with myself. A mind game I often play. If someone I expect to come does not come, or something I expect to happen is delayed, I know it is only my perception so I focus more on what I can do in the meantime. I believe that when I myself am ready, then things will move forward.

My game involved asking myself what else I needed to do before going to bed. Brush my teeth? Prepare my bag for tomorrow? Put some oil on my sore muscles? … The staff still hadn't come. What else then? Put the grapes in the fridge. Clean the two dirty cups. Switch off the desk lamp. … Still no-one. What else? There must be something more. I saw my earrings lying around – ooops, we don't want that. I placed them safely in their box. And then, the phone rang. I picked it up and it was the 'in-dining service'.

"Hello, could you please open your door? There is someone outside your door, but they don't want to ring your bell as you have the 'DO NOT DISTURB' sign on".

I smiled. "Of course! Thank you," I answered.

I'm thinking I should write another book about how often we wait for things to happen while we are not yet ready ourselves. We wonder why our goals and hard work do not materialise as quickly as we would like them to. We only need to make ourselves available and turn off our 'do not disturb' sign. We expect things to come to us even though *we* are the only ones these 'things' are waiting for.

I had the end of the book now and I re-started my laptop to put it into words. This was the day; Everyday NLP would become whole. I was ready.

One hour later, it was done. I looked at the city lights from inside my hotel room and enjoyed closure. This was the month I was due to turn fifty years old. A landmark for me, a special period. Being in Manila was significant as I felt so much at home there and after completing the course, I would touch down at home again, in Kuala Lumpur. These two countries had taught me many valuable life lessons about going with the flow, of acceptance and kindness, and being of service.

And then my thoughts drifted again back to Amorgos; Florence and I gazing at the sunset every evening with our toes in the sand, looking back at the blessings of the day, our achievements and fun moments, getting ready for the new sunrise the next day, celebrating the cycle of days and memories that make up our life.

I was now ready for bed, when Florence called.

Florence: "How are you, darling?"

Eleni: "Well, I've finished it, my lady!"

Florence laughed: "I sensed it! "

Nature does not hurry, yet everything is accomplished.

Lao Tzu, Chinese philosopher and writer.

Everyday Thinking and Doing ... Consider This

Ask yourself about the goals you have. Are they your idea?

- How enthusiastic are you about them?
- How committed are you?
- How motivated are you?

The higher you score yourself on these three questions, the faster your goals will materialise.

Then take your goal or outcome through this process and notice what happens:

The Well-formed Outcome Pattern

State Your Goal/Outcome in the Positive

1. State the objective in the positive (i.e. not what you 'don't want'– what do you want instead of that?). Check if it is in your control i.e. a self-maintained goal, not dependent on anyone else.

Define the Outcome in Sensory Specific Terms

2. Now imagine you are at a point in time where you have achieved what you really want. How will you know when you have achieved it?

   What will you be seeing ...what is the quality of light and shadow? What colours can you see? Is it clear or hazy?

   As you become more aware of what you can see, allow yourself to notice the sounds......What is the volume? How is it quiet? What is the nature of the sound you hear: loud soft, distinct, faint? Are the sounds outside you or within you?

   What are your emotions of being here? What would make this feeling even better for you? Make it better. How do you experience these feelings?

   Is there anything else you want?

3. Where do you want it? When? With whom? Where do you not want it? When? With whom?

Check the Ecology (how it affects every area of your life)

4. What are the benefits of achieving it....to you and the other people in your life, home/work?

If not a benefit to others, what would have to change/develop for this to be the case? (allow time for this)

What are the benefits of not achieving it?

What else do you want to achieve? Is there a conflict here?

5. What resources do you need to achieve this? (Mental and physical)

6. What is the cost (not just financial) of doing this – for you and others? Are you/ others prepared to pay this?

Make It Compelling

7. What will happen when you have made the decision?

   What will happen if you don't?

   What won't happen when you do?

   What won't happen if you don't?

Gather Resources and Take Action

8. If this is something you really want how come you don't already have it?

   What is the pay off of not doing it? (this may take a bit of time)

   How can you fulfil this need by letting go of your present state and setting yourself on course to achieve this future one?

   Achieving what you want usually comes at a price.... are you prepared to pay it?

   Are you willing to act on this outcome? If so, what is the first step? What are you going to do?

   Now step into your paradise!

Glossary for Everyday NLP

A

Accessing Cues – Behaviours such as eye movements and gestures which indicate both which representational system a person is using and also helps them to access that system.

Acuity – keenness of thinking and/or perception. (Sensory acuity)

Anchor – Anchors are a naturally occurring stimulus/response pattern e.g. our response to blue flashing lights. In NLP we can deliberately set an anchor to bring an immediate recall to a positive state. An anchor can be: set on part of the body, it can be an object, clothing, music, photograph, a smell, a taste etc, where seeing, touching, hearing, smelling or tasting the stimulus will recall a positive feeling response.

Associated – this is the experience of recalling a memory or event and being back in it, experiencing the emotions as if they are happening in the present.

Auditory – the representational system relating to the sense of hearing.

Auditory Digital – the representational system dealing with logic and self-talk. Anything expressed in language that is non-sensory.

B

Beliefs – ideas or generalisations about ourselves, others, the world based on our experiences. They can be Empowering and allow us to be the best version of ourselves or Limiting which in some way hold us back or sabotage our efforts.

C

Calibration – the skill of reading unconscious non-verbal clues to 'measure' an individual's state.

Cause and Effect – where we choose to place ourselves in considering a situation. At Cause is an empowered position where we take responsibility for achieving an outcome, at Effect we see others as the cause, and therefore feel disempowered to effect change.

Cognitive Dissonance – the mental discomfort experienced when someone simultaneously holds two or more contradictory beliefs, ideas, or values. In 1957, Leon Festinger proposed a theory that we have an inner need to hold our attitudes and beliefs in harmony, so processes like Collapsing Anchors or SWISH, force the brain to restore that harmony.

Congruence – when the behaviour of an individual matches their words and voice tone in a positive way. The person is in rapport within themselves.

Conscious mind – the part of the mind we are aware of in the present minute.

Chunking – breaking experiences into larger or smaller pieces. Chunking up involves moving to a higher level of abstraction and is useful to achieve agreement. Chunking down involves more detailed information and is useful to agree specifics.

Cybernetics – an umbrella term for actions taken from feedback to achieve a goal more often referred to as 'systems thinking'.

D

Deep Structure – our pure sensory experience held unconsciously.

Dissociated – this is the experience of recalling an event where you see yourself in the picture i.e. you are observing yourself in the situation and therefore less emotionally involved in the action.

Dopamine – a neurotransmitter involved in reward, motivation, memory, attention and movement. The brain is programmed to seek more of it, hence giving positive feedback is likely to encourage more of that behaviour.

E

Ecology – where we consider the wider impact of our actions, not simply the effect on ourselves. Ecology Frame is one of the NLP frames used with the express purpose of considering the wider consequences of a decision or action.

Environment – the external context in which our behaviour takes place i.e. anything outside us.

F

Filters – the means by which we manage and interpret information coming in from our senses. The filters referred to in the NLP Communication model are: Deletion, Distortion and Generalisation. Metaprograms, beliefs and values are also filters.

Future Pacing – mentally rehearsing a future situation to help the desired behaviour become the natural response.

G

Gestalt therapy – a form of psychotherapy where the patient is encouraged to become aware of their feelings in the present moment. It is interested only in the patient's past only in respect of how it is affecting them in the present.

Gustatory – the representational system relating to the sense of taste.

K

Kinaesthetic – the representational system relating to feelings tactile or emotional.

L

Logical Levels/Neuro Logical Levels – an internal hierarchy model developed by Robert Dilts based on the work of Gregory Bateson.

M

Meta – originally the name for what became known as NLP. It comes from the Greek (!) meaning above or beyond. It is usually used as a prefix indicating a higher level of abstraction.

Meta Model – the first formal model of NLP. It defines language patterns also known as Meta Model violations where someone has deleted distorted or generalised, and the questions by which this limiting thinking can be challenged.

Metaphor – how we express or explain one thing in terms of another. Stories that convey a message to the listener are metaphors, but they can also be physical like Tony Robbins 'Fire Walk' with the powerful message of triumphing over adversity or fear.

Metaprograms – filters inside our head that influence our perceptions, responses and actions.

Milton Model – the model of hypnotic language developed from studying the hypnotherapist Milton Erickson. It is the mirror image of Meta Model and is artfully vague to induce trance or agreement.

Mirror Neurons – a specific class of brain cell that fires when both observing an action or performing the action.

Modelling – the process of coding how someone does something with excellence for the purpose of replicating their results.

N

Neuro Linguistic Programming (NLP) – a model and set of skills and techniques developed in the early 1970s by Richard Bandler, John Grinder and Frank Pucelik. The basis of which was observing and modelling the patterns of excellence of experts in their fields.

Neurons – nerve cells in the brain.

Neuroplasticity – or brain plasticity. The brain's ability to form and reorganise connections as a response to learning, experiences or damage.

Neurotransmitter – a chemical in the brain that transmits messages between neurons and are therefore important in learning.

O

Olfactory – the representational system relating to the sense of smell.

P

Pacing – matching and mirroring the behaviour of another over a period of time to build rapport.

Parts – a metaphorical way of describing our different behaviours, strategies and thinking patterns. E.g. part of us may want to eat cake and part may want to eat healthily.

Predicates – words which indicate the representational system that someone is using.

Presuppositions of NLP – one of the underpinning theories of NLP, they are central principles or beliefs of NLP which derive from thinkers and modelling subjects.

Prime Directives of the Unconscious – the duties and features of the Unconscious mind as collated by Tad James.

R

Rapport – a harmonious relationship where those in rapport understand each other and communicate well.

Reality – who knows?

Reframing – looking at a situation or behaviour in a different way to change the meaning or interpretation. Context reframe looks at how an undesirable behaviour could be useful in a different context. Meaning reframe is looking at an alternative meaning for an undesirable behaviour that enables interpretation in a more benign way.

Representational Systems – also known as sensory modalities, refer to the senses through which we experience the world: sight, hearing, touch, smell, taste. Auditory Digital is also a representational system that is non-sensory.

S

Secondary Gain – where an undesirable behaviour has a positive function on some level e.g. smoking enabling the person to be calm.

State – our way of being in the moment from our emotions, our thinking and our physiology.

Strategy – the physical and mental steps involved in achieving an outcome.

Submodalities – the finer distinctions of the Modalities i.e. Visual, Auditory, Kinaesthetic, Olfactory and Gustatory. For example if a visual picture is clear or fuzzy, monochrome or colour etc.

Surface Structure – the words we use to describe the deeper level pure experience.

Synaesthesia – where two sensory modalities are linked e.g. seeing a particular person evokes a feeling.

T

Timeline – this is the term used for how we internally represent time in a linear way. Some people's timelines go in front and behind them and they are referred to as 'In-time'. For others their timeline is all in front of them going left to right (or vice versa) in a straight line, curved or V shape. They are referred to as 'Through Time'.

Timeline Therapy® – this is a specific approach to Timeline developed by Tad James.

T.O.T.E. – a model originally developed by Miller, Galanter and Pribram. It stands for Test-Operate-Test-Exit and is a basic feedback loop to guide actions.

U

Unconscious mind – the part of the mind that is 'offline' at any time i.e. we are not consciously aware of it.

Utilization – a pattern of Milton Model (hypnotic) language where the person inducing the trance improvises to use the client's experiences to deepen the trance. E.g. As the door slams…

V

Values – things that we deem to be important to us e.g. honesty, integrity, compassion.

Visual – the representational system relating to sight.

W

Well Formed Outcome – a process for setting goals that makes them more likely to be achieved by exposing conflicts, problems with ecology or secondary gain (the benefits of not pursuing or achieving the goal).

Wheel of Life – a powerful self -development tool which enables someone to highlight areas of strength and for improvement.

Sources and Further Reading:

ACKERMAN, D **A Natural History of the Senses** Vintage Books USA (1991)

ANDREAS, S and ANDREAS, C. **Change Your Mind and Keep the Change** Real People Press (1988)

BANDLER, R. **Using Your Brain For A Change** Real People Press (1985)

BANDLER, R., GRINDER, J. **Patterns of the Hypnotic Techniques of Milton H. Erickson,** M.D. Volume 1 Meta Publications (1975)

BANDLER, R. and GRINDER, J. **Frogs to Princes** Real People Press (1979)

BANDLER, R., GRINDER, J. **The Structure of Magic, Vol. 1** Science and Behavior Books; Highlighting edition (1989)

BANDLER, R., ROBERTI, A., & FITZPATRICK, O. **How to take Charge of Your Life. A User's Guide to NLP** Harper Collins Publishers (2014)

BODENHAMER, B.G., HALL, L.M. Ph.D. **The User's Manual for the Brain** Crown House Publishing; Revised edition (2000)

BURGESS, F. **The Bumper Book of Modelling** Kilmonivaig Publishing (2014)

COVEY, S.M.R. **The Speed of Trust: The One Thing that Changes Everything** Free Press; Reprint edition (2008)

CAULFIELD, M. **The Meta Model Demystified** Create Space Independent Publishing Platform; 2nd edition (2014)

DILTS, R.B. **Visionary Leadership Skills** Meta Publications Inc (1996)

DILTS, R., DELOZIER, J. **The Encyclopaedia of Systemic NLP & NLP New Coding NLP** University Press (2000)

DILTS, R.B., DELOZIER, J., BACON DILTS, D. **NLP II The Next Generation** Meta Publications (2010)

DISPENZA, J. PhD **You Are the Placebo: Making Your Mind Matter** Hay House (2014)

DOSTOYEVSKY, F. **The Brothers Karamazov** Penguin Classics; Rev Ed edition (2003)

DWECK, C. **Mindset: The New Psychology of Success** Random House (2006)

DWECK, C. **Mindset: How You Can Fulfil Your Potential** Robinson (2012)

EAGLEMAN, D. **Incognito: The Secret Lives of The Brain** Canongate Canons; Main – Canons edition (2016)

EAGLEMAN, D. **The Brain: The Story of You** Canongate Books (2016)

GALLWEY, W.T. **The Inner Game of Tennis** Pan Books, Revised (2015)

GAWAIN, S. **Creative Visualization** New World Library; New edition (2002)

GOLEMAN, D. **Focus: The Hidden Driver of Excellence** Bloomsbury Paperbacks (2014)

GOLEMAN, D. **Social Intelligence: The New Science of Human Relationships** Arrow Publishing (2007)

GRAVES, C. PhD **The Never Ending Quest: Dr. Clare W. Graves Explores Human Nature: A Treatise On An Emergent Cyclica** ECLET Publishing (2005)

GRINDER, J. **The Origins of NLP** Crown House Publishing; First Edition (2013)

GRINDER, J., BOSTIC ST CLAIR, C. **Whispering In The Wind** John Grinder & Carmen Bostic; 1st ed. edition (2001)

HANNAFORD, C. PhD **Smart Moves: Why Learning Is Not All In Your Head** Great Ocean Publishers (1995)

HARARI, N.Y. **Sapiens: A Brief History of Humankind** Vintage (2015)

HINCKS, A.T. **An Author of Life: Volume Book 1** Books Mango (2018)

JAMES, M.B. MA PhD **Integrate The Shadow, Master Your Path** Balboa Press (2014)

JAMES, T. MS PhD and SHEPHARD, D BSc DES **Presenting Magically** Crown House Publishing (2001)

JAMES, T., WOODSMALL, W. **Timeline Therapy and the Basis of Personality** Crown House Publishing; New edition (2017)

KIMSEY-HOUSE, H., KIMSEY-HOUSE, K., SANDAHL, P., WHITWORTH, L. **Co-Active Coaching: The Proven Framework For Transformative Conversations At Work And In Life** Aladdin (2018)

KISHIMI, I., FUMITAKE, K. **The Courage To Be Disliked: How To Free Yourself, Change Your Life And Achieve Real Happiness** Allen & Unwin (2019)

KNIGHT, S. **NLP At Work** Nicholas Brealey Publishing; Third Edition (2009)

LABORDE, G.Z. PhD **Influencing With Integrity** Crown House Publishing; Reprint (1998)

LAWLEY, J.D. and TOMPKINS, P.L. **Metaphors in Mind: Transformation Through Symbolic Modelling** Developing Company Press (2000)

MADDEN, F. **The Intention Impact Conundrum** Florence Madden Associates (2018)

MALTZ, M. MD FICS **Psycho-Cybernetics** Perigee Books; Updated and Expanded edition (2015)

MEHRABIAN, A. **Silent Messages: Implicit Communication of Emotions and Attitudes** Wadsworth Publishing Company, 2nd Revised edition (1981)

MOLDEN, D. **Managing With The Power Of NLP** Pitman Publishing (1996)

O'CONNOR, J., SEYMOUR, J. **Introducing Neuro-Linguistic Programming** Harper Collins Publishers (1990)

OWEN, N. **The Salmon of Knowledge: Stories for Work, Life, the Dark Shadow and Oneself** Crown House Publishing (2009)

RAMACHANDRAN, V.S. **The Tell-Tale Brain: Unlocking the Mystery of Human Nature** Windmill Books (2012)

RICARD, M. **Altruism: The Science and Psychology of Kindness** Atlantic Books (2018)

ROBBINS, A. **Unlimited Power: The New Science of Personal Achievement** Simon & Schuster UK; New edition (2001)

SAMPLES, B. **The Metaphoric Mind: A Celebration of Creative Consciousness** Jalmar Press Inc. (1992)

SARANTINOU, E. **Perception Projection: 9 Principles To Empower Your Team** Black Card Books (15 April 2018)

SHEDD, J.A. **Salt From My Attic** Mosher Press (1928)

SILVESTER, T. **WordweavingVolume1 The Science of Suggestion** The Quest Institute (2003)

SOOSALU, G., OKA M. **mBraining: Using Your Multiple Brains To Do Cool Stuff** CreateSpace Independent Publishing Platform (2012)

STRAUSS, N. **The Game and Rules of the Game** Canongate Books (2011)

SULLIVAN, W. and REES, J. **Clean Language: Revealing Metaphors and Opening Minds** Crown House Publishing (2008)

What Our 'Everyday' Reviewers Say...

They say it takes a village to raise a child and as this book is our 'baby' we would like to acknowledge our 'villagers'. We are grateful for the encouragement and support through the various drafts of our book from the following people, who have given us their time and now their feedback:

Florence and Eleni have combined their warm styles and extensive experience to take you on a thoroughly enjoyable learning journey. Artfully delivered, feeling more like a chat with a friend, you will come away with a solid foundation of NLP and practical tips on how to apply an NLP approach in everyday life. Who wouldn't want a deeper understanding of yourself and how to make the most of what life gives you ?

Alannah Britz, NLP Trainer, Coach and Communications Consultant

"What we learn with pleasure, we never forget." Alfred Mercier

This book was both a pleasure to read and absorb, and a huge learning experience for this teacher! Both Florence and Eleni captivate and educate with every chapter. As a complete beginner and novice in NLP, I found this book accessible, user friendly and an invaluable tool to add to my kitbag of life! It has allowed me to reflect on aspects of my job and my relationships where I am already successful and shown me ways to improve them further... shone a light on areas I struggle with and given me the confidence to approach them differently! Thank you both for this 'must read' guide to a fascinating subject!

Alyson Renwick, Nurture Practitioner and Teacher

What an excellent book. I liked Florence and Eleni's style and as an NLP student I have found this book easy to read and understand – a recommended read for those of us who like real everyday examples in their learning. This book is a must read for all NLP students. A book that makes sense of the complex theories and leaves you wanting more.

Andrea Pattinson, Human Resource Consultant and Business

This is the 'exceptional' one of the many NLP books I've devoured! All anyone needs to know about NLP and the ease of applying its fundamentals into one's own life! A must read for anyone if you are READY & looking for that EMPOWERING, REAL, SIGNIFICANT and HAPPY change in your life!

Angie Ong, Master NLP Coach

What Our 'Everyday' Reviewers Say…

If I were to recommend one contemporary book to someone new to the field of NLP it would be Everyday NLP. Florence and Eleni take the reader through a journey of discovery of the concepts of NLP in a contemporary way, beautifully weaving theory into daily life by sharing their own life experiences, experiences many of us share. For both new and seasoned professionals in NLP, Everyday NLP is engaging and quite simply an empowering experience. Thank you both.

Bibian McRoy, HR and OD Professional

This book is a joyous mixture of learning, openness, honesty, fun, and is a unique representation of NLP. Both authors delve deeply into their own experiences of everyday life and share their most authentic learning. In doing so, the learning makes so much sense and in reading the book, I had so many moments of "…that's me!! I recognise that in me."

Florence and Eleni are seamless in their integration with each other in writing this book. The movement from one author to the other flows gently and their connection, bond and shared, deep understanding of NLP is clear. It truly is about Everyday NLP. Whether you're new to NLP or have a deep understanding of it, this book shines a day to day lens on the subject that really brings it to life, in a way that is easy to understand. This is an inspiring read full of wonderful insights and learning.

Carol Moor, Leadership and Transformation Coach Glow for Success Coach and NLP Master Practitioner

There is always a bright line each time a dark area comes across with a luminous one. That's what a painter told me years ago. And that's what the content of this book is about. It's about learning the ways of giving life to our unique bright side each and every day.

Christina Spyropoulou, Lawyer, Master NLP Coach and Artist

A simple but genius guide to everyday life! It enlightened my 10 years of NLP studying, reading books, seminars, trainings, psychotherapy, reiki and every other self-improvement method I have come across. This book does so by giving me simple examples (so that my mind understands), exercises (so my unconscious mind learns new habits), and all of that in a funny, exciting and humorous way (so my heart enjoys the change)! A really inspiring, energizing, amazing and yet 'down to the earth' book, with a scientific background to improve life, work and relationships!

Eleni Kotopoulou, NLP Master Coach

What Our 'Everyday' Reviewers Say…

This comprehensive and easy-to-read book on NLP has inspired me to look at issues I had so far neglected in my life. While reading Eleni and Florence's book I felt empowered to take action and apply some of the clearly outlined NLP principles to my everyday attitude towards myself and others. The examples presented, the clear and well written text, the personal testimonies of the authors themselves, make this a very pleasant and enjoyable read as well. Thank you for sharing this valuable material on NLP with the world ladies!

Eleni Nikolaou, Primal Health Coach

'I am the one wearing Silver necklace and Gold shoes combined! Yes! I have been a participant to every Eleni's training program, from NLP Practitioner, to Master and NLP coaching, and I wish there are more and more! It was a blessed moment in my life. It was the most fantastic destination I have ever reached and God knows how much I travel. Reading this book, immersed me back into the NLP courses and the amazing energetic spirit. Reading through the chapters of the book I could remember how I experienced these concepts of life. There is not a day I don't apply one of the NLP's powerful tool and insights. The book talks about ideas that change one's life and at the same time Eleni & Florence make them so easy to understand.

Flavie Fournial, Master NLP Coach, Health Coach & Yoga Instructor

I have the privilege to know Eleni and Florence, both experienced NLP trainers and coaches. Their book provides a framework for clear unambiguous communication, which is critical to me as manager in a high tech company. It also serves all of us in today's world in which (mis)information is spread with lightning speed.

Frederike Hofstra, Senior Manager, Global Social Customer Care

It's amazing how Eleni and Florence continue to pursue their passion to reach out to people about NLP. I wake up for, I breathe, eat, think, walk and talk NLP. This book will be my 'go to' NLP toolbox for literally all areas of my life. Thank you for this treasure box! And congratulations and thank you ladies for making this available, well done!

Harry KH Ong, Managing Director Tyson Foods Malaysia

I still remember the first time Eleni came to Amorgos island in Greece to host her first seminar and brought great energy and knowledge to the island and to Aegialis Hotel & Spa. Congratulations my dear friend Eleni to you and to your associate Florence, for this great achievement! It is an amazing book! One can learn and benefit so much by reading it!

Irene Giannakopoulos, Owner & CEO Aegialis Tours - Aegialis Hotel & Spa

What Our 'Everyday' Reviewers Say…

Having completed NLP training with Eleni in Malaysia and learning life changing techniques, I was beyond excited to read Everyday NLP. This book is the tipping point for understanding and grasping the tools and techniques that help us manage our emotions and beliefs for a life by design. Eleni and Florence's ability to bring NLP theory into life is like a jolt of electricity. Weaving everyday stories and exercises into the specifics of NLP, make this an inspirational, educational and thought provoking read. I wish I had read this book in my late teens and recommend it for anyone seeking a deeper connection to their past, current and future self.

Jennifer Elliott, Creator of Smayver (Smart Saver – making saving fun for children)

The "how to guide," to living your best life: thoughtful, fun and practical.

Your "impossible," becomes "I'm possible." Your "try," becomes "I will," and your reasons to smile and succeed increase ten-fold as you create your personal choices for life, work and relationships.

Gift yourself this easy to read, action orientated book and have the life you dreamed of, become a reality.

Jenny Mackness, HR Manager px Group

Florence and Eleni have created a real gem! This book is engaging to read. It demystifies the jargon making NLP readily accessible in everyday life. They freely share their experiences as exemplars which serves to unlock your thoughts. There are poignant moments when the material has particular resonance for the individual; a light bulb moment. It is a valuable resource for those new to NLP as well as NLP scholars. Highly recommended!

Jill Pinington, Coach and NLP Practitioner

This is another great read and compliments The Impact Intention Conundrum perfectly. The exercises make it a valuable resource and self training aid. Written in a style that is easy to follow with real world examples of how NLP can help us all be more effective and resourceful in our everyday life.

Jim Maguire, NLP Master Practitioner, Development Coach and Mediator

What Our 'Everyday' Reviewers Say…

This is a warm and welcoming book that draws you in as two experienced professionals share their personal journey with NLP in authentic style of writing and in full technicolour! An enjoyable read that brings the principles and benefits of NLP to life through sharing potent and at times funny anecdotes that leave you reflecting on your own NLP learnings and life in general. This book is suitable for everyone regardless if you are new to NLP or have a deep understanding there is something in there for everyone acting as a real thought provoker. An easy read that had me reading chapter after chapter in one sitting and then at the end wanting to read more so a book I would highly recommend.

Katie Woods-Ruddick, Head of HR px Group

Florence and Eleni bring together their individual personalities and perspectives beautifully in this book, allowing the reader a journey which is both enjoyable and informative. Capturing the very best of NLP techniques and theory, the book is accessible and user friendly for both those with NLP understanding and those new to the field. An excellent read and fantastic addition to the field of NLP literature.

Laura Cadman, Executive Coach and NLP Master Practitioner

A beautiful book on NLP – easy to read, lovely visuals, and packed full of anecdotal experience that helped me to understand how I too could use these wonderful principles in my everyday life to make it even more meaningful.

Maureen Tallis, Head of Employee Development, Baxi Heating UK Ltd

It is easy to get lost in the breadth of learning and experience that underpins and forms the substance of NLP. For my own learning I have been lucky to find passionate mentors and tutors who have shown me that NLP is an approach to being and one that is both familiar and accessible, if only I pay attention to the right things. Florence and Eleni both have this quality – they are guides at my side whenever I find that I am in need of help, for myself or others. I close my eyes and hear their voices or see their faces as they invite me to find the thing I already know but have not yet accessed. I have the same feelings and sense of compassionate guidance when I read this book. Clear, concise, coherent and congruent, this is a book that I will turn and return to as I continue to learn all that NLP offers me.

Mike Rawlins, Coach, Leadership Development Practitioner and founder of Six Inches 2 The Right (and bon viveur)

What Our 'Everyday' Reviewers Say…

Everyday NLP is my manual for a fulfilling life – the way I want it. You have it next to your bed and you read it every day- and then you reread it and you just go to the chapter you need to work on more. Fluid language between the two writers, very direct to the reader and clear explanations for everyday people – us – on how NLP works and how it can change our way of thinking, and therefore our lives. Thank you, Florence and Eleni.

Mina Apostolidis-Maitre Chocolatier, Owner and founder of MINA Handmade Chocolates

It is an honour to give a testimonial to such a fantastic book. I apply NLP in my daily business since my practitioner training 20 years ago. Reading this comprehensive, yet easy to digest book, is a great reminder for me on the NLP tools and how to implement them even more deeply at my work. Everyday NLP is a real treasure as it contains the introduction and the key elements of NLP you need to know. However, what I like the most is the personal and practical approach and the ideas for immediate application. The book is what NLP stands for: Fast – Easy – Effective.

Peter Wyss, Group CEO PMCC Corporation

This book serves as a mental GPS, a guide to your own mind map, to help you achieve your true potential in life! The map is already there – the NLP GPS tells you where and how to go, to meet your personal goals!

Simon Spalas, Cards Portfolio Manager at Alpha Bank Greece

I am a big fan of self-help books and since I started my own NLP and coaching journey some years ago, I have read almost everything worthwhile on the subject. But I have rarely found something that is quite so inspiring and motivational as Everyday NLP. Full of fresh, well-documented information and personal stories, Everyday NLP is written in a simple and clear fashion that's designed to get right inside your head and stick; it really works! Whether you're a novice or an experienced NLP Practitioner, this is a must-have to improve your relationships – with those around you, and yourself.

Simonetta Roma, Talent and Transition Coach

About Eleni Sarantinou…

Eleni was born in Greece, she is an NLP Trainer, a NLP Master Coach, a wife, a mother, a world traveller. She is a keen chess player, enjoys meditating and playing the guitar. Having gained her bachelor degree as an economist, she has worked as a technical analyst in large IT corporations in Europe, Middle East and Australia before moving into what she calls her calling: personal development.

She is all about inspiring people to take action and take control of their lives. She is passionate about personal growth and her mission is for everyone to reach their potential.

Don't let your progress be a hindrance to your progress!

Eleni Sarantinou.

It is a combination of her deep understanding of human desires, working with people from many cultures and understanding of business processes which have resulted in her successfully coaching many individuals as well as bringing corporations to a higher level.

She is a Master NLP Coach, a Marshall Goldsmith Stakeholder Centered Coach and Internationally Certified NLP Trainer. Eleni's focus is on helping her clients make that important next step in the direction they desire and helping them to become leaders in every way. Her work focusses on creating practical and supportive strategies that will make the client's conscious mind realise their goals. Using the brain tools of today she helps people to make the difference in their organizations and their lives. Her style is best described as up close and personal, supportive, results oriented and FUN !

She travels the world and speaks about all life and business spheres. In addition to Everyday NLP, she is the author of *Perception Projection: 9 Principles to Empower Your Team, and co-author of Change 6* with Jim Britt and Jim Lutes.

Working With Eleni...

Her love for different mindsets takes her all over the world training individuals and consulting companies in more than 10 countries, 6 continents and in 4 different languages.

In addition to one to one coaching, she delivers NLP & Master NLP Practitioner, NLP Coaching, Time Line Therapy™ and Hypnosis Certifications courses, Leadership Programmes, Communication & Sales Workshops, Team Building, Family & Business Constellations. NLP Certificated programmes are run both in-house for organisations and on an open basis in various locations over 6 continents!

For full details:

www.life-spheres.com
or contact her on es@life-spheres.com

About Florence Madden....

Florence is a native of Northern Ireland and is an NLP Trainer and coach based in Cumbria in the UK. Living near the Lake District she is a keen walker, a rugby fan, loves reading history and has had a lifelong love of animals. She has a degree in Economic History from Queen's University Belfast and held various management and Human Resources roles before setting up her own management development business in 2002.

At the core of her work is her belief in our ability to learn and grow at any stage in our lives, and so this informs her approach to developing others; whether that is coaching one to one, or in group environments. She sees that how we relate to others, not simply one's technical skill, as the key to effectiveness in any part of our lives:

There is often a gulf between our good intentions and our impact on others – our effectiveness is determined by how well we bridge that gap.

Florence Madden.

Indeed, she has written a book on the subject The Intention Impact Conundrum which is based on her open course that she runs in The Lake District.

Florence is an Accredited NLP Trainer, a New Code NLP Practitioner and Coach, a Generative Coach, a Thinking Partner (Coach) and an Edward De Bono Six Thinking Hats Trainer.

Working with Florence....

She runs open NLP courses in The Lake District and in Greece. She also works all over the UK developing and delivering bespoke training solutions for organisations in the private, public and third sector. She develops and delivers programmes on leadership, team effectiveness and coaching as well as the full range of management skills. Clients

can expect a business partner with programmes and solutions tailored specifically to their needs, as well as full ongoing support prior to, during and after any assignment.

Her passion is seeing people and organisations thrive and succeed and is passionate about the part that development plays in that!

For full details:

www.florencemadden.co.uk

or contact her on:
info@florencemadden.co.uk

We want to say thank you …

Thank you from Florence:

Writing a book is a journey with twists and turns, whose destination only becomes clearer with each step. So, while there were many encouraging voices along the way, none more so than my husband Pat and I want to thank him for his boundless love and belief in me. And of course, I also want to thank Eleni who has made this an unforgettable experience in so many ways: her energy, her insight, her provocation, her wisdom and her fun! She took my throwaway remark of 'let's write a book' and turned a spark into a flame – and now here it is.

Thank you from Eleni:

How lucky for me to create this book together with my dear friend Florence: 'Thank you, co-author for your kindness, humour, resilience, your exquisite taste and instinct and your love!' Florence goes the extra mile in every sense of the word. A big thank you to my husband Gerard! For the last 25 years, he has held the space and time for me …to expand! His encouragement and love, I carry as a treasure in my heart, always. Our Isabelle and Victor, our shining stars, held my hand every step of the way, asking the tough questions and contributing in every way! Thank you!

Thank you from both of us:

There are so many people who have contributed to and inspired this book. Each chapter has stories of real people in everyday life: friends, family, teachers, course delegates and simply the people we have met along the way. Their stories have enabled us to show that NLP is simply part of our lives whether we recognise it or not – it is everyday! A special thank you to those who have read the various drafts and given us encouragement, feedback and testimonials.

And then you wish for editors who get you and we were blessed with two of them. Lucy and Maria were the epitome of angelic patience, clear-eyed savviness and sweet embrace … and they both got us! They have done more than simply correct our punctuation or word choices! And then, Philippa who has been both graphic designer and typesetter – unfailingly patient and wonderfully creative. A true blessing to have someone who cares deeply about what we envisioned and as committed to bring this vision to life!

And here you are reading it – so perhaps our greatest thanks is to you our readers for being curious to find out what we had to offer and we hope you have been happy that you did! We would love to hear your stories and how you have used your learning!